UPGRADING BOOK
DISTRIBUTION IN AFRICA

PERSPECTIVES ON AFRICAN BOOK DEVELOPMENT

Titles in the series

UPGRADING BOOK DISTRIBUTION IN AFRICA

EDITED BY
TONY READ, CARMELLE DENNING
   & VINCENT BONTOUX

WITH CASE STUDIES FROM
FRANK SEGBAWU
GAULPHINE NYIRENDA
DAVID MUITA
FRED MATOVU
MAMADOU ALIOU SOW
ETIENNE BRUNSWIC
JEAN VALERIEN
AMADOU WAZIRI
JEAN-PIERRE LEGUERE
GEORGES STERN
LESEDI SEITEI
ABDULLAH SAIWAAD

WORKING GROUP
ON BOOKS AND LEARNING MATERIALS
ASSOCIATION FOR THE DEVELOPMENT OF EDUCATION IN AFRICA

Published by the Working Group on Books and Learning Materials of the Association
for the Development of Education in Africa c/o DFID Education Dept, 94 Victoria
Street, London SWIE 5JL, United Kingdom

First published 2001

ISBN 1901830 15 2

Distributed by the African Books Collective Ltd,
The Jam Factory, 27 Park End Street, Oxford OX1 IHU, United Kingdom
Tel: + 44 [0] 1865-726686
Fax: + 44 [0] 1865-793298
E-mail: abc@dial.pipex.com

Printed and bound by
Unisa Production Printers
University of South Africa, Pretoria, South Africa.

CONTENTS

ACKNOWLEDGEMENTS

Book distribution continues to be a major preoccupation of the ADEA Working Group on Books & Learning Materials because of the continuing weakness of this crucial part of the book chain. The impetus for this piece of research came from two members of the Working Group's Steering Committee, Mitch Kirby of USAID and Jean-Claude Balmès of the French Ministry of Foreign Affairs. It followed on from an earlier study of textbook distribution in selected West African countries, which had drawn attention to the need for a more extensive study.

Thanks are due to Mitch Kirby for designing the original research proposal with a wider scope and scale, in terms of questions to be addressed and range of country experiences. We are also grateful to International Book Development (IBD) and Danaé-Sciences for their painstaking commitment to the task, having been invited by the ADEA *Books* Working Group to undertake the study after a competitive tender involving a number of organisations and consultancy firms both inside and outside Africa.

The ADEA *Books* Working Group would like to congratulate Tony Read, Carmelle Denning and Vincent Bontoux of IBD, and Etienne Brunswic, Jean Valérien, Jean-Paul Leguéré and Georges Stern of Danaé-Sciences for raising so many thought provoking issues, and for enabling us to benefit from such an impressive wealth of experience. In addition to the two organising teams, the other writers of the maxi and mini case studies (Frank Segbawu, Gaulphine Nyirenda, David Muita, Fred Matovu, Mamadou Aliou Sow, Amadou Waziri, Lesedi Seitei and Abdullah Saiwaad) merit gratitude for completing their contributions to a high standard, within the deadline.

We should also like to thank Veronica McKay and Mary Patrick for additional editorial assistance, and the production team at Unisa for their technical input. Everyone concerned with both the content and the production of this study has answered requests for additional information, clarification and modification with good will and patience, in our common endeavour to ensure a worthwhile outcome.

Finally, we should like to thank the French Ministry of Foreign Affairs, USAID and the UK Department of International Development for providing technical and financial support for the study.

Carew Treffgarne
ADEA Working Group on Books & Learning Materials, December 2000

EDITORIAL NOTE

From the outset the editors believed that it was important that the case studies, which form the foundation of this book, should have some common elements in order to achieve a useful level of comparability. To this end a set of basic guidelines was prepared to assist the contributors in the preparation of their case studies. The guidelines did not attempt to impose a common structure on the case studies and stressed that every case study should provide an overview of the total book distribution system from the local point of view. The guidelines requested that all studies should include some common topics, but only if they were considered to be relevant in the individual country situation. The proposed common topics were specified as follows:

- An introductory paragraph providing basic demographic details including educational roll numbers and the size of the private education sector at all levels, if relevant and available.
- A description of the most important organisations and companies concerned with book distribution in the different market sectors.
- A brief history of the evolution of the national book trade and the current book distribution system from independence up to the present and, where appropriate, an indication of the comparative roles of the state and private sectors in the evolutionary process.
- A description of the way in which books are currently distributed in the different market sectors with any specific problems highlighted.
- The impact of funding agency investments and government policies on national book development in general and on distribution and other book trade activities in particular.
- The role and significance of external book trade companies (multinationals and regional companies) in the national book trade and their impact on book distribution specifically and on book development in general.
- The significance of, and limitations to, the regional trade in books.
- Any recent policy changes or initiatives from either government or funding agency (or even book trade initiatives), which are likely to have an impact on overall national book development and specifically on distribution.

- Any issues not covered above which the authors feel have particular importance or significance in their own national case study.
- Any ideas, proposals or suggestions that the authors feel could improve the current position and performance of book distribution nationally or regionally.

In the editing, there has been no attempt to 'force' any of the case studies into a particular form of presentation, but the guidelines have obviously influenced the way in which many of the case studies have been presented. In some case studies the authors have organised their material differently and have created their own emphasis, but most of the topics specified above are still present in one form or another. Thus, for example, all case studies provide information on the national education system and list the main players in book distribution. They all comment on the regional trade in books and all case studies (except Botswana) comment upon the impact of funding agency investments and policies on the development of the book trade in general and on book distribution capacity in particular. In all of these examples there are considerable differences both in the significance of the facts presented and in the viewpoints of the contributors. It is these differences, and the reasons for them, which make these particular case studies so valuable as a source of reference and information on book distribution systems and problems in Africa.

The editors have adopted a deliberate policy of editing as lightly as possible and much of the editorial work has been concentrated on normal text editing, plus the standardisation of terminology wherever appropriate, plus some text reorganisation to allow for easier comparisons of key issues. As an example of the reorganisation of text, a 'Basic facts' box now precedes each case study. These boxes were originally developed from the background country details provided by each author. In some cases the background information was gathered together in one place; in other cases the basic information was spread throughout the text. Because no two contributors produced the same list of country indicators the editors unilaterally decided to place all the background information together in the same place, at the beginning of every case study. We then decided to create a standard package of background information using the same data sources for every country wherever possible. The editors are also responsible for the great majority of the many footnotes included in the case studies. These have been added to provide additional important information, or clarifications to the text, or to highlight important comparisons with other case studies without disturbing the flow of the main text. In every case where an editorial change has gone beyond basic copy-editing, a draft of the full and final edited study has been submitted to the author for final checking and approval to make sure that the views expressed in the case study remain those of the author alone. Finally, wherever we did not understand the significance or context of a comment or statement, we have asked questions of the authors. The answers to these requests for clarification have also been absorbed into the case study texts where relevant and necessary.

ABOUT THE CONTRIBUTORS

Frank Segbawu was educated at St Theresa's Preparatory School and the Presbyterian Boys Secondary School in Accra, Ghana, before completing his schooling at the Sevenoaks School in Kent in the UK. He took his degree at the University of Bath in the UK. He worked as a publisher for Longman Zimbabwe and also worked for Longman in the UK. He left publishing for a time to work with Johnson's Wax in the UK before joining SEDCO Publishing Ltd., in Accra as Sales and Marketing Director, a position he still holds. He is 35 years old and is married with three children.

Gaulphine Nyirenda majored in Mathematics and Physical Sciences and graduated with a Diploma in Education from the University of Malawi in 1974. She taught in a number of secondary schools up to 1990. From 1978 to 1985 she also sold school textbooks on behalf of Mallory International, a UK based library supplier and export bookseller, to projects funded by agencies such as the World Bank and the African Development Bank. In 1985 she also took on the representation of the school textbook and reference list of Oxford University Press in Malawi. She opened Maneno Enterprises Ltd. in Lilongwe in 1995 and very rapidly established a reputation as one of the leading educational booksellers in the country. In 1998 she added the Cambridge University Press school and children's book list to her representational portfolio. In 1999 she started co-publishing with Oxford University Press and managed to get four junior secondary textbook series approved for use in Malawian secondary schools. With CUP she also has published a number of local language reading books in Chiyao, Chilomwe, Chinyanja and Chitumbuka. She is currently an office bearer in both the Booksellers' Association of Malawi (BAM) and the Book Publishers' Association of Malawi (BPAM).

David Muita was born in Githunguri in Kiambu District in Kenya in 1952. He attended Githunguri Primary School before moving to St Josephs for 'O' levels and Njiri High School for 'A' levels. He obtained a B.Ed(Sc) from Nairobi University in 1977. From 1977 to 1984 he was a Biology teacher at Kangema High School and then at Mary Hill Girls High School before being promoted to Deputy Principal at Njumbi High School. He joined Macmillan

Kenya (Publishers) as a sales executive in 1984 and rose to the post of General Manager by 1987. In 1990 he was promoted again to become Executive Director, the post he currently holds. He has been the longest serving member of the Kenya Book Publishers' Association Council – from 1987 to the present. He has served as Council Member, Secretary, Vice Chairperson and has been the KPA Chairperson since November 1997. He has also served on the Board of the Kenya National Library Service and is currently the Chairperson of the Reprographic Rights' Association of Kenya (KOPIKEN). He is married with four children and is a keen golfer.

Fred Matovu has a BSc in Education from Makerere University in Kampala and an MA from Stanford University in the USA. He taught mathematics at senior secondary school level in Uganda from 1974 to 1976 before becoming a mathematics curriculum specialist at the National Curriculum Development Centre (NCDC) in Kampala from 1977 to 1988. In 1989 he established a bookshop (Matovu Books and Stationery) in Kampala and also became the local representative for Longman in Uganda. From 1992 until the present he has been managing director of Kamalu Ltd, one of the most important Ugandan educational publishing houses and book distributors and the co-publisher with Longman UK of many textbooks and supplementary materials for the Ugandan educational market. He is currently the Chairperson of the Uganda Publishers' Association (UPA), the Vice Chair of the National Book Trust of Uganda (NABOTU) and the Vice Chair of the Book Development Council of Uganda.

Mamadou Aliou Sow was a postgraduate student at the University of Conakry in 1976 and chose to write his dissertation on the subject of *'The Production of Instructional Materials'*. His work experience overseas as well as his position as head of the Department for Instructional and Multi-Media Support *(Appui pédagogique)* at Conakry's National Institute for Pedagogic Research and Policy (INRAP) from 1988 to 1994 have provided him with a deep knowledge of textbook-related issues. All aspects of textbooks have been his concern since 1993, when he became Managing Director of the publishing house Éditions Ganndal in Conakry. He also heads the Guinean Book Professionals' Network (REPROLIG), which advocates the creation of a national book development policy for Guinea. Today, Mamadou Aliou Sow is widely considered to be one of the most recognised publishers of his generation, not only in Guinea and but also in Francophone West Africa.

Amadou Waziri is a senior civil servant at Niger's Ministry of National Education and a member of the Permanent Secretariat of the National Committee for Teaching and School Reform. He is currently in charge of the textbook component of the World Bank's Education III Project. As INDRAP's (National Institute for Curriculum Research and Development)

Publishing Manager, he has also published several primary textbooks in national languages. He is a member of the Curriculum Committee of the PFIE (Environmental Training and Information Programme).

Etienne Brunswic, formerly a Director at Unesco, and **Jean Valérien**, a retired senior civil servant from the French Ministry of Education, are both distinguished experts in educational technology. They have teamed up to study textbook-related issues. In 1996 they ran the seminars and workshops set up in Libreville and Lomé by the Agence de la Francophonie to define its new textbook policy. Unesco's IIEP called on them to design and teach training modules for education planners in order to help them supervise the development of textbooks and to develop a distance education approach to textbook development policy and planning.

Jean-Pierre Leguéré is the founder and Director of Danaé-Sciences, a Paris based consultancy company specialising in editorial support, training and written communication. As a publisher, journalist and writer, he has long experience of Africa. He has trained numerous publishers from Africa and the Maghreb within the African Centre for Publishers' Training. He has also carried out various assignments in Africa on behalf of Agence de la Francophonie in support of textbook development, particularly in Chad and Niger. Finally, he is also a specialist with Agence de la Francophonie in the assessment of grant applications submitted by African publishers.

Georges Stern has in-depth experience in book distribution. He was previously Deputy Book Director for the Hachette group and the International Manager of The French Publishing House Flammarion. As such, he was in charge of African exports, and travelled extensively to Africa as part of his job, especially to Côte d'Ivoire, Senegal, Cameroon and Guinea. He has also carried out several assignments in Africa on behalf of the French Ministry of Foreign Affairs and the Agence de la Francophonie. Within CAFED, he has trained several groups of publishing executives from Africa and the Maghreb in book distribution. He is a consultant with Danaé-Sciences on publishing assistance.

Lesedi Seitei was born in Botswana in 1961. He graduated from the University of Botswana with a BA in Humanities and a Postgraduate Degree in Education. In 1997 he was awarded an MBA. He was a secondary school teacher in Botswana from 1985 to 1990 before joining Heinemann Botswana as an educational sales representative. From 1992 he was the Heinemann Sales and Marketing Manager in Botswana until he was promoted to General Manager in 1994. In 1999 he was appointed as the Managing Director of the company. He is currently also the Secretary of the Botswana Publishers' Association.

Abdullah Saiwaad graduated with an Honours Degree in Education from the University of Dar es Salaam in 1977 and also has a Post-graduate Diploma in Publishing from Oxford Brookes University in the UK. He worked initially as a teacher in Tanzania for four years but since then he has worked continuously in publishing in Tanzania from 1981 up to the present. He was first Publishing Manager, then General Manager of East Africa Publications Ltd up to 1993, when he became General Manager of Diamond Publications Ltd. From 1994 until the present he has been Managing Director of Readit Books. He has also occupied the position of Executive Secretary of the Publishers' Association of Tanzania from 1996 up to the present. His numerous publications include *Copyright Law and Authorship in Tanzania* (Editor) published by the Tanzanian Institute of Education, numerous books and articles in Kiswahili and, most recently, *The Publishing Industry in Tanzania* for the *Family Mirror*.

Carmelle Denning started her educational publishing career in the education department of Cassells Publishers in the UK and then went on to Evans Brothers Publishers where she was Editorial Manager of the Overseas Education Department and specialised in publishing textbooks for Africa and the Caribbean. She joined the British Book Development Council in 1982 as the Director of the Development Agencies Projects Service. She has been involved in educational publishing for almost 32 years and has been deeply involved in textbook development project work in Anglophone, Lusophone and Francophone Africa and the Caribbean for the past 20 years. She has travelled and worked on textbook issues extensively in Africa where she has a unique experience of the publishing and textbook provision systems. She has particular knowledge and experience of Gambia, Sierra Leone, Cape Verde, Senegal, Guinea, Niger, Mali, CAR, Burkina Faso, Liberia, Nigeria, Cameroon, Côte d'Ivoire, Rwanda, Zaïre, Ethiopia, Eritrea, Kenya, Uganda, Tanzania, Zanzibar, Madagascar, Zambia, Zimbabwe, Algeria, Tunisia, the RSA and Mozambique. Carmelle was one of the co-authors of the '*Summary Report on African Book Sector Studies*'.

Vincent Bontoux graduated in 1982 in political science, economics and sociology from the Paris Institute of Political Studies and took his Masters degree in 1983 in Project Management. In 1985 he qualified as an advanced translator from the Ecole Superieure d'Interpretation et du Traduction. He started his career as a strategic planner in the French construction industry. From 1990 to 1999 he was the Head of the Global Strategic Planning Department at France Edition. He joined IBD in 1999 as a Textbook and Publishing Development Specialist, with special responsibility for Francophone African countries and Latin America and the Caribbean. He has worked on book trade and book development assignments in Latin America, North America, Western Europe, East Asia and the Former Soviet

Union; and in Africa, he has worked in Côte d'Ivoire, Madagascar, South Africa, Lesotho and Malawi.

Tony Read graduated from St Catherine's College, Oxford University in 1962. He spent a year as a secondary school teacher in Sussex before moving to Cape Coast, Ghana, where he taught in St Augustine's College and Adisadel College for the next eight years. In his spare time he worked in adult education and also wrote and published several novels. He then moved on to Oxford University Press where he was successively Deputy Head of the UK Education Division, the Manager of OUP New Zealand and finally OUP's International Director. In 1979 he was appointed to be the Director of the British Book Development Council where he firmly established his strong interests in book development policies and schoolbook and library provision systems in the developing world and the transitional economies of the former socialist bloc countries. In 1990, in association with close friends and colleagues, he established International Book Development as an independent international consultancy and advisory company on all issues concerning books and information. He has worked in very many countries worldwide on book policy development, research issues, project design and project implementation and is a regular writer and contributor on book, publishing and educational topics. Tony Read has a special interest in book development issues in Africa and was a co-author of the *Summary Report on African Book Sector Studies* which was used as the core working document of the 1991 Conference on textbook provision and Library development in Africa held in Manchester. He has also worked extensively on curriculum, educational financing, school management, teacher-training and private sector issues. In recent years he has undertaken numerous assignments for many governments and funding agencies in many African countries including Gambia, Sierra Leone, Liberia, Ghana, Nigeria, Eritrea, Ethiopia, Kenya, Uganda, Tanzania, Zanzibar, Angola, Malawi, Zambia, Lesotho and South Africa.

ABBREVIATIONS AND ACRONYMS
USED IN THE CASE STUDIES

ABC	African Books Collective
ADEA	Association for the Development of Education in Africa
ADP	*Agence de Diffusion de la Presse* / News agents (in Senegal)
AFCLIST	African Forum for Childrens' Literacy in Science & Technology
AfDB	African Development Bank
AFNIL	Publishers' Association of Niger
AIF	*Agence Internationale de la Francophonie* / International agency for Francophone countries
AKF	Aga Khan Foundation
APMLCI	Association for the Promotion of the Book Trade in Cote d'Ivoire
APE	Parent Teacher Association (in Francophone countries)
APNET	African Publishers' Network
ASAL	Arid & Semi-Arid Lands (in Kenya)
ASSP	African Social Science Programme (a US initiative of the 1960s and 1970s)
BAM	Booksellers' Association of Malawi
BBC	Botswana Book Company
BODECU	Book Development Council of Uganda
BOP	Balance of Payments
BOPIA	Botswana Publishing Industry Association
BP	*Banque Populaire* / Popular Bank
BPAM	Book Publishers' Association of Malawi
BSBS	Book Scheme for Basic Schools (a MoE/DFID project in Ghana)
CAFED	*Centre Africaine de Formation à l'Édition* / African Centre for Publishing Training
CDD	Curriculum Development Division (of MoE in Botswana)
CDSS	Community Day Secondary School (in Malawi)
CEDA	*Centre de Distribution et d'Éditions Africaines* / Centre for African Publishing and Distribution (Côte d'Ivoire)
CEPER	*Centre d'Édition pour l'Enseignement et la Recherche* / Publishing Centre for Teaching and Research (Cameroon)
CF	*Coopération Française* / former French Technical Co-operation
CFA	*Communauté Française d'Afrique* / Economic Community of Francophone Countries (Common currency zone)

CFO	Chief Financial Officer
CIA	Chief Internal Auditor (in Uganda)
CIDA	Canadian International Development Agency
CIS	Chief Inspector of Schools
CLAIM	Christian Literature Association in Malawi
CNPMS	*Centre national de Production des Manuels scolaires* / National Centre for Textbook Production (Bénin)
COD	Cash on Delivery
COMESA	Common Market for Eastern and Southern Africa
CRC	Camera Ready Copy
CRDD	Curriculum Research and Development Department (of the MoE in Ghana)
CSS	Conventional Secondary School (Malawi)
CUP	Cambridge University Press
CWO	Cash with Order
DAAF	*Direction des Affaires Administratives et Financières* / Division of Financial and Administrative Affairs (part of the MoE in Guinea)
DANIDA	Danish International Development Agency
DDP	District Development Project
DEC	Distance Education Centre (in Malawi – now replaced by the CDSS)
DEO	District Education Office(r)
DFID	Department for International Development (of the British Government)
DoE	Director of Education (Kenya)
DPMP	*Direction de la Production des Moyens Pédagogiques* / Division for the Production of Teaching Aids (Burkina Faso)
DSE	Danish Support to Education (Danida pilot project in Malawi)
DSE	German Foundation for International Development
DSPS	Danish Sector Programme Support (Danida education project in Malawi)
DTP	Desk Top Publishing
DUP	Dar-es-Salaam University Press
EACT	East African Co-operation Treaty
EAEP	East African Educational Publishers (in Kenya)
EALB	East African Literature Bureau (defunct since 1970)
EAPH	East Africa Publishing House (in Tanzania)
ECD	Early Childhood Development
ECOWAS	Economic Community of West African States
EdSAC	Education Sector Adjustment Credit (in Ghana and Kenya)
EFA	Education for All
ELT	English Language Teaching
EMAS	Educational Methods and Advisory Service (part of the MoESC in Malawi)

EMIS	Education Management Information System
EMP	*Education en Matière de Population* / Population studies (Burkina Faso)
ESIP	Education Sector Investment Programme (in Uganda)
EU	European Union
FCUBE	Free Compulsory Universal Basic Education (in Ghana)
FEMEN	*Fonds d'Édition des Manuels de l'Education National* / Textbook Publishing Fund (Senegal)
FLT	French Language Teaching
FPE	Free Primary Education
FUPE	Free Universal Primary Education
GBDC	Ghana Book Development Council
GBPA	Ghana Book Publishers' Association
GBS	Ghana Book Supplies Ltd
GCBA	Gold Coast Booksellers' Association
GER	Gross Enrolment Ratio
GES	Ghana Education Service
GNP	Gross National Product
GPC	Ghana Printing Corporation
GPO	Government Purchase Order
GTZ	German Agency for Co-operation
GUP	Ghana University Press
HDI	Human Development Index
HERP	Health & Education Rehabilitation Project (in Ghana)
HRD	Human Resource Development
ICB	International Competitive Bidding
IDEC	*Imprimerie de l'Éducation et de la Culture* /Education and Culture Printers (Guinea)
IFC	International Finance Corporation
IIEP	International Institute for Educational Planning (UNESCO, Paris)
IMF	International Monetary Fund
IMU	Instructional Materials Unit (of the MoES in Uganda)
INDRAP	*Institut de Recherche et d'Animation Pédagogique* / National Institute for Curriculum Research and Development (Niger)
INEADE	National Institute for Curriculum Development (Senegal)
INFRE	National Institute for Curriculum Development (Bénin)
INRAP	*Institute National de Recherche et d'Action Pedagogique* / National Institute for Curriculum Research and Development (Guinea)
IPB	*Institut Pédagogique du Burkina* / National Institute for Curriculum Development (Burkina Faso)
IPM	*Imprimerie Papeterie Moderne* / Modern Printing and Paper Company (Guinea)
IPM	International Professional Managers (Botswana)

IPN	*Institut Pédagogique National* / National Institute for Curriculum Development (Mali)
ISSE	*Institut Supérieur des Sciences de l'Éducation* / Higher Institute of Education (Chad)
JICA	Japanese International Cooperation Agency
JKF	Jomo Kenyatta Foundation (in Kenya)
JSS	Junior Secondary School
KIE	Kenya Institute of Education
KLB	Kenya Literature Bureau
KPA	Kenya Publishers' Association
KSES	Kenya School Equipment Scheme (now defunct)
LDC	Less Developed Country
LIMUSCO	Librairie des Mutuelles Scolaires du Togo / School Bookshop Co-operative (Togo)
LPO	Local Purchase Order
MBD	Methodist Book Depot (in Ghana)
MBS	Malawi Book Services (now defunct)
MCDE	Malawi College of Distance Education
MEBA	*Ministère de l'Enseignement de Base et de l'Alphabétisation* / Ministry of Basic Education and Literacy (Burkina Faso)
MIE	Malawi Institute of Education
MK	Malawian Kwacha (unit of currency)
MoC	Ministry of Culture
MoE	Ministry of Education
MoES	Ministry of Education and Sports (Uganda)
MoESC	Ministry of Education, Sport & Culture (Malawi)
MoEST	Ministry of Education, Science & Technology (in Kenya)
MoF	Ministry of Finance
MOF	Milton Obote Foundation (in Uganda – now defunct)
MoGYCD	Ministry of Gender, Youth and Community Development (in Malawi)
MoLG	Ministry of Local Government (in Tanzania)
MoLGL	Ministry of Local Government and Lands (in Botswana)
MRH	Maternal and Reproductive Health
MTEF	Mid Term Expenditure Framework
MTER	Mid Term Expenditure Review
MUK	Makerere University in Kampala
MUPEC	*Mutuelle des Personnels de l'Enseignement du Cameroon* / Educational Staff Co-operative (Cameroon)
NABOTU	National Book Trust of Uganda
NCDC	National Curriculum Development Centre (of the MoES in Uganda)
NEI	*Nouvelles Editions Ivoiriennes* / New Ivoirian Publications (Côte d'Ivoire)

NGO	Non-Government Organisation
NIE	National Institute of Education (at Makerere University in Uganda)
NIK	*Nouvelle Imprimerie du Kaloun* / New Printers of Kaloun (Guinea)
NLS	National Library Service
NURP	Northern Uganda Reconstruction Project
OE	*Opérateurs Economique* / Economic operators (Cameroon)
OGL	Open General Licence
OUP	Oxford University Press
p.a.	per annum
PABA	Pan African Booksellers' Association
PASE	*Programme d'Ajustement Structurel Éducation* / Structural Adjustment Programme for Education (Guinea)
PATA	Publishers' Association of Tanzania
PCU	Project Co-ordination Unit(s) (Kenya)
PDEF	*Plan de Développement de l'École Fondamentale* / Development Plan for Fundamental Education (Senegal)
PFIE	*Programme Formation Information pour l'Environnement* / Environmental Training and Information Programme (Burkina Faso)
PIF	Project Investment Framework
PIU	Project Implementation Unit (Uganda)
PMU	Projects Management Unit (Ghana)
PNGT	*Programme National de Gestion des Terroirs* / National Programme for Land Management (Burkina Faso)
PoP	Pockets of Poverty (Kenya)
PPP	Pilot Project for Publishing (Tanzania)
PTA	Parent Teacher Association (in Anglophone Africa)
RDE	Royal Danish Embassy (in Malawi and Uganda)
REPROLIG	Guinean Book Professionals' Network
RNE	Royal Netherlands Embassy (in Kenya and Uganda)
RSA	Republic of South Africa
SAEC	*Société Africaine d'Édition et de Communication* / African Publishing and Communications Company (Guinea)
SALIPACI	*Société anonyme de Librairie et de Papeterie de Côte d'Ivoire* / Ivorian Bookshop and Stationery Company
SBDC	School Book Distribution Company (a private sector wholesaler in Malawi)
SEP	Secondary Education Project (in Malawi)
SIDA	Swedish International Development Agency
SLD	Schools & Logistics Division (of the MoE in Ghana)
SNIES	*Service des Infrastructures et Equipements Scolaires* / Service for School Equipment and Infrastructure (Guinea)

SNLP	National Federation of Booksellers and Stationers (Côte d'Ivoire)
SODIL	*Société de Distribution du Livre* / Guinean company for Book Distribution
SOGUIDIP	*Société Guinéenne de Distribution de la Presse* / Guinean Press Agency (Guinea)
SSS	Senior Secondary School
SSU	School Supplies Unit (of the MoESC in Malawi)
STCF	Save the Children Fund
SUPER	Support for Ugandan Primary Education Reform (a USAID project in Uganda)
TA	Technical Assistance
TAB	Textbook Approval Board (of the MoE in Tanzania)
TAC	Teachers' Advisory Centre (Kenya)
TAZARA	Tanzania Zambia Railway
TBC	Textbook Centre (a Kenyan bookseller)
TBS	Times Bookshops (Malawi)
TDC	Teacher Development Centre (in Malawi)
TDEC	Textbook Development and Evaluation Committee (of MoE in Botswana)
TES	Tanzania Elimu Supplies
TIE	Tanzania Institute of Education
TMC	Textbook Management Committee (in Guinea)
TPH	Tanzania Publishing House
TPP	Textbook Pilot Project (in Uganda)
TRC	Tanzania Railway Corporation
TRF	Textbook Revolving Fund or Textbook Rental Fee
UBA	Uganda Booksellers' Association
UBE	Universal Basic Education
UNEB	Uganda National Examinations Board
UNESCO	United Nations Educational, Scientific and Cultural Organisation
UNICEF	United Nations Children's Fund
UoB	University of Botswana
UPA	Uganda Publishers' Association
UPABA	Uganda Publishers' and Booksellers' Association (now defunct)
UPE	Universal Primary Education
UPH	Uganda Publishing House (now defunct)
UPT	Uganda Press Trust (now defunct)
USS	Uganda School Supplies (now defunct)
VAT	Value Added Tax
VSO	Voluntary Services Overseas
WB	World Bank
ZEPH	Zambia Educational Publishing House

Chapter One

INTRODUCTORY ESSAY
BOOK DISTRIBUTION IN AFRICA:
THE DAWN OF A NEW ERA?

By Tony Read; Carmelle Denning & Vincent Bontoux

Background

The ten case studies that form the foundation of this book have been authored (or co-authored in some cases) by some of Africa's most distinguished publishers, booksellers and educationists. All are highly successful current practitioners with strong track records in their own countries. Many occupy senior positions in national, regional or international book trade organisations and can thus, to some extent at least, comment not just from their own point of view but also on behalf of the local book trades and education systems as well. All have experiences and viewpoints that deserve careful, sympathetic but judicious consideration, particularly by decision-makers in governments and the funding agency community.

The African contributors are also drawn almost exclusively from the private sector book trades of the case study countries. The only representative of a state-owned book development institution is Amadou Waziri from Niger. As a result of this weighting toward the African, private sector book trade, competitive and practical perspectives tend to inform the views and opinions expressed in the case studies. A set of case studies on book distribution authored largely by Ministry of Education officials or by state or parastatal publishing and distribution houses from the same countries almost certainly would have produced a different set of perspectives.

It is important to note, however, that times are changing and that Ministers and senior government officials in many countries now openly acknowledge and welcome the increasing involvement of the private sector in educational book provision activity. It is for these reasons that the private sector viewpoints represented here are particularly important, because for many years they were either muted or ignored completely. If state-organised textbook distribution generally had worked effectively throughout the continent over the past twenty-five years then the current study would not have been necessary. It is precisely because state-organised textbook distribution has a pretty poor track record in most countries (at least in terms of getting good textbooks efficiently into classrooms) that this alternative set of appraisals and viewpoints is both timely and important.

In almost all African countries the heart of the book trade is in school textbook supply and in all of the case study countries, school textbooks represent

80–90%, or even more, of the total book market available to local publishers and booksellers. In these circumstances, the decisions taken by government and development partners on the nature and form of school textbook provision systems have an overwhelming impact on every facet of the book trade. These decisions will usually determine the nature, effectiveness and coverage of the national book distribution system, even in sectors that, at first sight, do not seem to be connected in any way with school textbooks.

It is for this reason that some of the case studies may make uncomfortable reading for both governments and development partners. In some case study countries, government and development partners seem to have combined in a series of interventions that have been strikingly unhelpful (and in some cases notably destructive) to the national book trade, while offering little in the way of effective national textbook distribution. The Guinea case study makes for particularly disturbing reading in this respect. This introductory essay will attempt to highlight the key policy issues involved and to explain the most likely implications of different kinds of policy approaches and decisions.

The case studies cover all kinds of book markets in each country, and thus a variety of different types of book distribution. However, it is the school textbook distribution systems that form the core of all of the case studies for the reasons stated above. Therefore, it is school textbook distribution that is the central thread in the analysis contained in this essay.

The Coca-Cola distribution syndrome

There is a fairly widespread current viewpoint that textbook distribution in Africa should be much easier than it is and that the process of national textbook distribution is in urgent need of demystification. According to this viewpoint, which has been perpetuated for many years without exposure to serious analysis, Coca-Cola, beer, matches, rice, sardines, tomato paste, plastic buckets, washing powder, exercise books, envelopes, pens, etc.[1] are easily accessible to almost every village throughout Africa. Thus, if these articles can be reliably and efficiently distributed on a national basis at acceptable cost, then it should be possible for Ministries of Education, publishers, distributors and booksellers to learn from the companies which distribute these articles and to establish equally reliable and comprehensive systems as a result.

There is some validity in the argument that textbook distribution in Africa could have been much more effective in the past. Textbook distribution is not rocket science and the basic principles, inputs and systems required to operate textbook distribution services effectively are very widely known. In the context of state-organised distribution of free textbooks the key factors are:

- Adequate and timely financing of the distribution process.
- Good current information on school locations, roll numbers and book requirements.

---

1 These are all consumer priority products where daily sales are pretty much guaranteed and are usually highly predictable.

- Effective, trained and experienced management using good (and preferably computerised) management systems.
- Access to adequate and appropriate storage and transport facilities.
- Effective monitoring and supervision of the whole process.
- The willingness and ability to correct errors and omissions.

Coca-Cola versus textbooks – is the comparison valid?

There are many differences between the commercial distribution of Coca-Cola (and similar consumer priority products) and the commercial distribution of textbooks. These differences invalidate the direct comparison of distribution effectiveness and the argument that the successful distribution of one product automatically ensures that the successful distribution of another, radically different, product is possible. Some of these differences are listed below.

- Coca-Cola is a product in daily demand; textbooks are highly seasonal (except for replacements).
- If Coca-Cola supplies are late the market for the product still exists; the late supply of textbooks can significantly reduce sales.
- Consumers of Coca-Cola will purchase very regularly, perhaps more than once a day; consumers of textbooks will purchase only occasionally, perhaps once a year.
- Sales of Coca-Cola are high priority purchases for an established, even addicted, clientele; textbooks are rarely high priority purchases for a majority of the customer base.
- Coca-Cola sales are relatively predictable; textbook sales are characteristically highly unpredictable.[2]
- Because Coca-Cola is a reliable 'sale', retailers are prepared to operate on a firm sale, cash with order basis; commercial textbook distribution can only rarely operate on a firm sale basis. Thus credit is not a serious problem for Coca-Cola but it is a major issue for commercial textbook distributors. This usually leads to serious under-stocking of textbooks, particularly in rural areas. Commercial textbook sales are far less certain and predictable and there are few local traders who can afford to invest in textbook stock to the extent required. For example, a village primary school in a rural area with an enrollment of 400 students might require a starting stock of 2,400 books (6 textbooks per student) at an average unit cost of $3 per book. This would require a local trader to invest in stock to a value of $7,200 less 25% discount = $5,400 in order to fulfil the needs of one average sized village school. The average annual income

---

2 In Kenya, in January 2000, the school textbook selling season was brought to an abrupt halt two months early because of public debate following the publication of a report on the possible introduction of a new curriculum. Although the curriculum reform was two or even three years away, public fear of purchasing redundant textbooks halted sales immediately. Pleas from booksellers and publishers to the Kenyan government to provide a positive statement that would resolve the uncertainty fell on deaf ears and substantial losses resulted.

of such a trader in a rural village might be only $300–400. Obviously, such an investment level is impossible for an under-financed village trader, even without the risk element involved in the purchase of textbook stock on a firm basis. In contrast, the village trader might purchase 144 bottles/cans of Coca-Cola at an average investment of $0,25 per can = $36,00. The trader knows from past experience that all stock will be sold in a week. At a profit of $0,05 per can the trader has recouped the original investment, has made a profit of $7,20, and is ready to re-invest in stock for the next week. This activity will provide a safe and reliable income for the trader of $374,40 per year. This example illustrates graphically the illogicality of the *commercial* comparison between Coca-Cola and school textbook distribution. It also illustrates the critical roles of credit, stock financing capacity and risk in the development of commercial textbook distribution networks. It shows the benefits of small but reliable daily/weekly sales in comparison to a narrow, annual selling season. It shows why textbooks are often not availabile in local bookshops.[3]

- Coca-Cola is never dependent upon unreliable government financing. Primary school textbooks are now mainly dependent upon government/agency financing in most African countries – and it is the unreliability and inadequacy of this funding that underpin many of the distribution problems.[4]
- Coca-Cola is not forced to attempt deliveries to high cost, low return, difficult access locations, whereas textbook supply is expected to reach every part of a country, no matter how remote, difficult to access and costly and often without compensatory price increases to cover additional costs.
- Coca-Cola is not expected to achieve on-time, total national supply; textbook distribution is judged on its ability to achieve on-time, simultaneous, national coverage once a year – often in the middle of the rainy season when many communication links are impassable.
- Coca-Cola is supplied in durable bottles or cans that are not subject to weather damage or deterioration in store; textbooks are made of paper and are thus highly susceptible in use and in store to water (including humidity), fungus, dust, insects, direct sunlight and vermin.
- Coca-Cola distributes perhaps three or four different branded products; a typical primary school might require up to 100 different textbooks and

---

3   The Uganda case study provides an example of this factor in the use of school-based capitation funds allocated for supplementary reader purchase. A high proportion of these very large funds are not used for their designated purpose because basic levels of appropriate books are not available in local bookshops. The lack of availability results from the poor stock financing capacity of the booksellers, their inability to accept the risk of non-sales by buying firm in advance and the refusal of the publishers to supply on credit because of a history of unpaid debts.

4   For example, any distributor who invested in a distribution network to serve the 14 districts of the RNE primary textbook project in Kenya would have suffered badly when the project was prematurely cancelled after one year despite generally very encouraging results.

teacher's guides, thus requiring more complex and sophisticated stock records and picking/packing systems.

- Coca-Cola users are not required to achieve long book life, undertake repairs, practise conservation and protect against loss and damage in order to afford to purchase; all of these are issues which are of considerable importance to textbook distribution, storage, usage and system affordability.
- Coca-Cola distribution staff are well-trained and well-supervised and have reliable operational budgets because Coca Cola is highly profitable; none of these advantages typically applies to the average textbook distributor in Africa.
- Coca-Cola distribution is not subject to swings in national policy; textbook distribution policy is frequently in a state of flux and change (see the Guinea case study).

The problems of state-organised textbook distribution in Africa

In state-organised textbook distribution systems the key tasks are usually restricted to collecting information on needs, ordering and allocating supplies and moving the supplies in good time and acceptable condition to widely dispersed school locations in fulfilment of school requirements. Most African countries have access to reasonably effective and reliable commercial trucking and freighting companies.[5] Thus, the sub-contracting of textbook warehousing and transportation services to commercial freight and storage agencies might have provided more effective delivery results if good and up-to-date information on school locations, pupil numbers and stock needs had been available.[6]

This, of course, is an over-simplification. The selection and contracting of a reputable and effective freighting company to deliver book stock requires well-constructed, publicly transparent and well-run competitive tendering procedures, plus good contracts with detailed and accurate technical schedules and realistic and enforceable penalty clauses to ensure good performance. Contracting out to a specialist freighting company still requires that good information be provided to the contractor, and government (or publishers/booksellers) still requires well-designed monitoring systems to check that the freighting company has performed adequately according to contract prior to final payment. With these caveats there is no reason why school textbooks (or any kinds of books) should not be moved efficiently to their intended destinations at the right time so long as finance is available to pay the bills. A number of the case studies, and particularly Malawi and Ghana, provide

---

5   The Tanzania case study describes some of the problems inherent in achieving good and reliable national coverage using local commercial freighting services.
6   Unfortunately, these three fundamental EMIS requirements are either lacking or seriously out-of-date in many, if not most, of the continent's education systems.

excellent examples of occasional book supply projects that testify to the speed and effectiveness of commercial consolidation, warehousing and transportation services if properly managed and controlled.

Inefficiency

In reality, however, state-organised book distribution systems in Africa have only very rarely contracted out the warehousing, stock consolidation and transportation functions to professional freighting companies. Governments, frequently strongly supported by funding agencies, for many years combined to fund state-owned central, regional and district level warehouses and bookstores plus fleets of lorries and trucks. But it was very rare that any of the state textbook distribution organisations had access to professionally trained and experienced logistics experts and the basic inventory control and stock movement and management systems were usually either inadequate or not well maintained.

The management and staffing of the state run distributors usually comprised teachers transferred from schools or bureaucrats on short-term postings. Distribution as a professional skill was rarely appreciated. Basic information on school roll numbers and needs was often not available, or it was inaccurate or out-of-date. At least two of the Francophone case studies note textbook stock losses of up to 65% per year during warehousing and transportation to schools performed by state run distribution systems. This scale of stock leakage from the system must be symptomatic of very poor system management. It certainly makes it impossible for any country to afford a basic textbook provision system. Quite apart from any other consideration, examples such as these, in countries that are already very poor, represent a criminal waste of scarce resources. It is difficult to see how governments and donors can continue to support systems that operate to these levels of inefficiency.

Under-funding

Under-funding by the state of the annual operational budget for textbook distribution achieved almost legendary status in many countries. Thus the transport fleets were not maintained or replaced (often they were diverted to completely different purposes), warehouse structures, equipment and systems were allowed to run down[7] and staff training and supervision were seriously neglected. In most cases there was little or no management of the total system and the HQ of the state textbook distribution organisation in the capital city often had no idea about what was really happening at regional, district, zonal and school levels. Stock loss and damage (from theft, lack of care, lack of experience, lack of equipment, poor stacking, rainwater damage, termites and vermin, etc.) often reached catastrophic proportions.

---

7   Leaking roofs, lack of racking and pallets and lack of basic warehouse equipment plus poor stock maintenance and poor security often caused high levels of stock damage in the warehouses even before books reached schools. No commercial company could have survived with the level of stock loss and damage that was common in the stores of some state textbook distributors.

Remote schools

Perhaps the most serious problems arose (and still arise) in moving book stocks from district or zonal stores down to individual schools. Districts or zones in most poor countries usually suffer from even more serious budgetary constraints than central and regional stores. Thus, book stocks often get stuck at the district or zonal levels because there is no transport (or budget to hire transport) to move the stock down to individual schools.

Schools close to the district stores find it relatively easy to come to collect stock and frequently take far more than their official allocations (even if these were correctly estimated in the first place). Church schools, which often have access to transport, also tend to get more than their fair share of available stock and there are well-documented cases of vehicles driving from region to district to zone to collect the maximum possible textbook stock from a variety of different stocking locations. Funding agencies and NGOs are also often guilty of using their muscle to get a greater share of the available textbook stocks for the schools that they are supporting.

Schools in rural or remote locations may not even realise for some time that books have arrived in their district. By the time that they find out and eventually visit the District Education Office (DEO) (usually when they come to collect salaries) they discover that much of the key stock has already been taken. They are also faced with additional bills to transport their books over long distances back to their schools. The Tanzania case study describes some teachers from rural schools carrying a few books back to their schools each month when they come in to the DEO to collect their salaries. In these circumstances there is neither equity of supply nor equity of cost. The rural and remote schools usually receive less and pay more.

This is not inevitable. The Instructional Materials Unit (IMU) in Uganda, as part of the USAID-funded Support for Ugandan Primary Education Reform (SUPER) project, managed to organise state run textbook consolidation and distribution down to the level of individual schools quite efficiently from 1994 to 1998, even though many schools did have to pay the costs of collection. The now defunct Malawi Book Service (MBS) in Malawi also had quite a good reputation for distribution efficiency, although not for financial management. State textbook distribution to primary schools also rates quite well in the Botswana case study.

But these are relatively rare islands in an ocean of incompetence. Few of the case studies have anything good to say about state-organised textbook distribution and particularly the process of moving books from districts to schools. It could be claimed that the case study contributors are biased, but most independent surveys have reached broadly the same conclusions.

On the other hand, the Royal Netherlands Embassy (RNE) pilot textbook project in Kenya provided schools with their own purchasing power and encouraged them to select their own private sector bookseller supplier. The schools discovered to their astonishment that local private sector booksellers, competing fiercely for their business, were prepared to deliver books direct to schools without additional charge (in one case over a distance of 160 kilometres of very bad tracks). The booksellers were also prepared to offer discounts off published prices of up to 10% plus, in some cases, premium offers as well.[8]

The Malawi case study also demonstrates that contracted private sector booksellers will deliver free to schools and will compete strenuously for contracts via discounts and high levels of offered service. When all the costs of state and private sector distribution are identified and compared it is probable that private sector distribution generally competes well on cost and would almost certainly score more highly on service. This conclusion is at odds with the accepted truth of the 1960s and 1970s. The introduction of state distribution was commonly justified at the time because it was perceived to be cheaper than private sector distribution. In most cases it was only seen to be cheaper because all of the real costs were not properly identified or accounted for.

Mistakes in supply

One of the most fundamental problems associated with state run distribution systems was (and is) that payment for distribution services has never been dependent upon results in terms of the right quantities and titles of books in schools, supplied at the right time and in good condition. Because state distributors were always paid in advance, rather than on proven successful fulfilment, mistakes in supply were rarely corrected in most state run systems. There was no financial incentive for the state distributor either to distribute correctly in the first place or to correct errors once these had been discovered.[9] Most state financed distribution systems were strongly supply-side oriented and most of the recipient schools had no idea what stock had been allocated to them, so that checking for errors against delivery notes and packing lists often never took place (frequently because there were no delivery notes or packing lists).

David Muita's Kenyan case study describes the mismatch between textbook supplies and school requirements, the accumulation of much-needed textbook stock in district stores rather than in schools and the high operational costs that were characteristics of the Kenya School Equipment Scheme (KSES) before it closed. The Malawi case study describes the lack of good warehousing, the inadequate budgets at every level of the system and the absence of effective control over the totality of the distribution chain. Several of the Francophone case studies (and Guinea and Niger in particular) testify to consistently late

---

8   One bookseller offered a free dictionary with every school order.

9   One of the other side benefits of the RNE textbook pilot project in Kenya was that booksellers corrected errors in supply immediately. Schools had copies of their orders and knew exactly what had to be delivered. If mistakes were made or stock was damaged the suppliers corrected quickly because the schools wouldn't pay until the order had been fulfilled. Suddenly, after years of being ignored, schools discovered that their purchasing power put them back into the driving seat and that they could therefore demand and expect good and efficient service.

supplies and staggering losses through theft and other forms of attrition during normal state run distribution activities.

The simple process of the transportation of known quantities of books to specified locations should never have been a major problem. But state textbook distributors rarely sought to contract out to specialist transport and warehousing companies, except as a last resort, preferring instead the maintenance of inefficient and under-funded state corporations or ministry departments. When contracting out did take place it was often too late, uncontrolled and with insufficient budgets.

Closure of the retail book sector

State control over textbook distribution frequently destroyed or seriously damaged the existing private sector book wholesalers and retailers while not providing a reasonable alternative textbook service to schools. This is perhaps the most tragic aspect of the state domination of textbook distribution in Africa over the past 40 years.

The Ghana case study describes the near destruction of the national book distribution systems operated efficiently by religious bookselling groups until the announcement of the state textbook monopoly. In Malawi, the MBS was supported by heavy, low-cost state investment and government decisions that concentrated all supplies into one state-owned company. As a result, the commercial book trade was reduced to a shadow. When MBS[10] finally collapsed there was nothing left in the private sector to replace it and national book distribution has been a major problem in Malawi ever since. The confinement policy in Tanzania and the operations of the state-owned Tanzania Elimu Supplies (TES) have reduced the effective commercial bookselling trade in 2000 to around 10 creditworthy booksellers to serve a country of 32 million people, and most of the operational booksellers are located in Dar-es-Salaam. The Niger case study characterises the current state distribution system for primary school textbooks as follows:

- poor planning, frequently resulting in late print ordering and stock deliveries
- the diversion of transportation funds to other purposes
- poor security and high rates of loss both in storage and in distribution
- poor storage conditions and security in schools
- no funding for deliveries down to school level
- non payment for distribution services provided
- distribution rated as less important for the donors than production
- the concealment of the real costs of textbook distribution within other government spending, thus making donors and government believe that state distribution was cheap in comparison to commercial distribution services

---

10   MBS at least had a reputation for operational efficiency even if its financial management was widely considered to be unsatisfactory and the major cause of its demise.

The establishment of Uganda School Supplies (USS) in Uganda, plus continued state oriented textbook distribution policies even after its closure, also seriously undermined national private sector book distribution systems. The Uganda book trade was sufficiently damaged that even today it still can't cope with school-based purchasing of supplementary materials except in the capital city, Kampala.

In Kenya, state companies posed extremely serious threats to the very existence of private sector publishing and bookselling. It was only the collapse of KSES in 1984 that provided a lifeline. It is interesting to note that in Kenya and in Ghana the failure of the state distribution companies to perform adequately provided a market loophole, which enabled the commercial book trades to survive. It is, of course, axiomatic that if the state controls the income from the critical textbook market then there is little other market available for the private book trade sector. In Africa, national bookshop networks depend absolutely on the income from textbook sales. If there is no income, because the system is controlled by the state, then there is no national bookshop network. The absence of a national bookshop network reduces the potential for all other kinds of national publishing including local language books, drama, poetry, fiction, trade books of local/national interest, children's books, vocational and technical publishing and even support for literacy and HIV/AIDS programmes.[11]

The destruction of bookshop capacity has always been worse in the rural areas than in the cities and thus has been more damaging to the poor than to the rich. It can be argued that the growth and development of reading societies in many African countries has been seriously hampered by the lack of national retail bookshop networks. It can also be argued that this situation can be laid squarely at the door of the post-independence proliferation of state-owned textbook distribution organisations, usually supported by donor funding.

Varying distribution patterns between Francophone and Anglophone Africa

In both Anglophone and Francophone Africa the book market is overwhelmingly a textbook market and government and funding agency policies toward textbook provision therefore determine the nature and form of book trade development. Despite this common starting point there are a number of significant differences between the experiences and emerging policies of Anglophone and Francophone countries in Africa.

Enrollment and free books

The case studies demonstrate that the Gross Enrollment Ratios (GER) of most Francophone countries are significantly lower than those in many Anglophone

---

11 Religious publishing and bookselling have always survived better than other kinds of publishing in Africa because of the highly developed internal sales networks and the captive markets, which characterise many of the churches. These have carried on largely unaffected by the loss of the state textbook distribution monopolies.

countries and that book markets are therefore generally considerably smaller. In this context it is worth noting that Malawi, Uganda and Botswana have already virtually achieved Universal Primary Education (UPE) and that this is a major target of educational policy in most other Anglophone countries.

Affordability and sustainability are constant factors in policy development all over Africa but the case studies suggest that policy in Francophone countries is moving in a different direction. Many of the countries covered by the case studies appear to have given up on the concept of free and universal primary textbook provision (for example Bénin, Senegal, Côte d'Ivoire, Togo and Cameroon have all moved away from free primary textbook provision to parent-funded provision, normally via sales to parents). Where parental sales systems develop they are often (but not always) via private sector bookshops. In Senegal the failure of parent purchasing to achieve equity of provision has led to an interest in textbook loan and rental schemes. Textbook loans are also a feature of policy in Togo. In Guinea, Niger, Burkina Faso, Mali and Chad, agency funding continues to support at least partial free textbook provision at primary level.

School versus student ownership of books

In Anglophone countries there is a strong preference for good quality paper and binding, etc. in order to achieve long book life and maximum cost amortisation. This in turn is expected to result in the lowest recurrent annual expenditure on textbook provision. To achieve this, school ownership of textbooks (as opposed to student ownership of textbooks) is considered crucial. Agency/government financial support is therefore increasingly provided to schools in the form of per capita purchasing power budgets (for example Botswana, Uganda, Kenya).

By contrast, in those Francophone countries where free book provision to primary schools has been abandoned, the tendency is towards parental purchase and student ownership rather than school purchase and school ownership. Similarly, agency support to most Francophone countries tends to be in the form either of free 'safety net' supplies or to publisher (producer) or household (consumer) subsidies. Producer subsidies create supply side distribution systems and tend to distort the market and hinder competition and choice. Household subsidies prevent school ownership and loan scheme development by focusing on student-based ownership and the development of second hand sales.[12]

Decision-making

It is also noticeable that book policies in Anglophone countries increasingly emphasise competition and choice with the school as the decision-maker in the selection of course materials. In Francophone countries primary textbooks are still dominantly monopolistic with the ministries of Education, rather than the school, being the decision-maker.

---

12   It is very noticeable that none of the case studies has referred to second-hand textbook markets as significant factors in national book (or even textbook) distribution.

The case studies seem to suggest that Francophone book development policies are more interventionist with more emphasis on the development of state publishing and the increased use of local printing and production facilities. Some of the distribution policies (for example in Togo and Cameroon) positively support the development of NGO and Parents and Teacher Association distribution systems at the expense of private sector distribution. In Anglophone countries, the emphasis is increasingly on market-oriented systems and competitive trading environments in which the roles of government and donors are perceived to be those of the rule makers and referees. In this model the government is responsible for curriculum, minimum book specifications, the evaluation and approval of competing books and the supervision and monitoring of the total system. Private sector booksellers and publishers, usually via their trade associations, become partners in the operation of the system rather than adversaries. State distribution still exists, to some extent at least in Botswana, Malawi, Tanzania and Ghana but the policy trend in most cases is to shift toward private sector distribution as soon as possible. In this environment, private sector distribution is not perceived to be uncontrolled and unmonitored but as free and competitive within rules acceptable to all parties.

Impact on retailers

In Francophone Africa the state run textbook distributors seem to have had less impact on the demise of national bookselling networks. With the exception of Côte d'Ivoire and Senegal, most Francophone countries did not have the well-developed church and private sector bookshop networks, which characterised many Anglophone African countries after independence. Also, the state was probably less dominant because of the maintenance of a strong tradition of parental purchase of textbooks, which always permitted some book trade access to the core textbook market. The operation of the subsidised *Communauté Francaise d'Afrique* (CFA) maintained imported book prices at artificially low levels and thus supported far higher levels of textbook importation in French speaking countries.

Local publishing

The Francophone case studies also seem to underline the experience of Ghana and Kenya that poor performing state systems provided market opportunities, which the private sector was able to exploit to survive, even if not to prosper. It is also probably true that there was far less local publishing in Francophone Africa, because the tradition of publishing for Africa from the colonial base continued far longer in Francophone countries than in Anglophone countries. In contrast, the opening of many local companies owned by or affiliated to British publishers onwards and the development of wholly locally owned publishing houses, reflect the rapid development of local publishing in Anglophone Africa from the 1950s. The local titles produced by these locally based publishing houses reflected production standards that were more affordable to the economic realities of the countries concerned. They also frequently contained subject matter of greater interest to the local reader. This local publishing output was widely affordable and saleable in the economies of the period and it could easily have supported a rapid expansion in local reading if national bookshop networks had not been simultaneously destroyed or depressed by state interventions.

It is interesting that the case study on Francophone West African countries (see page 177) concludes that there is an urgent need in Francophone countries to reduce the current high production values (case bound, four colours) of imported textbooks to make them more affordable and accessible to local parents.

Development partner involvement

It is interesting to note that most of the Anglophone case studies complain about too much funding agency interference in textbook distribution. In the Francophone countries the complaint is that funding agencies are too little concerned with investing in book distribution systems and are much more interested in front-end investments in book development, publishing and production, often via state facilities.

The broad differences outlined above need to be taken into account in the analysis of key issues and the development of new strategies for book distribution in Africa.

Developing improved book distribution systems

Given the difficulties and contrasting realities described above, textbook supply in many African countries represents a difficult but not absolutely intractable problem. The case studies demonstrate that there have been many interesting and hopeful developments in the past five to ten years and that there are now clear signs that the right lessons are being learned by many governments and funding agencies. Current policies and approaches in many countries now seem to be moving slowly in the right direction.

Certainly, there is no universal panacea or quick fix for the creation of effective and sustainable book distribution systems, which will provide timely, accurate, and cost-effective teaching and learning materials to schools in Africa. Each country represents a different set of educational, political, social, economic and infrastructural factors, which in turn require detailed and specialist analysis prior to decision-making. The development of good systems may well take time and may need well-planned transitional policies, particularly where commercial wholesaling and retailing networks have to be re-created.

The following key issues have to be taken into account in the development of good textbook distribution systems and are each dealt with in detail below:
- Predictable systems and regular funding.
- Financing policy.
- Competition and selection mechanisms.

- Publishing issues and their impact on distribution.
- Distribution systems.
- Reconstructing national private bookselling capacity.
- The regional book trade and other book markets.

The decision-tree for policy-makers in Chapter 4 provides a summary of the key policy decisions required in the development of an effective textbook distribution system.

Predictable systems and reliable funding

These two factors are absolute requirements for the development of reliable and improved distribution systems. It is obvious that rapid changes in national financing, selection, publishing, and distribution policy for teaching and learning materials are not conducive to the development of stable distribution systems that are well adjusted to market circumstances. Key policies must be well thought out and soundly based on good analysis, and must then be maintained for a sufficient period of time to allow all participants to become experienced in their operation.

The Guinea case study, with constant and frequent changes in textbook distribution policy, is a classic example of the pitfalls of unpredictability. Similarly, systems that are financed irregularly, or via very large government/ agency funded procurements that only take place infrequently, do not allow for the development or maintenance of good distribution systems.

Unfortunately, many funding agencies appear to have preferred very large book procurements at irregular intervals rather than the steady, annual release of funding which is essential to the development of stable and effective systems of supply. Big bang, front-end, one-off book procurements may fit internal agency disbursement requirements but they rarely help to develop and maintain local educational publishing and distribution systems.

The development of local publishing and distribution requires regular and predictable funding. Large, one-off, irregular, procurement financing, however organised, usually tends to favour multinational over local publishers and distributors because:

- The turnover possibilities of multinational publishers are well spread over a number of different national markets.
- Multinational publishers gain experience of bidding through operating in many markets.
- If the bid is big, the much larger financial resources of the multinational publishers tend to dominate the outcomes.

The local publisher is restricted to the national market and is not well served by 'feast or famine' funding policies. Big bids often effectively sideline local publishers and booksellers who have to operate in the context of high interest rate local financial markets.[13] Book markets can be small and still operate

---

13   Interest rates of 25 to 60% are not uncommon. Publishers, with no collateral, would in any case find it difficult to raise investment finance from local banks for a large competitive bid. Most local bidders would probably fail to qualify for a bid on their financial capacity alone.

efficiently. But if they are irregular and unpredictable it is very unlikely that good local distribution (or publishing) systems can be maintained or that adequate private sector investment in distribution will take place.

The impact of financing policy on distribution systems

This is one of the most crucial issues underpinning the type and performance of textbook distribution systems. The type and efficiency of the financing system, the sources of financing, the point at which financing is applied and its regularity and reliability all determine the type of distribution mechanism which is possible and its ultimate effectiveness.

Textbooks are usually financed from one or more of the following sources: government, funding agencies, parents and/or sponsorship.

Agency funding is normally considered to be a temporary variant of government funding rather than a genuine alternative source of funding because it is usually applied via government. Sponsorship as a significant source of textbook funding is rare in Africa but in other parts of the world it is developing as a source of funding, particularly for very poor students, (for example the Former Soviet Union). It should at least be considered in the future as a possible source of textbook financing in Africa. Various types of combination funding are common using some or all of the above financing sources. For example:

- Government funding for primary; parental funding for secondary.
- Government funding for textbooks; parental or sponsorship funding for libraries.
- Government funding for rural areas; parental funding for urban areas.
- Government funding for core subject textbooks; parental funding for other textbooks.
- Government funding for 'safety net' supplies; parental funding for the rest.
- Parents purchase at subsidised prices; producer subsidies provided by government.
- Parents purchase but government subsidies target the poorest students.
- Initial supplies funded by Government; replacement and maintenance funded by parents.
- Government funding for the poorest; parent funding for the richest; mixed system for the majority, etc.

Government funding can be often notional rather than real and severe under-supply is common in some government-funded situations. Thus, in Malawi, Ghana, Tanzania, Uganda and the Sahelian countries, the current free primary textbook provision policies are only sustainable with substantial and on-going donor support. When agency funding is not available, free textbook supplies are severely constrained and textbook distribution becomes ineffective simply because there are insufficient textbooks to service the system requirements. The announcement of 'free textbook policies' is often the precursor to inadequate government funding and low levels of book supply unless other, non-governmental financial support is well tied-in. In these circumstances parents quickly come to realise that 'free' textbooks can often mean 'few' or even 'no' textbooks.

The key issue about the 'source of financing' policy decision is that it should produce the kind of reliable and predictable long-term financing profile that has been referred to above. Adequate and reliable financing is not only the foundation for distribution effectiveness but also the basis of adequate provision of teaching and learning materials into the education system.

Affordability and cost analysis

Book provision systems *must* be affordable to be sustainable and acceptable levels of affordability to either government or parents have to be established for each market. This may well involve investigating a full range of cost reduction possibilities (for example, fewer required titles,[14] extended book life, reduced book to pupil ratios, the use of textbook rental systems, short loan library-based lending, reduced use of colour, and sensible decisions on extents and formats, etc.). Affordability and cost analysis are essential components of a financially sustainable system and thus they underpin all effective distribution systems.

If the textbook provision requirement, however financed, is basically unaffordable then there will be inadequate supplies of books, inadequate funding of the distribution system and inadequate provision in schools. This is a very fundamental issue but it is often overlooked, particularly when new primary curricula specify textbook requirements of ten or more subject textbooks per grade level plus teacher's guides, teaching aids, etc.

All new curricula should be required to specify the minimum teaching and learning materials required to deliver the curriculum effectively. These should then be costed and analysed for affordability. For example, the Uganda case study refers to the proposed new curriculum structure and government and donor concerns about its expensive minimum textbook requirements. In this context, funding agency/government partnerships in funding textbook provision need to be very realistic. Short term agency support can encourage short term textbook financing policies, particularly immediately prior to elections, which in turn may have to be reversed when continued donor support ceases to be available.

There are signs of this kind of problem emerging in Kenya where development partner support for primary textbooks in a number of districts was recently withdrawn. In Ghana, the planned introduction of a new primary curriculum, a new generation of textbooks and a new competitive primary textbook provision system is currently without committed donor support and is thus at risk. In Malawi in 1995, it was the prospect of the termination of development partner funding for textbooks that led to a government decision to license state developed

---

14 Reduced textbook requirements are essentially a curriculum issue.

textbooks to private sector publishers for commercial sale to parents. In 1996 when a new funder offered to fund textbook supplies the licensing policy immediately went into reverse at considerable cost to the publishers (and book distributors) involved. Agency funds are widely considered to be temporary, stopgap, financing mechanisms that are limited in time, even if there is a commitment to support teaching and learning materials for ten to fifteen years into the future. Often, they may provide a breathing space in which to create more sustainable and realistic systems.[15]

Some agencies and NGOs apply pressure on governments for the introduction of new primary school subjects, which fit the wider developmental policies of the funding agencies concerned. Funding in these cases is typically provided for the origination and development of course materials for new curriculum subjects, but not for their production or on-going sustainable provision, which then becomes a recurrent burden on government. The primary curriculum grows, as do the cost implications of textbook provision.

Government funding is often unreliable and is subject to wider economic factors and to perceived, and often changing, government priorities. In an ideal world all textbook provision to schools should be free at both elementary and secondary level, but, in reality, alternative sources of textbook financing always have to be considered in the search for reliability.

Producer versus consumer financing

Producer financing (funding publishers or printers to manufacture *or* supplies units to procure and/or state distributors to distribute) often, but not inevitably, creates supply-oriented distribution systems and Ministry-based decision-making on the books to be used in, and supplied to, schools. These, in turn, frequently result in inaccurate supplies, which do not coincide with school needs. Producer financed systems can also undermine school management and decision-making capacity. Producer financing often acts against competitive publishing and school-based book selection. In producer funded textbook systems the procured or manufactured books are typically delivered free to schools.

Consumer funding occurs when textbook financing is provided in the form of purchasing power (rather than books) to the end-user, which in the case of textbooks, is usually, and most effectively, the schools. Some of the Francophone countries are interested in the concept of household subsidies, but accurate targeting and reliable fund delivery to the households are serious problems. The main types of consumer financing that can be provided by government/donors to schools are:

- The provision of cash textbook budgets to schools (for example, Kenya).
- The provision of textbook budgets to schools via vouchers or local purchase orders (LPOs) for example, Kenya and perhaps Uganda.

---

15   There are countries in the case study (for example, Malawi, Uganda, Tanzania, Ghana) where donor support for textbook financing has been forthcoming for many years.

- School-based purchasing power using order forms and centralised procurement and delivery (for example, Uganda and the World Bank-funded Secondary Education Project in Malawi).

It should be noted that there are very few examples of consumer based funding in the Francophone case studies.

Cash is probably the easiest and cheapest method to administer but has the greatest problems with accountability. Order forms are the most administratively complex to administer but are relatively accountable. LPOs often suffer from difficult operational problems (for example, long delays in achieving reimbursement from cash strapped and bureaucratic government offices).

Consumer financing can also be provided to schools by parental contributions. This normally occurs when parents pay textbook rental fees that are held in schools (rather than remitted centrally) and used to purchase the school's teaching and learning materials requirements. Lesotho and Gambia (which are not case studies in this book) both operate on the basis of parentally funded primary textbook fees, which are used to create centrally administered textbook 'revolving funds'. In Lesotho, an attempt has been made to give schools ordering responsibility, but not against a known annual budget. In Ghana, small textbook fees are collected but these are remitted centrally and are not available for schools to spend.

Senegal and Togo have both attempted to establish sustainable fee based, textbook loan systems, but the contributions from parents were set at unrealistically low levels and the funds have not proved to be sustainable. Ghana is a part parental contribution system but it is *not* consumer financing in the sense that schools have control over the use of the funds that they receive. Malawi has a parentally funded textbook rental contribution at secondary level, supported by government/development partner matching funds. The funds are maintained in the schools and joint committees of teachers, students and the community decide on the use of these funds for textbook and school library purchases and remain accountable for how the money is spent.

The selected source of textbook financing is frequently associated with particular forms of supply. Thus government financed textbook provision has, in the past, often been associated either with monopolistic state publishing and distribution (Malawi and Tanzania), or monopolistic state procurement from the private sector and state distribution (Ghana and Botswana). In either scenario, the funding has been applied to the 'producer' end and supply-oriented distribution systems tended to be the result.

In the primary sectors in Tanzania, Ghana, Botswana and Malawi government/donor financing systems applied to producers have all resulted in supply-side distribution systems, which in turn have demonstrated a number of built-in disadvantages. But this situation is not inevitable. Uganda and Kenya have both experimented very successfully with government/development partner textbook financing at the primary level that has been applied to the consumers (schools) via the provision of school-based purchasing power. This has resulted in demand-led ordering and distribution systems combined with centralised procurement.

Similarly, in Malawi's secondary schools a new system of parental financing via annual textbook fees has been introduced recently. The fees are maintained within each school and create school-based purchasing power, which is then supplemented by government/development partner matching funds. This is a very interesting example of combination financing for school textbooks, which still enables financial and selection control to be maintained at the level of each individual school.

The Kenyan (primary) and Malawi (secondary) approaches are being used to create demand based ordering systems, which will match the use of available budgets accurately to the fulfilment of school needs. In Kenya and Malawi the new systems are being used also to re-involve the commercial book trade in school textbook distribution and thus to support the development and maintenance of national systems of private sector supply. In Côte d'Ivoire, parental financing is used to support demand-based provision systems via private sector booksellers.

Textbook financing based on parental contributions typically assumes either that parents purchase textbooks from the commercial book trade or that parents make contributions via the payment of annual textbook fees. Parental purchase via local booksellers automatically creates demand-led distribution systems. Parental rental fees can create demand led distribution systems if the fees are maintained in schools (as in Malawi secondary schools) and are used to purchase supplies from local booksellers.

In Ghana, parental rental fees are very small in comparison to the real cost of books and this situation is echoed in Senegal and Togo. The rental fees in Ghana are collected by schools but are remitted to a central point and are used to offset the costs of procurement. Thus, they do not support demand-led distribution and the involvement of local booksellers. Perhaps more significantly, many schools and parents do not feel that they are in control of funds that are remitted away from the school and are thus less motivated to pay because they cannot see the link between the payment of textbook fees and the benefit to their own children. Fee payments that are maintained within the schools and are thus under the supervision and control of both school and parents are much more likely to be supported by the community simply because they can see the benefit to their own children.

One of the recurrent problems with rental fee systems of textbook financing is that governments often resist increasing parental textbook fees in line with inflation for political reasons. The common result is that fee-based purchasing power rapidly becomes negligible and worthless (for example, secondary textbook fees in Malawi had not been increased since 1976 and in 1999 were worth only two and a half cents per student per year). This level of fee made it impossible for Malawian secondary schools to afford any kind of textbook purchase for many years. A majority of parents would willingly have paid more to ensure better levels of provision but there was constant resistance from government over a period of almost 25 years. In 2000 the secondary textbook fee levels were increased to US$4 per student per year and the latest reports indicate a very high level of parental support. If parental textbook fees are to be effective, they must be maintained at realistic levels relative to what they are expected to provide. Thus, if the curriculum requirement increases, the rental fees must increase in parallel. If the local currency is devalued, then fees must be increased to cope with local currency price increases.

The point at which funding for textbooks is applied – either centrally to producers or devolved via individual schools – once again has a critical impact on the kind of distribution system that will emerge and this is the second crucial policy issue which has an impact on textbook distribution systems. Closely associated with this issue, but only applicable when consumer funding is the favoured option, is the type of consumer funding system that is used.

Cash or voucher budgets to individual schools will strongly encourage the participation of local booksellers. In Kenya, with a strong local book-retailing sector, the selection of these types of consumer funding was easily possible. In Tanzania, where the local textbook retailing sector is very weak after years of the 'confinement policy' and state supply, the use of cash budgets or vouchers is not an option that has been considered.

Order form systems with district level order consolidation, procurement and delivery, theoretically provide schools with management control over their selection decisions but do not encourage local bookselling. They do, however, strongly support local publishing development because the publishers receive annual, bulk orders paid centrally by government or donors and without the requirement to distribute or establish comprehensive distribution systems. Countries where local textbook retailing is not well established on a national basis, or where publisher/bookseller credit is a difficult issue, would tend to find order form systems more suited to their needs. But order form systems and central procurement and distribution do little to help local bookselling development. The authors of the Francophone case studies argue that private sector publishers (and specifically the multinational publishers) have made no investments in local book distribution systems. But this is only possible if three basic conditions exist. These are:

- There is an available market that is large enough to encourage and support a significant investment in distribution.
- The market is reliable and predictable enough to warrant a significant investment.
- The textbook provision policies actively require publisher funded distribution systems.

Where these conditions exist, as in Côte d'Ivoire, private sector investment in distribution systems has taken place and has been substantial. Where the conditions don't exist, as in Guinea, there has been very little private sector investment in book distribution systems.

There is no reason why order form systems and cash/voucher systems shouldn't exist in parallel. Districts with good booksellers could operate cash/voucher systems, but districts without access to good booksellers could operate on an order form basis. It is likely that emerging distribution policy in Kenya will move in this direction. It is possible to have centralised funding and procurement associated with de-centralised control over decision-making, but only when a conscious decision has been taken to implement such a policy. The Ugandan case study clearly demonstrates that such a system can operate successfully for primary schools. In this context, recent policy decisions in Uganda described in the case study are interesting. From 1994 up to 1998 the centralised procurement of textbooks was consolidated and delivered by the Ministry of Education under the supervision of the Instructional Materials Unit. In 1999, Ministry-organised consolidation and delivery was replaced by a competitive bid to the private sector book trade. This is another symptom of the change in approach to book distribution systems that is now becoming apparent in many African countries.

Competition, choice and selection

A variety of textbook selection possibilities exist and the choice of textbooks can be offered in different ways and made at different levels in the system. The kinds of systems that are used for selecting and choosing teaching and learning materials have a profound impact on the type of distribution systems that develop and the way in which they are required to operate. The following are the basic types of choice available:

Free and unrestricted choice

Any school can choose any course book without constraint. There is no Ministry approval or approved list. Such systems usually apply only in highly developed textbook publishing countries where teacher sophistication in exercising choice without supervision or guidance via an approved book list is well established. This is not a system that is likely to have much attraction in many African countries in the foreseeable future.

Limited choice

The Ministry creates an evaluation and approval system, which results in an approved textbook list from which individual schools can choose. This kind of system provides inexperienced and untrained teachers with essential support because they know that every book on the approved list conforms to the curriculum requirements and is suitable for use in their schools. It also provides Ministries with control over the quality of textbooks to be used in schools.

Uganda and Kenya currently have limited choice systems and Ghana is in the process of developing such a system for its new primary curriculum textbooks. Malawi is actively considering such a policy for primary schools but already has a sophisticated evaluation and approval system and an annual

21

approved textbook list for secondary schools. Tanzania has a limited choice in theory but to date there are only two subject/grade textbooks where alternative choices are available. Botswana operates without a choice of textbooks but this is perhaps inevitable bearing in mind the very small size of the school population.

There are still problems with the actual mechanics of evaluation, selection and approval in some of the case study countries. Uganda has a threshold system of evaluation and approval. This means that any title that achieves the minimum required standards will be approved for use in schools. This probably has resulted in too many titles being approved. Some teachers are overwhelmed by choice and print runs have been reduced and unit costs increased. The Botswana case study indicates that there are problems with the transparency of the selection process. Ghana has yet to finalise its evaluation and approval system, etc.

Monopolistic choice

The key characteristics of this approach are periodic selection by the Ministry on the basis of submissions by publishers. One course will be selected as the monopoly course for a fixed period after which reselection applies. Monopolistic choice is often suitable for countries with very small school enrollments where competition could fractionalise the market size, reduce print runs and increase unit costs (for example, Botswana and Lesotho).

No choice

Usually associated with monopolistic state publishing or single title selection systems. Many of the Francophone case study countries operate 'no choice' systems.

The possibilities of choice are affected mainly by the following factors:

- Roll numbers and print runs: large market size and good print runs enable increased choice. Similarly, small markets with low print runs inhibit choice because of the lack of economies of scale.
- Multiple languages of instruction can reduce print runs, increase origination costs and reduce economies of scale, thus affecting the effective level of choice.
- Full-colour books require larger print runs to achieve economies of scale and can thus also reduce the effective level of choice.
- Long book life and low loss and damage rates: both of these factors can reduce print runs by significantly reducing and delaying replacement. Both can thus limit the level of choice. It should be noted that very long book life reduces potential annual sales volume and thus has a potential impact on the viability and attractiveness of commercial book selling. Similarly, increased costs through reduced economies of scale also have an impact on prices and thus sales potential and thus the viability of commercial bookselling.

The general advantages of competition, choice and school-based selection of titles can be summarised as follows:

- Choice is the basis of competition.
- Competition tends to improve quality and prevents publishing inertia (many state publishing systems with no competition tended to delay new editions for very long periods).
- Good marketing in support of competition, choice and school-based selection can provide better information to teachers on books, methodology and content at no cost to the Ministry of Education.
- Competition improves services to schools because schools will often decide which title to use or which bookseller to contract on the basis of the quality of service that they have received. The Kenya case study notes the improvements in services to schools caused by shifting from supply via KSES to supply via local booksellers.
- Competition can maintain pressure on prices.
- Choice can act to change examination systems because the memorisation and repetition of specific passages from a single monopoly textbook can no longer be used as the basis of an examination if more than one title is approved for use in schools. Competition tends to shift examination requirements away from the rote recall of content towards the demonstration of skills, concepts and understanding.
- Choice empowers schools and encourages decision-making.

There are some advantages also in monopolistic single copy supply:

- It maximises print runs and economies of scale.
- It reduces waste in the supply system (for example, the risks of overprinting but underselling are greatly reduced).
- It reduces supply and stock risk and it reduces the complexity of supply.

There are some aspects of choice that will have an impact on distribution systems. Thus school-based choice makes publishers and distributors work harder. It also requires more investment in local staff and facilities to handle sales, promotion, warehousing, distribution, accounts and credit to fulfil the requirements of choice. Local publishing and distribution companies are often disadvantaged in school-based choice because they may lack finance to support the considerably increased servicing requirements demanded by this kind of system. While this is hard on publishers' costs and overheads, it is good for local employment. However, special conditions may need to be created to counter this problem so that small local publishers and distributors are not disadvantaged. Thus, nationally organised book fairs, to which local schools are invited and national approved book lists enable small local suppliers to meet their market with the minimum of investment in time and money.

In Malawi, the move to school-based title choice at the secondary level has led to significant increases in locally employed staff to service the sales and marketing requirements. School-based choice also tends to be more reliable in satisfying school needs. Centralised book selection and supply decisions can lead to inaccurate or inappropriate supply, which does not fulfil school needs. Approved textbook lists may also have an impact on distribution. Approved lists will provide guidance on stocking for booksellers and distributors but regular updating of the lists encourages new publishing. This can increase stock risks for distributors. A minimum period of title approval (five years is common) encourages reasonable stock holding by distributors and retailers because it reduces risk. Predictable curriculum revision and review cycles are essential to protect distributors from stock losses caused by sudden changes in the approved list.

Publishing issues and their impact on distribution

The key issue is probably state publishing versus private sector, commercial publishing. State publishing usually implies some kind of monopoly or market distortion, which acts against free choice. State publishing was historically linked in Africa with state distribution systems and often with state printing facilities. But in the past decade all of this has begun to change. The Tanzanian case study demonstrates that since 1991, the Tanzania Institute of Education has lost its manuscript development monopoly, Tanzania Publishing House, East Africa Publishing House and Dar-es-Salaam University Press have lost their publishing monopolies and the state run distribution company, Tanzania Elimy Supplies, has been de-monopolised and is no longer the source of supply to schools. Private sector publishers now have access to the primary textbook market and state-owned printing houses no longer have a monopoly of production.

Similar radical shifts away from state centralism towards private sector, market economy operations are now beginning to emerge all over Africa. In Kenya, the favoured positions of the parastatal publishing houses, Jomo Kenyatta Foundation and the Kenya Literature Bureau have been removed and these organisations now have to compete on equal terms with private sector publishers for approved textbook status and for sales. In Côte d'Ivoire the state equity in *Nouvelles Editions Ivoirennes* is steadily decreasing and will soon be completely divested.

Perhaps the most visible sign of this change is the publication in the past few years of a series of national textbook provision policies. These policy documents renounce state involvement in publishing, printing and distribution and require the fullest possible involvement of the private sector in every aspect of the provision system – including distribution and supply. New policy documents have already appeared in Uganda, Kenya, Tanzania and Malawi and are in process in Ghana and Botswana. Thus all six of the Anglophone case study countries have new, market-oriented, textbook provision policies, although not all require private sector involvement in distribution.

Uganda has the renaissance of a national bookselling infrastructure as a policy objective but has not yet instituted specific policies that involve local private sector bookselling in the textbook distribution chain, although these are probably imminent. Tanzania's policy development has reached a similar stage. Malawi and Kenya both have policy documents that require private sector involvement in schoolbook supply and both countries have policies that will force change in this direction. Botswana excludes private sector distributors from primary supply but includes them at the secondary level. Only Ghana, of the six Anglophone case study countries, is still clinging to state textbook distribution policies.

In the Francophone case study countries there are no published national textbook provision policies as such but the authors of the case studies strongly support the development of national policy documents.

However, the case studies also demonstrate that a strong, competitive, commercial publishing sector does not always support commercial distribution. Sometimes the publishers sell direct to governments or states (for example, Uganda, Botswana, Ghana and perhaps Tanzania[16]) or supply direct to schools. The case studies reveal that government and donor policies have tended to concentrate on the involvement of commercial publishing in textbook supply systems, but that distribution and printing involvement tends to be a rarity rather than a norm. Under these circumstances it is likely that some form of state textbook distribution will continue for much longer than state textbook publishing.

It should also be noted that there is no reason why state-owned publishers cannot compete on equal terms with commercial publishers so long as there is a 'level playing field' with no favours or hidden subsidies. In Kenya within the past four years, the JKF and the KLB have lost their status as the only publishers of core textbooks. Both of these state publishers now compete on equal terms with commercial publishers and supply through exactly the same private sector bookselling outlets.

State publishing will, perhaps, continue to have a role in a limited number of market situations such as:

- Markets that have no existing commercial publishing sector.
- Markets that are unattractive for foreign investment (because the market is too small or unstable or financially constrained, or requires unknown linguistic requirements).
- Markets that have little possibility of rapid local or regional private sector development (markets with a very small effective population base, little or no local investment capacity, no local publishing skills, or high political risks).
- Markets with a strong anti-commercial sector political philosophy (these are noticeably fewer in number than even five years ago).

The Anglophone case studies also demonstrate that the heat appears to have gone out of the (sometimes difficult) issue of international/multinational versus

---

16 Tanzanian primary textbook procurement policy had not been finalised at the time of going to press, but it seems likely that in 2001, districts will buy direct from publishers and schools will collect from the districts. There is thus unlikely to be a role for booksellers or book distributors.

regional versus national publishing. At primary level it now appears to be widely accepted that all types of publishers are required to fulfil market requirements and that all can work together more or less easily via their national trade associations. The Malawi case study provides an interesting list of current educational publishing houses, annotated to show a wide range of different types of ownership and operations. The need to source textbooks from international or regional locations (this is usually typical of secondary and tertiary textbook supply and is probably more common in southern and central Africa than in West Africa) will usually require significant stock financing and the ability to handle foreign exchange and import regulations. The weaker commercial book trade networks may find this too onerous and local publishers' stockholding warehouses may be required to fill in the missing parts of the infrastructure. Publishers who don't trust local booksellers will often create direct school supply operations thus keeping local booksellers out of the picture completely.

The Francophone case studies suggest that the issue of international/ regional/national publishing involvement in textbook provision is much more alive and emotional than in Anglophone Africa.

Supply and demand-led distribution systems

In the case studies, supply-led, primary level, distribution systems now operate only in Malawi and Ghana and in most of the Sahelian countries. The coastal states of Francophone West Africa, plus Uganda, Kenya and Botswana operate demand-led systems but only Kenya is actively considering cash or voucher based purchasing power budgets and supply via the local book trade.

Supply-led systems are generally associated with state monopolistic distribution systems. They are characterised by the Ministry of Education (or the state distribution organisation) deciding what supplies schools should have. These decisions are typically based on gross percentage allocations of existing stock based on frequently out-of-date and inaccurate data. As a result:

- Supplies may not be aligned with school needs.
- Schools may have difficulties in getting supply errors corrected.
- Service levels may be lacking (because payment does not depend upon quality and speed of service).
- The long lead times between statistics collection and delivery often exacerbates supply inaccuracies.

In demand-led distribution systems, schools order their requirements against a school-based purchasing power budget. The delivery mechanisms can be very diverse and can include:

- State/MoE/District distribution organisation (for example, Uganda, Ghana, Tanzania).
- Wholesale and retail bookseller chains (for example, Botswana secondary, Kenya, Côte d'Ivoire, etc).
- Direct from publisher(s).

- Via specialist consolidators/truckers (for example, Supplementary Reading Materials in Ghana; Danida Community Day Secondary Schools supply in Malawi and World Bank Conventional Secondary Schools supply in Malawi).

Supply tends to be faster and more accurate and mistakes can be corrected more quickly when schools can resist payment until supplies are correctly completed. Demand-led systems where schools can control payment almost universally work better than state-run, supply-led systems. Service tends to improve when distributors have to compete for school contracts.

Reconstructing national private sector bookselling capacity

The case studies demonstrate very clearly the devastating impact of state centralism on private sector book wholesaling and retailing. Only three of the case study countries (Kenya, Botswana and Côte d'Ivoire) still have national private sector book supply networks capable of undertaking national textbook supply. Private sector bookselling only survived in Kenya because of the large market size, continued access to the secondary school market and the introduction of the cost sharing policy in 1988. This required parents to contribute to the costs of textbooks[17] and thus enabled them to choose the books that they wanted rather than the books prescribed by the state. In Botswana, until the late 1980s, the efficient and capable local bookseller, Botswana Book Centre (BBC), was responsible for all primary textbook distribution. This changed when another commercial company, International Professional Managers (IPM), was awarded the primary textbook tender out of the blue. According to the case study, IPM turned out to be both dishonest and incompetent. Schools did not get their books, the government lost large sums of money and supplying publishers had to write off huge debts. Instead of returning the contract to BBC at the end of this disastrous experiment, the government instead established a unit within the Ministry of Local Government to undertake textbook supply to primary schools. This department has worked well, but no better than BBC, and a government department replaced a well-functioning private sector system.

At independence, all six Anglophone countries had some form of national book distribution capacity – most often rooted in a number of different and competing religious bookselling chains. Within a few years of independence the national capacity in Kenya, Uganda, Tanzania, Malawi and Ghana had been destroyed, seriously reduced or diverted into other, less profitable, activities as a direct result of the tidal wave of state centralism that swept over textbook supply in all five countries. Only in Malawi did the state-owned distributor operate relatively efficiently, although expensively. The case studies comment very unfavourably on the performance of state-run textbook distribution in Niger, Guinea, Ghana, Uganda, Kenya and Tanzania, etc.

In Ghana, Tanzania, Malawi and even in Kenya, a number of funding agencies strongly supported inefficient state publishing, printing and distribution

---

17   Significantly, if parents were paying they wanted control over selection and thus started to reject many of the state approved core texts in favour of commercially published books.

for many years and must take their share of the blame for the collapse of previously competitive systems and their replacement by generally inefficient and usually more expensive systems.[18] In recent years, as the aid pendulum has swung back in favour of the advantages of competitive, private sector involvement, donors and governments have found it much easier to support local publishers than local booksellers.

In 2000, the real problem lies in the development and effective implementation of a strategy that will re-create, often almost from scratch, the national distribution capacity that previously existed. Unfortunately, it is much easier to destroy than to rebuild. Of the case study countries, Botswana receives no current external aid for book supply or development but has a national working party comprising government and the private sector that is moving toward more private sector involvement in school textbook distribution. In Malawi and in Kenya there are positive donor policies to re-create private sector distribution chains. In Uganda there is a clear objective and a clear strategy, but it has been decided that it is still too early to move toward de-centralised distribution via local booksellers except on an experimental pilot basis. Nevertheless, if the pilot is successful there is a clear target for de-centralised systems that could require the full involvement of local booksellers by 2003. In Tanzania there is a policy objective to involve local booksellers in textbook distribution, but local bookselling is very weak throughout most of the country and there seems to be no clear strategy to achieve the policy objective. In Ghana there is, perhaps at best, a vaguely expressed intention to involve booksellers – but no clear strategy as yet. In Togo and Cameroon, teachers' mutual societies have been encouraged to enter textbook distribution at the expense of private sector development. In Guinea, three different donors appear to have three different policy approaches.[19] In the Sahelian countries state distribution still appears to dominate government and donor thinking. In some of the coastal Francophone countries, local booksellers are seen as central to the textbook distribution process but in these countries parental purchase is the favoured method of textbook supply.

Throughout the case studies there are clear indications of the common problems facing the re-emerging private book distribution sector. The following is a summary of the most important issues that recur throughout most of the case study countries, although in Kenya, Botswana and Côte d'Ivoire the problems are significantly less acute and pervasive.

- Lack of bookseller finance to purchase required stock.
- Lack of bookseller finance to cope with stock risk (particularly true in competitive supply systems).
- Poor credit records with publishers who won't provide stock on credit terms.

---

18 Malawi Book Service charged a straightforward 20% commission on retail prices for warehousing and internal transportation to schools. Recent calculations by private sector freight agents in Malawi suggest that 5–7,5% would have been a more reasonable charge.
19 USAID supports free primary textbook supplies. AIF supports a parental purchase system. NGOs are supporting the development of school-based rental systems.

- Bad reputations with local schools that won't provide cash with orders in case the orders aren't fulfilled.
- Inadequate experience in schoolbook supply.
- Poor management and/or consolidation capacity.
- Inadequate financial management and record-keeping skills.
- Inadequate storage and display space and thus poor stock condition.
- The inhibiting lack of a substantial and well-funded textbook wholesaler.
- Head-on competition from publishers who supply schools direct. This is a problem not just for booksellers but also for small, emerging, local publishers who cannot compete with the direct sales capability of larger and better financed publishing houses.[20]

The list of problems provided above is extremely important. If there is to be a resurgence and renaissance in the establishment of national book distribution networks throughout Africa then this is the list of problems that must be confronted and resolved. Training is only part of the solution, although this can help with some of the issues listed above. But financing capacity is particularly difficult in countries where bank-lending rates are often punitive and booksellers do not rank as high priorities for bank loans and equity investment. Similarly, creditworthiness is a characteristic that has to be earned from suppliers. A government or donor cannot confer it without guarantees to cover bad debts.

The regional trade in books

There is a striking difference between West Africa on the one hand and Eastern, Central and Southern Africa on the other, in the responses to the development of a regional trade in books. For many years most African countries have tended to buy more books from Europe than from other African countries. This was partly the result of well-established trade links linking the book trades of Anglophone and Francophone Africa with the UK and France respectively and poor inter and intra-regional transportation and communication links within Africa.

The advent of the African Books Collective (ABC) and the African Publishers' Network (APNET) has done a great deal to change this situation. However, in Ghana, surrounded by Francophone countries, the regional trade in books in English and local languages is insignificant. In East Africa, with a developing common regional language in Kiswahili and the developing economic and political grouping of COMESA,[21] the potential for a regional trade in books is now becoming significant. The book trade associations of Kenya, Uganda and Tanzania now organise joint national book weeks and other co-operative

20   The Kenya Publishers' Association (KPA) recognised this issue from the outset and has committed itself to support booksellers by only supplying schools through recognised bookseller outlets. The longer-term perspective of the KPA in supporting booksellers is relatively rare, but it is one of the key factors that has created the strong bookselling sector in Kenya. This same strong bookselling sector provides a market for other types of publishing, so everyone benefits.
21   Common Market for Eastern and Southern Africa.

activities. Unfortunately Tanzania still imposes a 5% tax on books from Kenya and Uganda.

Botswana has a tiny local publishing industry because the market size is small and therefore regional imports are significant, although exports are not as important. Malawi, which shares a common local language with several neighbouring countries (Chichewa/Chinyanja is also spoken to some extent in Zambia, Tanzania, Zimbabwe and Mozambique) and has considerable agency finance available for secondary textbook purchases, also has significant regional trading links in books. The new, secondary school, approved textbook list contains secondary textbooks approved for use in Malawian secondary schools, which have been published in six other African countries.[22]

The Francophone countries appear to perform no better than Ghana in inter or intra-regional book trading, despite the existence of many common borders with other Francophone countries. According to the case studies, the main reasons for this are the low level of local publishing, the existing established trading links with Europe and the competitive advantages of importation from Europe traditionally provided by the subsidised CFA franc.

The lack of regional trading links throughout most of Africa is a significant problem because it limits the size of the regional book markets and inhibits the growth of regional publishers. The weak financial position of many national publishers and booksellers is also a serious inhibiting factor. Many local publishers cannot or will not extend credit for export sales to booksellers or publishers in other countries and, without credit facilities, few potential importers are willing to take the risk of purchasing significant stocks. Volatile exchange rates between different national currencies and slow and cumbersome banking procedures, which sometimes require local currency transfers to be exchanged first into and then out of an external hard currency, such as US dollars, are also serious barriers to the regional and continental trade in books. Multinational publishers with branches or associate/subsidiary companies widely spread throughout the continent have a considerable advantage in the development of regional trade because they can usually operate largely on the basis of inter-company trading, which is considerably safer in terms of credit risks.

Other book markets

The case studies reveal a number of other common factors. For all countries the school textbook market is dominant. Where private sector book distribution has a significant role to play in the school market it tends to be stronger and more active and has greater local coverage. Côte d'Ivoire, Kenya and Botswana all have these characteristics and the rapid growth of local bookseller participation in the secondary school market in Malawi bodes well for the future.

---

22   The six other countries supplying textbooks for Malawian secondary education are the RSA, Namibia, Botswana, Zimbabwe, Zambia and Kenya.

In most of the Anglophone case study countries, the secondary school textbook market is the most significant bookseller market in the absence of any access to primary school markets. In most countries, both Francophone and Anglophone, it is the secondary school market that has provided the opportunity for bookseller survival whenever the state has dominated primary textbook supply. This was certainly the case in Kenya before the collapse of KSES and the introduction of parental contributions to textbook provision via the 'cost sharing' policy.

Tertiary market access is significant for local booksellers in Anglophone countries only in Kenya and then only to a small extent but it is probably a more significant market in Côte d'Ivoire, Senegal and Cameroon. Highly specialist library suppliers and journal subscription agents operating out of the UK, France and the USA serve most of the tertiary book and journal markets in Africa.

Trade markets are good in Kenya and developing in Uganda, Ghana, Senegal, Cameroon and Côte d'Ivoire, but are still insignificant in comparison with the all-important school textbook (and library market). Only Kenya, Botswana and Côte d'Ivoire, of all of the case study countries, have bookseller networks that come close to providing national coverage. All other case study countries tend to be strong in the capital city and in one or two provincial urban areas. The rural areas tend to be largely unserved by competent private sector wholesalers or retail outlets. Only in Malawi has a major new book wholesaling operation come into being, and this happened purely to serve the rapidly growing, donor funded, secondary school market.[23]

Chapter Two and Chapter Three contain the individual case studies on which the analysis and arguments provided above are based. Chapter Four offers some basic conclusions and suggests some interim strategies, which should assist in the development of national book distribution capacity. It also includes a 'decision tree for policy-makers', ie a flowchart to assist government and development partners in the creation of policies and strategies, which will lead to a new era of efficient and cost effective book distribution on a national scale.

---

23 The new textbook wholesaler is a partnership between a UK based library supplier, three Malawian retail booksellers and a Malawian freight forwarding company. The company was established to serve the new secondary school textbook market created by new government textbook policies and the financial support of funding agencies.

Chapter Two

MAIN CASE STUDIES ON NATIONAL BOOK DISTRIBUTION SYSTEMS

Case study A: Ghana

By Frank Segbawu, SEDCO Publishing Ltd, Accra

Basic facts
- Located between Latitudes 5–11° N and Longitudes 3° W and 1° E.
- Bordered by Côte d'Ivoire to the west, Togo to the east, Burkina Faso to the north and the Atlantic to the south. All the neighbouring countries are Francophone.
- Population: 18,1 million (1998 estimate).
- Area: 238,500 square kilometres and a population density of 81 per square kilometre.
- 37% of the population is classified as urban.
- The capital city is Accra with a population of 1,7 million (1995 estimate).
- Per capita GNP: US$390.
- 30% of the population are Christian, 30% are Muslim and 40% adhere to traditional religions.
- Life expectancy is 60 years with female life expectancy at 62 years and male life expectancy at 58 years.
- A former British colony, independence was attained in 1957.
- English is the official language and there are 11 main local languages.
- According to the World Development Report (1999) 64,5% of Ghanaians are functionally literate. Of these, 77% of men and 57% of women are functionally literate.
- Main economic activities are aluminium mining, timber, agriculture (cocoa, rice, coffee, peanuts, maize, etc.) and tourism.
- Ghana is administered via ten regions and 110 districts.
- The unit of currency in Ghana is the Cedi. In January 2000, 3500 Cedis = US$1.

The education market

Table 1 Basic education statistics (1998)		
Type of instruction	**Number of institutions**	**Enrollment**
Pre-schools		
Public	5,553	Not known
Private	1,343	Not known
Total	6,896	573,306
Primary schools		
Public	11,765	2 027,026
Private	1,249	306,321
Total	13,014	2 333,347
Junior secondary		
Public	5,597	695,468
Private	282	42,589
Total	5,879	738,057
Senior secondary		
Public	456	188,908
Private	48	5,877
Total	504	194,785
Technical/vocational schools		
Public	22	–
Private	60	–
Total	82	14,547
Polytechnics		
Public	8	15,179
Universities		
Public	5	23,126
Private	3	3,000
Total	8	26,126

Pre-schools

The number of private pre-schools has grown rapidly in recent years, largely to prepare children for private primary school entry where entry requirements have become steadily more difficult. Until recently this sector was dominated by private schools. Apart from a few model pre-schools, there had been little public sector involvement.

From 1997, this situation started to change. Although there are still more private pre-schools than public pre-schools in the urban areas, the national figures now show that there is a large number of public pre-schools. This is because the government has, over the last three years, embarked on a nation-wide pre-school building programme. Even in Accra City and the Greater Accra region, (which is the most urbanised region) the balance between public and private pre-schools is changing in favour of public schools. In regions such as Upper East and Upper West, there are hardly any private pre-schools. All the pre-schools in these regions are public pre-schools.

There has been little direction from the Ministry of Education regarding syllabus/curriculum content or book policy. Sources of books and learning material are a combination of local materials produced by indigenous publishers and more expensive but better quality books mainly from UK sources such as Ladybird. There is an association of pre-school proprietors, which exercises loose control over its members. Schools are divided into grades based on the quality of teaching staff and the quality of facilities provided. Book supply to schools is generally via local bookshops and direct promotion/sales by publishers.

Table 2	Public and private pre-schools in Accra City and Greater Accra in 1999	
Region	**Number of public pre-schools**	**Number of private pre-schools**
Greater Accra Region	205	251
Accra City	104	145

Despite the rapid growth in pre-school numbers, this is not yet a significant market for publishers. There is a shortage of good, local, pre-school materials, although most local publishers have one or two titles on their list in acknowledgement of the existence of the sector. Two local publishers (Sam-Woode Ltd and All Good Books) concentrate on pre-school publishing but most publishers have not yet appreciated the potential of the sector. Nevertheless, the pre-school market has considerable potential. The private pre-school market is quite dynamic and provides better quality teaching and learning has lost few students to public pre-schools.

The current demand for pre-school materials is dominated by private school purchases. There is no government budget for materials for public pre-schools at this time but it is possible that this will change in the future. The impact that government purchases might have on current distribution arrangements will depend on the nature of the purchasing arrangements. If purchasing is organised through districts there could be a beneficial impact on the local book trade. If materials are ordered nationally then there will be little impact on booksellers.

Basic education: primary and junior secondary schools

Numerically there are far more public/government schools and students enrolled than there are private schools and students. However, overall performance and the quality of students is perceived to be poor to mediocre in public schools and is believed to be declining sharply. Recent Maths and English examination results demonstrate the decline in public school standards. The reasons for this include the lack of:

- Books and other learning aids.
- Adequate supervision of teachers by principals.
- Supervision of principals by school supervisors.

When government textbooks were first introduced all schools had to use them. This applied to both public and private schools. Schools were not permitted to purchase other titles in addition to the prescribed government textbooks. Government textbook production was agency funded and the quantities procured were considered to be sufficient for the needs of all private and public school students. Because syllabuses had been changed, at the time of the introduction of government textbooks they were the only ones that conformed to the new syllabus requirements. Private sector publishers were not permitted to have access to the syllabi.

Over time, and as the government programme failed to deliver in terms of both quantity and quality, alternative textbooks began to be re-introduced into the system. Certain private schools were the first to reject government textbooks. The rejection is not overt; private schools still receive government textbook supplies and pay the user fees but also purchase other more suitable textbooks and pass the additional costs on to parents in higher school fees. As the government programme continued to under-perform, some public schools also started to recommend the purchase of alternative books to parents. The Ministry of Education (MoE) continues to collect user fees and supply government textbooks and appears to turn a blind eye to the fact that alternative books were starting to creep into the schools. Within the public school system, secondary schools use far more alternative textbooks than primary schools – it seems that secondary school principals are able to exercise more discretion.

Having said this, the majority of schools, particularly state schools in rural areas, continue to rely solely on government textbooks because of the cost of private textbooks. Parents are reluctant to pay both a user fee and the purchase price of an alternative textbook. Private sector textbook publishers thus have some access to the school market but are still cut off from the majority of government schools.

Private schools tend to be based more in urban than in rural areas and are showing significant growth in the basic education sector. Parents who can afford to are keen to remove their children from government schools. The difference in performance between public and private schools is very striking and a majority of private school pupils gain entrance into senior secondary level. Therefore, as at pre-school level, the private sector sets the standards in terms of quality and performance but remains an elite minority.

Senior secondary schooling

The majority of senior secondary schools are public. These consist of:
- Traditional boarding schools set up by the state between 1960 and 1990.
- Schools set up by the various Christian denominations and now converted to Ministry of Education control.
- Newer community-based day schools (non-boarding).

The private sector schools at this level are characteristically small and not very successful. The main reason is that the tradition is for parents to send their children to boarding schools and especially the older, religious schools, which have a reputation for discipline and character building. Since most proprietors of private secondary schools do not have the funds to invest in boarding facilities they do not attract the better calibre of students and thus tend to have lower levels of performance. Principals in public senior secondary schools tend to be better qualified and more experienced so these public schools are therefore managed more effectively than those at the basic levels.

Tertiary education

The most prestigious tertiary institutions belong to the state. There are three new private tertiary institutions set up by religious organisations to provide alternatives to government funded institutions. These are currently in an embryonic state but their prospects appear to be good, as government budgets are inadequate to cope with all tertiary level financing requirements. The inadequacy of government tertiary level funding has led to frequent student unrest in government universities. The main problems the private universities face are accreditation and facilities.

The tertiary market is not a vibrant sector for local publishers. Very few local publishers have any product for the market and most of what is available is in areas such as Law, History and Accounting. Most of the prescribed titles originate from the developed world – mostly from the US. A few local booksellers (EPP for engineering and Readwide for law books) do stock key tertiary titles but the sector is generally unattractive to local booksellers as a result of high prices, lack of local purchasing power and a high level of illegal photocopying. Similarly very little academic journal business goes through the local book trade. Most tertiary institutions cannot maintain up-to-date journal collections. In theory institutions have annual budgets for journals but in practice very few journals are ordered, usually because the required funds are not released to the institutions. Diversion of budgets to pay for immediate needs such as salaries is part of the problem. Occasionally a funding agency provides funds for tertiary journal procurement but these are usually put out to tender and won by overseas specialist journal suppliers (for example, Blackwells). Other reputable academic institutions (for example, the Council for Scientific & Industrial Research) order through SEDCO, Mallory or SMI, etc.

37

Key players in the distribution and sales of books in Ghana

The Supplies and Logistics Division of the MoE

The Supplies and Logistics Division (SLD) is headed by a director who reports to the Minister of Education via the Director General of Education. SLD's mandate is to procure and supply textbooks for all schools nationwide (both public and private). They also supply supplementary reading materials for school libraries and consumables such as stationery. All students pay a textbook user fee collected by the schools and paid into a revolving fund that is used to replenish supplies as required.

By volume and value, this is the biggest organisation in the supply and delivery of books in Ghana. Until the 1980s, it was the largest importer of books. It placed orders mainly with overseas publishers (but also with some local publishers) for imported books to be supplied to schools. As a result of a change in policy in the early 1990s, the Ministry of Education now produces its own textbooks for primary and secondary schools and as mentioned above, turns a blind eye to the fact that schools buy other materials as well.

The occasional orders for supplementary reading materials for school libraries are quite insignificant compared to the textbook business although they do provide an occasional lifeline to local publishers that have been squeezed out of the core textbook market by the state monopoly.

The distribution of textbooks to schools by SLD has been fraught with problems:

- Most schools in the urban areas (including private basic schools, which import their own textbooks) receive their full allocation. However rural schools often do not get the books that they require. These schools are expected to go to government warehouses to collect their allocations but are not provided with the funding to transport books. In some remote areas, core textbook ratios are as low as 1:10 or worse.
- Reprints depend on the availability of agency funding. The procedure for international competitive bidding (ICB) is very cumbersome and time consuming. There is a perception that the procedure is also not free from corruption, yet printing contracts effected without ICB have been particularly problematic and it is considered unlikely that the anticipated cost savings have been realised as a result of non-transparency in the granting of orders and deliveries. In 1994 fire destroyed a warehouse where goods were supposed to have been delivered. The cause of the fire is still unknown.

The Projects Management Unit (PMU)

The PMU was set up to handle procurement and supply supported by development partner funding. Its mandate covers regular textbooks and also

Ghanaian language readers and money for school construction, etc. This body is widely considered to be more professional than the SLD because of the employment of a higher calibre of staff, better staff remuneration and adequate logistical backing in the form of computers and vehicles, etc. The PMU is funded by funding agencies and is headed by a Director General who reports directly to the Minister of Education.

Publishers

Longman. Longman is represented in Ghana by SEDCO Publishing Ltd. It maintains a trading account (for imported books) as well as a co-publishing programme (for local publications). Longman also trades directly with the MoE, and with other importers such as EPP and Readwide plus overseas library suppliers and consolidators. Longman has a long history of publishing in and for Ghana but its local publishing activity was effectively suspended after the government take-over of school publishing. However it has continued to be one of the main sources of supplementary readers, dictionaries and atlases for the school system. As schools in the secondary sector have began to show renewed interest in buying textbooks in addition to the government books, Longman has produced a mathematics course in association with SEDCO and the Mathematics Association of Ghana for senior secondary schools.

Macmillan. Macmillan is represented in Ghana by Unimax Ltd, which is also its main trading partner apart from direct ministry orders. It also trades direct with EPP (see p. 41). Macmillan also has a long history of publishing in and for Ghana. It has recently published a number of science textbooks for senior and junior secondary schools. The relative success of these privately published titles is an indicator of the problems in the current state publishing, production and distribution policies.

Oxford University Press, Heinemann and Evans. These UK publishers have not recently produced any textbooks specifically for Ghana but they are suppliers of supplementary readers and dictionaries to the MoE and to the private school sector. They are all maintaining a close watch on current developments in anticipation of the liberalisation of the book industry in Ghana. They all have local Ghanaian representatives who maintain offices in Accra. They all supply direct to local bookshops and distributors, for example, Readwide and EPP (see 41).

Far East, Middle East and African Publishers. There is little business being done with publishers from the East except for System Publications, which sells reference materials for primary and junior secondary schools. There is a growing level of local publishing activity with Indian companies however because Indian books are significantly cheaper than UK or US titles. Indian publishers are also perceived to be more willing to permit local adaptations with local Ghanaian imprints. There is very little inter-African trade at the moment although there have been discussions between a number of potential partners and collaborators.

SEDCO Publishing. SEDCO is one of the leading local publishers and aims to publish textbooks and supplementary materials for all levels from pre-school to senior secondary. The company maintains two retail outlets in Accra and in Tamale in the north. It supplies to wholesalers such as Readwide and to bookshops such as EPP and the university bookshops. It is a co-publisher[24] of the government's basic school science series, and the publisher of several successful senior secondary school textbooks in subjects such as mathematics, English, science, physics, chemistry and biology, etc. Like all local publishers the company has suffered in the past from the state monopoly of textbooks, but with the growing awareness in the better secondary schools that they cannot rely on government textbooks, there is a strong sales resurgence currently in progress.

Afram. This company is another leading local publisher with a range of well produced readers and is a co-publisher of the government English textbook, which it also produces for the open market. It has a small bookshop/showroom in Accra. It distributes its English textbook to schools throughout Ghana and supplies its books to other booksellers such as university bookshops and others.

Ghana Printing Corporation (GPC). This was the state printing and publishing corporation. It was the co-publisher of the government 'Mathematics for Basic Schools' series. The corporation hovers on the verge of being sold off and may not be a viable player on the book scene within the next year or two. GPC is a government owned corporation and is also the government printer. It therefore has considerable business potential and under normal circumstances should not be at risk. However:

- Many government departments doing business with GPC do not pay their bills.
- Many government departments prefer to do business with the private sector rather than with GPC because of the inducements offered by the private sector.
- The GPC labour force is oversized and highly unionised.
- GPC has an obsolete plant and has little or no investment in new equipment.
- GPC owns high value real estate that is reported to be more valuable than the company.

Other local publishers (Adwinsa/Samwoode/All Good Books, etc). The Ghana Book Publishers' Association has over 80 members, of which about twelve can be classified as significant companies. All have created niches as publishers of readers and supplementary textbooks at primary level. None of these companies

---

24   The MoE selected five leading local publishers as co-publishers. The selection criteria included volume of business, number of titles published, number of titles in print and financial capacity to act as a co-publisher. SEDCO pays 10% royalty to the MoE on sales revenues. Prices can only be changed with the authorisation of the MoE. Discounts to booksellers/customers are also fixed by the MoE. The current discount level is 20%. The co-publisher receives no financial assistance from government in the production and sales of co-published titles. The MoE retains the right (which it exercises) to print the same titles and supply them direct to schools as part of the textbook user fee system. The MoE does not produce titles for sale on the open market.

however can achieve full potential until the book industry (and particularly the critical school textbook market) is liberated. Most publishers maintain bookshops attached to their offices. A full list of GBPA member publishers is attached as Appendix 1.

Wholesalers/Retailers

University Bookshops. The bookshops of the main universities used to be the leading sources of textbooks not only for the university faculties and students but also as general bookshops for all of Ghana's literate society. Over the years, and largely due to mismanagement, the bookshops of Cape Coast University and the University of Science and Technology in Kumasi have fallen by the wayside and are unable even to satisfy the requirements of their own faculties. Under capitalised and perennially in debt, they are unable to achieve the critical mass of titles which would make them effective and attractive. Legon University Bookshop continues to be the premier bookshop in the country. It is, however, unable to satisfy the demands of some of its faculties for the less popular titles and journals. This is at least partly because it does not have the ability to transfer funds abroad.[25]

EPP. EPP Books Services is currently the largest bookselling chain currently operating in Ghana with five branches, of which three are in Accra. It has plans to expand further and stocks the largest variety of titles under one roof except for Legon University Bookshop. It deals mainly in imports from the UK and USA but will sell any title for which it can spot a market. Prices are kept low by purchasing heavily on the remainder market. Its outlets are, however, situated in urban areas like all of the other main book distributors.

Readwide. Readwide is a relatively new company, which concentrates on supplies to schools (especially literature and readers for secondary schools). It uses headmasters in each region for promotion. Because it has developed close ties with headmasters, it has taken advantage of the dissatisfaction of schools with the government textbooks to supply alternative textbooks from commercial publishers. It also hopes to move into publishing, although it is not clear whether this will be textbooks or readers. It has co-published a couple of titles with Heinemann. The proprietor is a senior lecturer at the School of Law and thus Readwide is also the major supplier of law books in Ghana.

Valco. The Valco Trust Fund was established to assist the educational sector through financial contributions from the Volta Aluminum Company. It aids schools with logistical requirements such as vehicles, books, scientific equipment, etc. and also makes book purchases from time to time in response to requests from schools. The criteria by which such requests are assessed is, however, not clear to would-be suppliers or prospective beneficiaries.

---

25 Legon University Bookshop is part of the University of Ghana. Sales income is paid into the university account. The University is frequently under financial pressure and often relies on proceeds from the bookshop to fund other activities. Opening a letter of credit to import stock requires tying up capital for at least 120 days before the ordered stock arrives and is sold. The University finances are such that this kind of investment is often impossible. Thus the bookshop cannot establish letters of credit and thus cannot order all the stock required by the faculties.

SMI/Mallory/Blackwells. These organisations are UK based library book and journal suppliers. They serve the market as and when funds become available to supply specialist books and journals to government departments/ministry libraries, etc. The source of funds is usually occasional agency support although they also do business from time to time with private organisations. Blackwells usually waits for the large funded library supply projects, which have been few and far between in Ghana in recent years – the last being in 1992.

Religious bookshop chains. From as early as 1870, several religious organisations were set up to provide books throughout the country and were once very successful. They imported books from overseas publishers and purchased from local publishers, as well as distributing religious material and bibles. With the advent of the monopolistic 'one textbook' system, with the government as sole textbook publisher and distributor, they lost the lucrative textbook market. Apart from the religious materials (which were not sold at much profit) they were largely reduced to selling stationary to survive. They were not permitted to be involved in the distribution of government textbooks although they had the capacity and expertise to play a very significant role. Because of capital restrictions[26] they are now unable to raise the letters of credit necessary to import books and have to rely on private sector importers such as SEDCO, Unimax, EPP and local publishers for credit and stocks. These booksellers are:

- **Methodist Book Depot (MBD)**. This organisation was founded in 1881. It once had nine branches in Accra, Cape Coast, Swedru, Takoradi, Kumasi, Berekum, Tamale, Tema, Oda and Tarkwa. The last two branches have now been closed. The MBD now deals in religious books, stationery, children's books, and textbooks from basic to tertiary/professional levels. The head office holds stock and distributes to branches nation-wide. Sources of finance are the church and the reinvestment of trading profits. MBD is now a limited liability company.
- **Presbyterian Book Depot**. Originally established in 1870 with nine branches. It still maintains all nine branches and currently is the strongest of the religious book chains.
- **Anglican Book Depot**. This is the weakest of the religious book chains with only two branches, very little capital and few business prospects.
- **Challenge Bookshops**. This organisation used to deal only in religious literature but is now fully involved in the distribution and retailing of textbooks published by the private sector. They have ten branches in regional capitals.

History of the book trade in Ghana

Religious evangelical bodies set up schools throughout the country during the colonial era. They had their own syllabi and book lists. They distributed the

---

26 Capital restrictions in Ghana are generally the result of lack of company finance and the high rate of bank credit (between 28% and 40% in 1999).

required books through their book depots, which operated nationally. They did not just distribute to schools but to the society as a whole and also served as distributors for many villages and rural based bookshops, which once operated at the grassroots level. The first blow to their operations (and to their capacity to hold stock regionally) came when the mission schools were co-opted into the new Ghana Education Service (GES). This reduced their turnover because the Ministry of Education now dictated what should be used and purchased for schools and it also replaced the religious bodies as the main distributor of textbooks. The second blow came when all schools, including the former mission schools, had to use one state published, produced and distributed textbook per subject per grade. With the weakening of the religious book depots, many small local bookshops closed down because their main source of stock declined sharply.

The Gold Coast Booksellers' Association (GCBA) was formed in the 1950s. It was a completely indigenous grouping. Very vibrant and successful, the members distributed books to the districts and rural areas. They joined the religious chains, for example, the Presbyterian, Methodist and Anglican Book Depots, which had been distributing books in Ghana for a long time. Members of the Association made a great deal of money and, at this time, the combination of the GCBA and the religious book chains provided a genuinely national book distribution capacity.

A socialist government followed Independence. Education was to be free to all. No school fees were payable up to the completion of tertiary education. All textbooks were free. They were used in schools but pupils were not allowed to take the books home. The nation had large foreign exchange reserves from cocoa exports and could afford it. This policy was crystallized in the Education Act of 1961, which was to have unfortunate consequences for local publishing development. People did not develop the habit of buying books because all educational materials were provided free of charge. Although widely regarded as an anachronism, successive governments have been unable to gather the political will to jettison the Act. Ghana Book Supplies Ltd was formed in 1963 to take charge of importing and distributing of school textbooks on behalf of the government. Purchases were made in bulk from publishers (mainly UK publishers) and delivered to schools. There was little indigenous publishing except for the GPC, which produced some readers: Ghana University Press provided support to tertiary level requirements and to the Bureau of Ghana Languages.

In 1975, the National Redemption Council government reserved publishing for Ghanaians. This led to the physical withdrawal of British publishing companies from Ghana although they continued to do business with the Ministry of Education and other government departments through their local agents/partners. The withdrawal of British publishers led to the birth of private indigenous publishing. Several local publishing houses sprang up and started to provide competition to some of the overseas publishers.

In the early 1980s the government of Ghana decided to adopt a 'one textbook' policy with all school textbook titles published, produced and distributed by the government. This was made possible only with massive donor support, which effectively sent local publishing and bookselling back into the doldrums. The overseas publishers lost business as well but coped because they had other markets to rely on. This was not the case for the local book industry. The situation was compounded by the economic collapse of Ghana in the 1980s. Since then local publishing and bookselling has only been able to survive by taking advantage of the failures of the government book delivery programmes and by living on the sales of readers, children's books and other supplementary materials.

Sales and distribution of general books was initiated by the missionary societies who set up book depots around the country (see above). Initially successful, and a vital source of books in the regions, the double effect of the economic collapse of the 1980s and the government textbook monopoly undermined the religious bookshops and thus affected the viability of general publishing (including local children's books) and book selling. Many bona fide privately owned bookshops folded at this time and it was not until the early 1990s that new companies such as EPP and Readwide emerged to take advantage of the increasingly obvious gaps and failures in the system.

Subsequent legislation has done little to support the local book industry. For instance, the legislative instrument published in 1991, which contained the Provisional National Defense Council (PNDC) Law 116, sought to confer incentives or benefits on enterprises in Ghana. Referring to publishing, it conferred 'exemption from customs, import duties, and other related charges in respect of inputs needed for the production and printing of books'.

Superficially, publishers might have sighed with relief that at last the government had come to their assistance. But this was not the case. In subsequent clauses, the law meticulously set down the modalities of conferring the promised blessing. To qualify for the exemptions, the publisher had to produce an income tax certificate covering the period from 1983 to 1987; evidence that the publisher had fulfilled social security obligations for the same period; and proof that the business had been duly registered. The legislation sought to use the exemption bait to make publishing concerns conform to the statutory requirements of business practice in Ghana. The result was that many publishing houses were in default of the requirements and could not take advantage of the exemptions. The few publishers who did qualify and who tried to claim exemptions found themselves in a quagmire of bureaucracy. The intrepid ones signalled that they would persist in their efforts, if only to test government sincerity. In the 1992 budget statement, corporate tax was reduced from 55% to 35%, but a withholding tax of 17,5% was imposed plus 10% import duty on paper. The book trade thus received very mixed signals.

The current book distribution system

School textbooks

The school textbooks system in Ghana at the moment is officially monopolistic and prescriptive with a supply-led distribution system. All funding from both government and agencies to support textbook procurement is provided to producers (printers) rather than to the schools – the consumers. The majority of textbook distribution is undertaken by a state controlled distribution system. **Pre-schools**. Although the public sector has expanded recently, book supply to pre-schools is relatively insignificant. Private pre-schools depend on local published materials and a few books from UK publishers imported through local agents, wholesalers and retailers.

Basic and secondary schools. Official, government policy is a target book to pupil ratio of 1:1. This is the core book market for Ghana but it is completely dominated by state publishing and distribution.

The Ghana Education Service (GES) estimates the annual quantity of books required for each subject and level based on its own statistics. Government textbook distribution in Ghana is thus a supply-led system. Because the textbook budget is never sufficient, the GES decides each year how many books per subject will actually be printed. Printers are invited to quote. Orders are placed. Printed books are supplied to the main GES warehouse in Tema. From here the GES sends the books to regional depots. The books are then sent on to district depots. The schools in the districts go to the district depots to collect their allocations. In years where aid funding is available it is the Projects Management Unit that handles the print tendering process. Once again the printed books are sent to the Tema warehouse for distribution to regions and districts. The students pay a textbook user fee for their book supply, which goes into a revolving fund to replenish the books. This revolving fund also covers stationery, chalk, etc. The textbook user fees for 1999 are provided in Table 3, below.

Table 3 Textbook users' fees in 1999		
Level	Public schools (Cedis)	Private schools (Cedis)
Primary	300 (US$0,085)	1 500 (US$0,428)
Junior secondary	500 (US$0,142)	2 500 (US$0,714)
Senior secondary	9 000 (US$2,57)	12 000 (US$3,428)

The textbook fees are based on an assumed average book life of three years. In practice actual book life varies from one to five years depending upon the book/pupil ratio – the more a book is shared, the shorter the life span.[27]

---

27 Physical textbook specifications require 70 gsm bond text paper and wire stitched bindings for primary and JSS books and perfect binding for SSS books.

Textbook distribution is therefore financed via a combination of funding agencies, government and parents (in that order of magnitude). In years where funding is available, agency funds can comprise about 70% of textbook financing, with the government providing 20% and parents approximately 10%. Where donor funding is not available the ratio is approximately 80% government funding with 20% from parents through the user fees. What this means in practice is that without agency support, government is unable to achieve or sustain satisfactory book:pupil ratios. It also means that what parents pay is only a tiny proportion of the actual cost of textbook supply. However, this is not made clear to parents, and those in the rural areas are not happy when schools ask them to consider the purchase of additional books. They do not see the need to buy books for their children and they have no idea of the real cost of books. It also means that the revolving fund is not, as it stands, a viable means of supporting and sustaining even basic book supplies. The administration of the fund is also not considered to be sufficiently transparent. Annual accounts are not made available to the public. The reliance on donor funding is a weakness in the system because it leads to great irregularity in supplies. Not even local printers benefit because they cannot compete with printers from India and Singapore.

The fact that the distribution system is supply driven has led to problems. Since the inspectorate division of the MoE is very weak, it has not been able to provide reliable information on which books are most needed and in which schools. This is why some urban schools achieve 1:1 ratios while some rural schools continue to have 1:10 ratios or even worse.

There is no element of choice. As a result many private schools are known to receive their government allocations and simply put them aside while schools source their own preferred books from local publishers or importers. Very often the books that are written for government schools are not sufficiently challenging to private schools or the better public schools. The same situation occurs in a minority of government secondary schools. It is this practice that has provided a lifeline to local publishers.

The government system of textbook supply theoretically has simplified and reduced the cost, complexity and sophistication of book selection and provision. A few officials in the MoE are able to make decisions and execute them. Immediate cost savings are made in the amount of time spent on these assessments. Schools and districts can concentrate on teaching without the distraction of book selection. Where donor funding has been made available large print runs are possible with attendant low unit costs. On the other hand the system has led to books getting out of date without being revised. This is a very common problem in *all* state monopolistic systems of book publishing and supply. People at the regional/district/school levels have lost the skills involved in the assessment of texts and now require workshops to be able to select titles for pilot projects. It has led to inertia in the publishing industry, which in turn has resulted in low levels of capitalisation and an emasculated local publishing and printing capacity. Book wholesaling and retailing have been driven to near insolvency and no longer provide genuinely national coverage in Ghana.

It is only the inefficiencies of the system in not being able to meet the needs of schools in terms of the quality and quantity of materials that currently enables local publishing and bookselling to survive. The supply-led system also creates great inequalities, particularly between urban and rural schools. Many of the books printed somehow do not seem to get to the schools. A study of the quantities printed with donor funding does not match the picture of book supply in the schools across the country. There is a large gap between textbook supply and the availability of books in the classroom, which has not been adequately explained.

The students are not allowed to take books home because school authorities don't want to be held responsible for losses. It is difficult to assess the real cost of the missing books or the real cost of distribution. The government warehouse facilities at regional and district levels are inadequate. Although there seem to be enough vehicles at the urban centres there are not enough to send books to schools. Schools with vehicles often claim they do not have funds to purchase fuel to drive to regional or district centres to collect their allocations.

For some primary and junior secondary subjects, private co-publishers are allowed to print and distribute to the open market in support of government efforts. Prices are fixed and can be changed only with government permission. These books are distributed through a network of local booksellers and this system seems to work relatively efficiently. Shortages are rare and short-lived. The element of choice is, however, still absent.

Tertiary books and journals

Faculties and departments make their own book choices. The GES/MoE has no influence on book selection at this level. Traditionally the university bookshops would place orders using their own import licenses. This is no longer the case as the bookshops have lost the mandate (or the capacity) to establish letters of credit. Currently a few local private booksellers such as EPP, Readwide, Unimax and SEDCO import titles to sell to students or to serve the very rare and very small orders from tertiary libraries.

Occasionally the MoE purchases a few titles for tertiary libraries from the local booktrade. This is neither regular nor reliable.

The last time tertiary institutions received a reasonable supply of books was in 1992 at the time of the last large World Bank tertiary project. The last journal supply was in 1997, which was possibly the last batch of the subscriptions originally placed in 1992. These orders were supplied through Blackwells, a UK subscription agent, and did not benefit the book trade in Ghana. There has recently been another programme to supply books to agricultural institutions and the University for Development Studies, which were supplied through a consortium comprising SMI, Mallory and SEDCO. Charitable donations are the other main source of tertiary books.

47

Trade books and magazines

The main players are the private booksellers such as EPP, SEDCO and Unimax, etc, which import books. Other retailers such as the religious bookshops, university bookshops and a few small struggling independent bookshops do supply imported books but these are sourced via EPP and SEDCO, etc.

The indigenous publishers have active publishing programmes for children's readers, which are sold through the local retail trade.

The biggest problem for booksellers is the lack of capital. Local books are at a disadvantage in terms of cost because they have to pay taxes on inputs such as paper, ink and chemicals. Imported books, however, are free from these taxes under the terms of international conventions. Commercial bank finance is not easily available. Publishers and booksellers are regarded as poor credit risks because their stock is not regarded as acceptable collateral. Also, the volume of their business and turnover does not usually justify loans. The local interest rate of 30% is also not very attractive as it easily exceeds the average industry profit margins.

There is no information available concerning the total cash value of the book and information sector in Ghana, nor on the relative value of the different market sectors.

The impact of donor investment

Although the World Bank started supporting Ghana's development activities in 1962, it was not until 1986 that the first credit was provided to the educational sector. This came after 50 loans or credits had been granted to Ghana in most other sectors for a total of more than US$1 billion. Since then seven credits in the educational sector have been approved for a total of over US$230 million.

The first education credit was for the emergency Health and Education Rehabilitation Project (HERP). The project was approved early in 1986 with a budget of US$5 million allocated to education. The project provided emergency supplies of text and library books, writing materials and other essential supplies. The Project Completion Report (Report No. 11080-GH) concluded that the project met its objective in getting the necessary materials into the school system in a short time. The project was followed by a series of programmes and projects to support the Government's 1987 education reform programme. In 1987, the First Education Sector Adjustment Credit (Cr. 1744-GH, which closed on 31 December 1991) for US$34,5 million was approved. This was a broad, policy-based Sector Adjustment Credit, covering the whole of the educational system, but with the resources generated from the credit being concentrated on the junior secondary level (Grades 7–9). The Project Completion Report (Report No. 12622-GH) concluded that the impact of the project was positive and laid a strong foundation for further reforms in the education system. It also emphasised the importance of project implementation activities falling under the direct and day-to-day leadership of a high level political appointee. In 1990, a Second Education Sector Adjustment Credit (EdSAC II) worth US$50 million was approved, based on the model of Cr. 1744-GH described earlier, but focused on the senior secondary and primary levels. All three tranches of this credit have been released, and the programme closed on 31 December 1994. In 1992, EdSAC II funds were used to finance a small pilot project in sixteen public and private vocational institutes and two clusters.

In theory the funding agencies do not interfere with policy. They provide funding for projects that meet their mandate. In theory, therefore, the agencies have had no impact on book policy as far as issues such as syllabus content and extent, and the element of choice versus prescription, etc. In practice, the willingness of development partners in the past (from at least the mid 1980s) to support a prescriptive and supply-led system of book provision has played a significant role in cementing the current monopolistic policy.

It began with support for a review of syllabuses. This was followed by USAID support for the writing of textbooks by the MoE for primary schools. Between 1987 and 1990 the World Bank and other funding agencies supported and funded the printing of these books. They also supported and funded the writing and printing of textbooks for junior and senior secondary schools. Apart from the financial support for origination and manufacturing, agency support was also necessary to distribute the books to regions, districts and schools via the provision of manpower, administration, vehicles, logistics and storage facilities at districts and schools. Agency funding therefore actively supported the current book policies of the government. Recently, the support of USAID for an experimental scheme to include cross-subject experiences called 'Linkages in Learning Sequence' in the school curriculum has led to its adoption by the MoE despite some disquiet from the curriculum division and other stakeholders. The changes will no doubt be implemented nationally in due course.

In the past few years, 90% of textbook funding has come from funding agencies. The agencies supported the institution of a textbook user fee to be paid by parents but it is acknowledged that this is only a token payment and is not commensurate with actual costs. No steps have been implemented to replace or phase out donor support. Ghana therefore remains totally dependent on donors to execute any exercise in book delivery.

The funder community has funded over 95% of educational publishing activity in Ghana with the MoE as the main beneficiary. This comprises 100% of the core textbooks supplied to schools since the early 1990s. The distribution of school textbooks also is completely dependent on agency funding. The ministry has little logistical capacity of its own. Indeed, there is little real current capacity anywhere within the public sector, but the agency funded PMU ensures that textbook procurement and distribution takes place with relative efficiency, although without involving Ghana's private sector booktrade.

In summary, from the viewpoint of project efficiency, the support of funding agencies may have been successful. The use of funds has been implemented at minimum cost, due to large print runs based on monopoly titles. In the long term funders have taken the easy way out. Agency funding has compromised the quality of materials supplied, maintained an inefficient state bureaucracy, avoided the issue of sustainability, ensured continuing dependency on foreign funding and failed to create choice or genuine local capacity.

Book scheme for basic schools (a recent DFID funded project)

The first year's programme (1999), valued at UK£8 million has been completed. The purpose was to provide supplementary reading material to basic schools to encourage reading habits and help students understand and feel comfortable with the English language. The source of book supply was local and overseas publishers.

The British Council, using rented warehouse facilities at Tema, managed the book distribution. Books were delivered direct to District Education Offices. The books were pre-packed in specially constructed book boxes and labelled individually for each school in each district. Head teachers were paid to come to the district depots to collect books for their schools. The success of the programme lay in the co-ordination of the arrival of the trucks in the districts, on the presentation days, so that the book boxes were distributed direct to head teachers so that no storage was necessary at district level. As such, implementation has been relatively successful. The lesson is that it is possible to effect efficient distribution of books in Ghana using the private transport sector. The one issue not yet clear is how the safe delivery of books to schools and the correct usage of the books are to be monitored. It is reported that the MoE does not wish the British Council to be involved in educational book distribution in the future because local distribution capacity should be developed.

The role of external publishers and multinationals on the book trade and distribution

Historically, UK publishers completely dominated Ghanaian publishing and prevented the development of local capacity. In 1972 publishing was reserved for local indigenous companies and many of the foreign companies, which then had offices, warehouses, bookshops, etc. withdrew and reduced their activity to dealing through local agents and partners. This led to a tremendous growth in local publishing, which filled the gap until the state decided (for cost and socio-political reasons) to introduce state publishing for school textbooks.

Foreign companies have remained the dominant suppliers of reference material such as atlases, dictionaries, pre-school children's books, etc. Now they operate in association with local companies with whom they continue to co-publish books for Ghana. These companies have little or no impact on distribution as none of them actually has offices in Ghana. They still remain the main source of tertiary books and journals. Indian publishers have recently made some inroads by having some of their titles adapted for local use. Should the school textbook market be liberalised, it is more than likely to result in a flurry of activity. Overseas companies will, however, almost certainly continue to work through local agents.

Unlike the post-independence period when multinationals completely dominated the scene and were physically present in Ghana, today their operation is more of a partnership with local publishers. Many current publications are joint efforts and this is likely to be a growing trend. Most multinationals have been affected by down-sizing and cost reductions; and are therefore compelled to rely more on local expertise in key areas rather than on UK-based staff. Local consultants are also cheaper. This process tends to intensify the training of the local workforce. With regards to distribution, multinationals have always relied on the local networks when these have been allowed to operate.

The significance of regional trade in books

There is insignificant inter and intra-regional trade. SEDCO, for example, co-operates and co-ordinates with Longman Nigeria from time to time in the management of regional stocks and a few local language texts are sold across the border with Togo. There is, however, a thriving trade in *pirated* books particularly from Nigeria to Ghana through small-scale traders who shuttle between the two countries. The fact that Francophone countries surround Ghana acts as a barrier and filter to keep pirated books down a little. There is very little book trade between Ghana and its neighbours for reasons of language, culture, currency differences, incompatible laws and a general mistrust despite attempts at inter regional trade through ECOWAS.

Ghana is a signatory to the UNESCO Florence Agreement. Books are therefore imported free of taxes and duties. There is no import licence system operating in Ghana. Exchange control regulations do not provide a hindrance to the book trade. The only requirement is that import consignments over US$5,000 in value should be subject to pre-shipment inspection. Without documentation proving compliance with this requirement it is difficult to transfer funds against goods through the banking system.

Recent policy initiatives

Free Compulsory Universal Basic Education (FCUBE)

This is a funder initiative for the reform of the basic educational system. The terms of reference go beyond the scope of the book industry. The goals of the proposed policy include:

- Timely production and distribution of books.
- Producing and distributing books at minimum cost without sacrificing quality.
- Building local capacity in textbook development and distribution in particular and the book industry in general.

- Enabling teachers, pupils, parents and other educational authorities to choose the textbooks that are used in schools.
- Achieving a book to pupil ratio of 1:1.
- Ensuring a sustainable system of book production and distribution.
- Fostering active private sector involvement in the implementation of a sustainable book production and distribution policy.
- Procurement of supplementary reader's, wallcharts and flashcards, etc. for schools.

The MoE will produce subject syllabuses through the Curriculum Research and Development Division. Publishers will then purchase syllabuses, indicate areas of interest, arrange for the writing designing and typesetting of the books, conduct pilot testing at their own expense and submit camera ready copies to the MoE for evaluation.

MoE will approve all suitable titles and recommend at least three titles for each subject and grade level. District book selection committees, in consultation with their schools, will choose between the three recommended titles for purchases by the MoE. Approved titles, which did not make the recommended list, can be sold on the open market. The period of validity of approval is five years unless syllabuses are reviewed earlier. Price will be a consideration in the approval criteria. Copyright will be vested in the publisher and authors. Negotiations for reprints will be between publishers and the MoE. Sixty percent of purchases by the MoE are to be printed locally. Publishers will be given one year's notice for delivery of books.

Funding will be through an education tax with initial support from funding agencies, which will be gradually phased out. Publishers will deliver books to districts and will submit delivery receipts from districts for payment by HQ. Cost of delivery will be invoiced at a mutually agreed rate. MoE will limit its role to monitoring. Booksellers will be encouraged to participate in distribution. Local authorship will be developed. Subject associations will be encouraged, trained and strengthened.

A stakeholders' conference was held in May 1998 to confirm and approve the above policy framework. There was unanimous approval from all participants. Reasons for this approval include:

- The massive injection of capital into the local economy from multinational publishers to authors, printers, illustrators, etc.
- The building of local capacity.
- The revitalisation of the whole private book industry.
- The introduction of choice, competition and dynamism.

The policy makes sense because there is already an existing commercial publishing sector ready to work. Overseas investors consider the market attractive. There is already a tradition of local publishing.

The big obstacle in the way of this policy is a covert anti-commercial sector sentiment within the MoE. Despite the lessons learned from the current prescriptive state publishing and distribution system there is reluctance to hand over to the private sector. Elements within the establishment are happier to deal with printers than with publishers. There also appears to be some influence from some multinational publishers who want to cash in on short term business as opposed to investing for the long term and who are happy to trade in copyrights for cash. There is therefore a reactionary lobby to maintain a one-book policy with the MoE retaining copyright privileges.

Suggestions and recommendations

Since the Government sector has failed to provide (after several years of operation and investment) a reliable, viable, sustainable book provision and distribution system the private sector should now be tasked to assume this role.

Production

The burden should be lifted off the public/agency sources. The private sector, both local and international, appears at last ready to take up the challenge. The structure proposed in the new draft policy appears quite suitable.

Distribution

Although the private sector has atrophied under the years of government distribution, the basic framework still exists. Publishers should be made responsible for getting books to districts and must be tasked to set up a distribution system in association with booksellers and particularly with the religious chains. This is a quite feasible and workable proposition. The role of government will be to monitor and audit and ensure that payments are effected only upon satisfactory completion. The local Publishers' Association and multinational companies could be tasked to draw up a master plan and draft agreements with the various distributors for assessments. Aid funding for such a project would be invaluable.

Tertiary intervention

Large aid packages are urgently needed to:
- Properly equip university libraries with modern equipment and up-to-date books and journals.
- Equip university bookshops with up-to-date infrastructure. The University bookshops should be re-capitalised and given the mandate to operate independently of university administration in the procurement and sales of books and journals. Apart from committing a percentage of revenue to the university and providing access to accounts, they should be run like any other business.

The suggestions made would have an effect on business activity in the general trade and children's book sectors because the fact remains that although this is not where the profit lies, it is where recognition and respectability lies for both publishers and booksellers.

Case study B: Malawi

By Gaulphine Nyirenda, MD, Maneno Enterprises Ltd, Lilongwe

Basic facts

- Located between Latitudes 5–17° S and Longitudes 32–36° E.
- Bordered by Tanzania to the north, Mozambique to the east, south and south-west and Zambia to the west.
- Population: 11 million (1998 estimate).
- Area: 306,874 square kilometres.
- Population density: at 112 persons per square kilometre it has one of the highest population densities in Africa and also one of the highest deforestation rates.
- 15% of the population is classified as urban.
- Per capita GNP: estimated at US$200 in 1998.
- 75% of the population are Christian (Protestant = 55%), 20% are Muslim and 5% are Hindu and other traditional religions.
- Life expectancy (1997) is 43 years, the lowest in Africa. Men and women have the same life expectancy.
- Independence from Britain was attained in 1964.
- English and Chichewa are the official languages and there are nine other languages of which three are reasonably widely spoken. These are Yao, Chilomwe and Tumbuku.
- According to the World Development Report 42% of Malawians are functionally literate (1995). Of this, 57% of males were literate but only 27% of females.
- Main economic activities are agriculture (tobacco, tea, coffee, cotton, maize), timber and tourism.
- Malawi is administered via three regions and 32 districts. Within the Ministry of Education, Sport and Culture (MoESC) the 32 districts are administered via six divisions.
- The unit of currency is the Malawi Kwacha (MK). The exchange rate in January 2000 was MK45 to US$1.

The education market

Table 4 Basic education statistics (1998)		
Type of instruction	Number of institutions	Enrollment
Pre school Public Private		
Primary schools (1997) Public Private	3,730 31	2 905,590 4,000
Secondary (1999) Government Community secondary Private	103 540 300	80,000 180,000 30,000
TTCs (1997) Polytechnic & Vocational (1999) Public	7 1	7,935 1,209
Universities (1999) Public	2	4,739

Pre-schools

There are very few state funded pre-school institutions. All pre-schools (including private pre-schools) are the responsibility of the Ministry of Gender, Youth and Community Development (rather than the MoESC). There are no reliable official statistics for private pre-schools, although a considerable number exist in the major urban centres. Local publishers and booksellers do not consider pre-schools to be a significant market sector at this time.

Primary schools

In 1994 the establishment of the policy of free primary education led to student roll numbers increasing from 1,9 million in 1993 to 2,9 million in 1994. Primary school enrollments have remained stable at around this level up to the present. This significant increase in student numbers created financing problems in the provision of adequate quantities of schoolbooks. Current textbook provision policy is established in the MoESC 'Project Investment Framework (PIF) Scenarios for Basic Education' (September 1999) which states:

A target book/pupil ratio of 1:2 for all subjects and all grades.
Eight core subject textbooks required per grade. An assumed book

life of two years. Unit textbook cost is assumed to be MK50 per book. Textbooks will be provided free to all students but parents are to be responsible for replacing lost and damaged books.

The 1992 primary school curriculum currently in use specifies eleven subjects requiring four textbooks for Standards 1–4, six textbooks for Standards 5–6 and eight textbooks for Standards 7–8. It is planned to introduce an additional subject (Life Skills) into the curriculum from Standard 4.

Currently, there is a single set of textbooks and teacher's guides for each subject and grade, which were originally developed and published by the Malawi Institute of Education (MIE).[28] The development costs of the curriculum, textbooks and teacher's guides were covered by a World Bank funded project, as were the costs of printing and distributing some of the first editions. The World Bank textbook funding terminated in 1994.

In 1995, the MoESC (via the Malawi Institute of Education) feared that no other funder would be forthcoming and without funding of its own to continue the free textbook provision policy, they licenced the commercial reprint rights for these textbooks to two local publishers – Macmillan Malawi and Jhango – for sale direct to parents. The publishers printed quantities of three core textbooks and teacher's guides for Standards 1–4. However, within a year of signing this contract, and before significant commercial sales could be achieved, the MoESC reached agreement with CIDA for a further programme of agency funded reprints and free textbook distribution to primary schools, which effectively terminated all private sector publisher involvement in the primary textbook market. Both publishers claimed to have suffered substantial losses as a result of the licencing agreements with the MIE, and the issue was a subject of dispute between publishers, the MoESC and the donor for several years.

The primary textbook market thus remains closed to all private sector publishers and booksellers, as it has been almost since independence. Sales of a few commercially published primary school courses are made to a few elite private schools. There is also a small market for sales of primary school supplementary readers, also to a limited number of elite private primary schools. Within the past five years DFID funded the procurement of primary school reading books from commercial publishers and their supply to all Malawian primary schools in small book boxes. This, however, was a one-off purchase only. In 1999 and 2000 a number of funders have combined to build and equip approximately 315 Teacher Development Centres (TDCs) each of which has a small primary teacher's library. This project has also provided a small market for private sector publishers. Very few of the agency-funded materials listed above have been procured from or distributed via local private sector

---

28 The MIE is an autonomous but state owned and financed institution, established by government decree and reporting direct to the MoESC.

booksellers[29], although in the past year there have been signs that donors are willing to buy from booksellers if they can provide stock to deadlines.

With the exceptions stated above, private sector publishers (with the exception of Dzuka – see below) and booksellers in Malawi have not been permitted access to the core primary school book market for the past 35 years. And yet the primary school market in every African country is widely considered to be the essential basis for all local book trade development.

Secondary schools

This consists of conventional secondary schools (both government schools and grant-aided schools) and the newly established Community Day Secondary Schools (CDSSs).

Until 1990, the secondary school market was the only significant educational market that was theoretically available for private sector publishers and booksellers. However, in practice, the secondary textbook market was dominated by two virtual monopolies. In publishing terms almost all approved secondary textbooks were originally published by Dzuka Publishing House, or were reprinted locally under licence by Dzuka, or were locally represented in Malawi by Dzuka. Dzuka was a private sector, publishing house entirely owned by the then life President of Malawi, Dr Hastings Banda. In terms of distribution, virtually all of the educational book sales to state secondary schools (and effectively to the tiny private school market as well) were made via Malawi Book Services – a state owned educational book distribution monopoly, which closed for financial reasons in 1994.

Up to the early 1990s, the secondary school market in Malawi was small and progression rates from primary to secondary school were very low. From 1989 until the present, enrollments in both state and private sector secondary schools have grown very strongly as the result of the lifting of the barriers to secondary education imposed by the previous regime. Thus, in 1989 the conventional state secondary school roll numbers were 29,326 against a 1997 official enrollment of 70,858 – a growth of 241% in eight years. The numbers of secondary school students enrolled in Distance Education Centres (DECs) run by the Malawi College of Distance Education (MCDE) rose from 19,596 in 1989 to 108,846 in 1997 – a growth of 555% in eight years. The overall secondary education growth rate was 367% for the same eight-year period.

Although the MCDE schools were called Distance Education Centres, by the mid 1990s it was clear that very little distance education was taking place in these schools. They had evolved into a type of safety valve in which the enormous demand for secondary education from parents and students could

---

29   There is also a limited market for children's books and junior reference and reading books to those parents who are both sufficiently affluent and motivated to be able to purchase reading books for their children. It is worth noting in this context that the Cambridge University Press series of local language reading books for primary grades (published in four local languages in Malawi) is selling particularly well to parents and to some local schools (usually private primary schools).

be partially provided with minimum financial inputs from government. The state provided the salaries for primary school teachers to teach secondary school subjects. Local communities provided buildings (often via afternoon/evening usage of existing primary schools). The government regulated tuition fees, but communities were free to levy boarding fees and other incidental charges. The tuition fees were supposed to cover the provision of sets of specially produced learning materials but MCDE was never provided with sufficient budget to print enough copies and most DECs operated with seriously inadequate supplies of learning materials. The reality of the DECs was recognised in December 1998 when DECs were renamed as Community Day Secondary Schools (CDSSs) and removed from the control of MCDE. The DEC/CDSS developments of the 1990s created a low-grade type of secondary school with very poor performance levels. In 1999/2000 Malawi's secondary schools achieved the lowest ever pass rate for the MSCE, the national senior secondary leaving examination. The 1999/2000 pass-rate was barely 3% in the CDSSs.

For many years secondary school students paid a returnable textbook deposit of MK5 for the four years of secondary school. The government also provided annual budgets to secondary schools for the purchase of textbook and library supplies from MBS. From the early 1990s onwards, budget provision declined sharply. Thus, the growth in student numbers, which promised a booming secondary school market, was counter-balanced by steeply declining textbook purchase budgets from the government. For a time the MoESC shifted its secondary textbook and library budgets to the School Supplies Unit (SSU) but once again budgetary provision was irregular and low-level and SSU was never able to supply school needs.

In 1997 there was a radical change in textbook policy by the MoESC. Dzuka had already lost its place as the virtual monopoly publisher of textbooks and the monopoly distributor, MBS, had closed. The old list of approved textbooks, which had operated virtually unchanged from 1976, was completely updated on the basis of competitive submissions from commercial publishers. A choice of three approved textbooks for each secondary form and subject was introduced and private sector publishers were allowed free access to the secondary school market for the first time for many years.

Two funding agencies, Danida and the World Bank, provided purchasing power to conventional secondary schools (CSSs) and CDSSs. In the two-year period 1998–1999, approximately US$5 million in agency funding was provided to secondary schools for the selection and choice of textbooks and library materials from an approved list of teaching and learning materials published by private sector publishers in Malawi, the southern African region and the UK. As a result, local publishing has boomed from three active local educational publishing houses in 1995 to thirteen in 2000.

Unfortunately, the local book distribution network was considered to be too weak to take on major book distribution activities and distribution and consolidation services from publishers to secondary schools was contracted out on the basis of competitive bids. The bids for Danida funded supplies to CDSSs and World Bank funded supplies to conventional secondary schools were won by overseas specialist consolidators working in partnership with local freighting companies. Plans are underway, however, to fully involve local book distributors in the next phase of secondary book market developments starting in 2001.

It is significant that local and regional publishers have responded extremely well to the provision of agency funded, school-based purchasing power and access to the secondary school market. For the first time in 25 years:

- New junior secondary school courses are being written and published specifically for the new junior secondary school curriculum.
- A new edition of the Malawi School Atlas has also been produced.
- Entirely locally owned publishers have competed successfully with large multinational publishers to achieve approved textbooks in core subjects and the local publishing industry is now widely profitable and thriving.
- New skills have been developed in the development and presentation of textbook submissions (on time against deadlines) for competitive textbook evaluations as the basis for a new, and annually updated, approved book list.
- The MoESC is also learning new skills as the creator and guardian of standards rather than acting as a monopolistic producer.
- The Malawian government no longer has to find investment finance for new title development.[30]
- The new textbook evaluation exercise is open and transparent with all results published and available for scrutiny and complaint if necessary.
- Secondary schools are now getting up-to-date teaching and learning materials.

The tertiary education book and journals market

As can be seen in Table 4 on page 56, the tertiary book and journal market is very small. It comprises six primary teacher-training colleges and one secondary teacher-training college (Domasi College of Education). The University of Malawi consists of Chancellor College in Zomba, Bunda Agricultural College, The Malawi Polytechnic specialising in engineering and business studies, Kamuzu College of Nursing and the College of Medicine, which produces medical doctors. Mzuzu University, as separate institution is based in the north of the country. The Ministry of Labour administers and funds Technical Colleges but the MoESC provides teaching personnel. There are also a limited number of private sector tertiary institutions.

---

30 Under the previous system very little new book investment finance was required because the monopolistic publishing system then in place was characterised by inertia and very few new titles were developed for Malawi from the mid 1970s up to 1999, when the new MoESC policy was introduced.

In 1997 the total tertiary sector had an official enrollment of only 14,000 students. Many of the tertiary institutions now have only tiny procurement budgets or no effective budgets at all and textbook, reference book and journal purchases are small. Under the previous system, tertiary level procurements were generally the sole preserve of MBS (unless competitive bidding was required) and no other local bookseller developed either market share or skills in tertiary level supply.

The collapse of budgets during the past ten years provides little incentive for local booksellers to become involved. There is very little local tertiary level publishing and most of the required materials are published overseas. Occasional agency-funded procurements are usually put out to competitive tender and are won by specialist overseas library suppliers.[31] Local booksellers do not have the necessary bibliographic skills or facilities, nor do they have the necessary investment finance to compete with specialist international library suppliers and specialist journal subscription agents for the tiny local tertiary market.

The general, public library and religious book market

The National Library, with its HQ in Lilongwe, has approximately a dozen branches in the main towns throughout Malawi. Most of the National Library book stock is provided by overseas donations, mainly from Book Aid International in the UK and from Canadian-funded book donation organisations in North America. Local discretionary budgets are tiny. In 1997 the National Library had sufficient discretionary budget to purchase only 300 titles from local publishers and booksellers for all its branches. In the past year there are signs of a slight improvement in the National Library purchasing power and new school textbooks have been purchased for central and regional textbook libraries. The quantities are relatively small however.

The religious book market is steady and is served by a number of specialist local publishing and bookselling companies including CLAIM, the Moni Bookshop, Popular Publishers and the Simon de Montfort Bookshop in Balaka. The religious market has sustained a number.of local publishing and bookselling companies for many years when few other markets where available to the private sector.

There is a small but steady tourist market served mainly by the Times Bookshop kiosks which are established in airports and the main tourist hotels. No information is available on the size of this market but it is thought to be small. It comprises international, regional and local magazines and newspapers, travel books, mass-market paperback remainders and some locally published fiction both in English and Chichewa.

---

31 Most of the leading international library suppliers have local agents in Malawi who watch for bidding and supply opportunities and inform the overseas principals and act on their behalf. Thus local companies do receive a percentage of the profits on competitive library supply contracts. Similarly, local freighting companies are often linked to overseas library suppliers and consolidators for the purposes of customs clearance, local storage and internal distribution and delivery.

The general and trade market outside the tourist kiosks is small. It comprises local fiction (and some non-fiction) publishing in both Chichewa and English, educational titles to richer parents and private schools, reference books mostly published outside Malawi (for example, dictionaries) and a limited number of coffee table books (often remainders) on African and wildlife themes.

Neither the Book Publishers' Association of Malawi (BPAM) nor the Booksellers' Association of Malawi (BAM) maintain any book trade sales statistics and it is thus impossible to estimate the current size of the book market with any accuracy.

Key players in the sales and distribution of books in Malawi

Publishers

Table 5 provides a list and a brief description of the main publishers currently active in Malawi.

Table 5 Main publishers in Malawi in 2000

Name of publisher	Type of company
Longman Malawi	Locally incorporated subsidiary of a multi-national publisher. It reports to Maskew Miller Longman in Cape Town. It publishes locally authored and edited textbooks and also markets regional and UK published titles of interest to Malawi.
Macmillan Malawi	Locally incorporated subsidiary of a multi-national publisher. It publishes locally authored and edited textbooks and also markets regional and UK published titles of interest to Malawi. Until recently there was some local equity. Also publishes Chichewa literature and African fiction.
Jango-Heinemann	Fifty-fifty equity joint venture between a local company and a multinational also publishing locally authored and edited school textbooks and marketing Heinemann regional and UK titles. Also publishes local children's and supplementary reading books and African fiction.

Dzuka	Wholly Malawian owned company still actively involved in local textbook publishing. It acts as local marketing agent for Nelson, Evans Bros (both UK companies) and for ZEPH based in Lusaka. Also publishes Chichewa grammar and literature titles.
Evans Bros	A UK based company legally represented in Malawi by Dzuka and now interested once again after a gap of many years in specialist local educational publishing.
Oxford University Press	UK based university press (charitable status) legally represented in Malawi by Maneno Enterprises. Recently published four new textbook series for the new junior secondary curriculum, which were locally authored and originated. This is OUPs first local publishing for Malawi for many years.
Cambridge University Press	UK based university press (charitable status) legally represented in Malawi by Maneno Enterprises and the publisher of an adapted title for the new JS curriculum. Has also recently published a series of local language readers in four Malawian languages which are selling well.
John Murray	UK based private publisher legally represented in Malawi by Macmillan Malawi and publishing locally adapted textbooks which have been recently approved for use in the new junior secondary curriculum for Malawi.
Nelson	UK based company legally represented in Malawi by Dzuka. Interested in local publishing for Malawi but has not yet succeeded in getting a course approved for the new curriculum.
CLAIM	Wholly Malawian-owned religious publishers and booksellers. Recently successfully competed to win approval for a junior secondary maths course against local, regional and multinational competition.
Popular	Wholly Malawian-owned company; affiliated to the Catholic Church. Recently successfully

	competed to win approval for a junior secondary religious education textbook course against local, regional and international competition. Also publishes Chichewa literature.
Tupokiwe Press	A wholly locally owned religious publisher.
Chancellor College Press	University Press owned entirely by the University of Malawi. It also has approved textbooks on the secondary textbook list.
Zambia Educational Publishing House	A Zambian parastatal publishing house publishing approved Chinyanja language titles and represented in Malawi by Dzuka publishers.

Book retailers

Table 6 provides a list of the key book retailers currently operating in Malawi.

Table 6 Main book retailers in Malawi in 2000

Name of bookseller	Type of company
Times Bookshops	The oldest bookshop chain in Malawi and currently owned by Blantyre Print and Publishing which was once part of Press Trust – the Banda family holding company. Blantyre Print and Publishing also owns Dzuka Publishing House. Times Bookshop is essentially a book retailer specialising in general trade and children's books but with an interest in selling textbooks and educational materials if there is an available market. Historically it shared the book market with MBS. Times Bookshops handled general books and MBS specialised in educational supply. It has its HQ in Blantyre and has branches in Blantyre, Lilongwe (2), Zomba, Mzuzu (2) and Kasungu. It also has hotel and airport kiosks.
Central Bookshop	Established in 1960. Essentially a general bookseller but interested in educational supply at school level if the market is available. Has some direct import business, mostly of remainder books. Has its HQ in Blantyre and one branch in Lilongwe.

CLAIM	Religious publisher and bookseller. Has its HQ in Blantyre and branches in Mulanje, Zomba, Malosa, Balaka, Mangochi, Lilongwe, Kasungu, Mponela. Nkhoma, Salima, Mzuzu, Karonga, Rumphi, Ekwendeni and Mzimba. Is starting to take an interest in secondary book supply with the opening up of the secondary school market as the result of the new 1997 MoESC policy.
Dzuka Publishing Company Bookshops	An educational bookseller concentrating on sales of Dzuka publications but also stocking other educational books in demand. Also stocks Chichewa literature and readers, etc. HQ in Blantyre and branches in Limbe and Lilongwe.
Maneno Enterprises	Well-established bookseller in Lilongwe specialising in educational, children's and reference books. Will open a new branch in Mzuzu in 2000. Local representative for OUP and CUP.
Moni Bookshop	Small religious and Chichewa language bookshop in Limbe owned by the Catholic Church. Recently interested in stocking educational books as a result of the new MoESC policy toward secondary education.
St Louis Montfort Bookshop	Catholic owned religious, general and educational bookshop in Balaka.
The Bookmart	General and educational bookshop in Blantyre.
Papermine	General and educational bookseller and stationer in Blantyre.
Odini Bookshop	Small general and educational bookshop in Lilongwe owned by the Catholic Church.

All of the book retailers listed here are officially approved book suppliers for the Danida funded Secondary School Textbook and Libraries Project. The Booksellers' Association of Malawi has approximately 30 member booksellers but the above bookshops represent the companies to which a majority of local publishers are prepared to extend some form of credit

Wholesalers

In January 2000 there were no genuine book wholesalers in Malawi. It is planned, however, that two well-financed textbook wholesalers will be created shortly to serve the newly established secondary textbook and library market.

One of the wholesalers[32] is a joint venture between a group of local booksellers, a local freight forwarder and a British consolidator. A local Malawi trading and freighting group will finance the other wholesaler. It is a symptom of the current dynamism in the Malawi book trade, created by the newly accessible secondary textbook market, that two competing and well-financed book wholesalers are in the process of formation.

The School Supplies Unit

The School Supplies Unit is a department of the MoESC based in Blantyre. It was established in the mid-1990s to fill the educational supply gap left by the collapse of the MBS. The SSU has the mandate to warehouse and distribute the full range of educational supplies, including books.

From 1996 the SSU was responsible for storing and distributing the millions of free textbooks and teacher's guides financed by CIDA and printed in Canada. The distribution methodology was very supply-oriented and there were delays, mis-supplies and damages.[33] Significant quantities of the free textbooks leaked into the commercial book trade and were sold. This is currently the subject of an investigation by the Anti-Corruption Bureau. There were also problems in clearing the free textbook supplies from the shipper's warehouse and very large demurrage charges accumulated, which were only cleared in 1998. CIDA is currently considering how further free textbook supplies for primary schools should be distributed in 2000 and 2001.

In 1996, school based secondary textbook budgets were diverted to the SSU so that the SSU could buy centrally, achieve good prices and distribute books efficiently to schools. Unfortunately, the budgets allocated by the GoM and requested by the schools were never made available and the SSU has not been a major purchaser of secondary school books.

Occasional small, agency-funded, book supplies are sometimes procured and distributed by SSU including a recent African Development Bank procurement for the basic textbooks required by seven new secondary schools. However the major agency-funded secondary textbook procurements of 1998 and 1999 from the World Bank and Danida were put out to competitive bid and were won by foreign specialist consolidators working in partnership with local freighting companies.

In the past, the SSU received training and specially developed stock management and inventory control software from USAID but the software is not currently operational and the hardware provided by the funder is also out of commission. A new CIDA funded textbook project was scheduled for lift off in 2000[34] and this may also finance hardware, software and training for the SSU.

---

32 Book Supplies and Distribution Company (BSAD).
33 Much of the damage in the past was caused in transit as a result of too many handling movements, a poorly specified carton and the lack of shrink-wrapping leading to water damage.
34 At the time of writing the CIDA project is suspended pending a final decision by the Canadian Government.

The SSU has a central warehouse in Blantyre rented from a commercial company. Shortage of SSU funding has led to closures of this warehouse in the past and an inability to access urgently needed stock because of late payment of rents and demurrage charges. In addition, the warehouse is too small for large consignments such as the CIDA primary textbook consignment and is inadequately equipped. SSU also operates two other regional warehouses in Lilongwe and Blantyre. Primary textbooks are supplied from central to regional warehouses on the basis of centrally calculated stock allocations. From the regional warehouses books are distributed to one of the 32 district education offices. This is another problem area because very few districts have adequate storage facilities.

From the districts the books are further delivered down the supply chain to one of 315 zones. Once again, zonal storage is inadequate and transport from districts to zones is dependent upon the availability of district level storage or district level funding for hired vehicles and/or fuel. The final stage in the supply chain is collection by the schools from the zones.

The above system is clearly ineffective.[35] It is a totally supply-led, top-down approach with nobody at the next stage of distribution knowing what will happen and when. The matching of centrally allocated book supplies to school needs is poor and supply errors to individual schools are rarely corrected. The whole system is dependent upon budget allocations that are either virtually non-existent (zonal and district levels) or seriously inadequate (regional and central level). There is a general lack of facilities, equipment and good management systems. In 1999 the SSU attempted to shorten the supply chain by supplying from regional stores direct to schools. This has helped to some extent but the fundamental supply problems described above still exist.

A history of book publishing and distribution in Malawi

Primary schooling always has the majority of pupil enrollments, and thus the print run volume and profit opportunity, which provides the financial platform for all other local publishing, printing and distribution development. In most developing countries local publishing (and logically therefore, book wholesaling and retailing) is usually focused on primary school textbooks, unless state centralist policies have intervened to create state run textbook provision systems. In Malawi, the following factors have made it difficult to maintain an adequate, private sector, book publishing and distribution system without private sector access to the main school markets:

- Low literacy rates.
- Very low parental purchasing power.
- The high local costs of investment and the under-capitalisation of local book trade companies.
- The lack of a tradition of reading and book buying.

---

35   Vide Fearnley R (July 1998) Primary Textbook Distribution in Malawi, CIDA for the Ministry of Education, Sports and Culture.

The situation before independence

Prior to independence almost all textbooks used in primary and secondary schools in Malawi (with the exception of Chichewa/Chinyanja language books) were published by British publishers either based in the UK or via branch offices in neighbouring countries. The exception was Longman, which had registered a local company office in Blantyre (Longman Malawi) in the early 1960s.[36]

There was no policy of free textbook provision under the colonial government and all school textbooks at both primary and secondary level were sold to parents via the local book trade, which at that time was dominated by Times Bookshops, the Africa Book Centre and by religious booksellers.

The post-independence educational book trade

Following independence in 1964, textbook fees were introduced at both primary and secondary levels. The fees were collected by government and were set against the costs of provision. Primary textbook fees were finally phased out in the 1990s with the introduction of free primary education, but secondary textbook fees continue up to the present.

Work also was started on the development of a new curriculum. It was intended that this curriculum would represent the national aspirations and culture of the newly independent Malawi. Longman Malawi and, to a lesser extent, Macmillan, published textbooks for the emerging new primary curriculum. Local authors wrote most of the primary textbooks. Longman also invested in secondary textbook publishing and there was a wave of local secondary publishing in the 1970s out of the Longman Malawi office, based on the adaptation of titles originally published in Zimbabwe (Secondary English, Secondary Maths, Secondary History Course, etc).

Despite the fact that the secondary school market in Malawi was very small, other publishers also invested in the development of secondary school textbooks specifically for Malawi. Thus, Macmillan published a secondary school Atlas for Malawi and Evans Brothers, based in London, published a junior secondary level Geography of Malawi. It is, perhaps, a comment on the inertia of secondary curriculum development in Malawi that most of the secondary school courses originally published in the 1970s are still in use now, although in some cases in recently updated, revised editions.[37]

With a static primary and secondary curriculum (even the secondary level literature set books have run for many years without change) there was little opportunity or incentive for local educational publishing activity after the initial burst of post-colonial textbook publishing from the late 1960s to the late 1970s.

---

36 Although the Longman Malawi company was Blantyre based and employed local editorial, marketing and distribution staff and developed local authors, it was nevertheless still wholly owned by the parent company in the UK.

37 The introduction of the revised junior secondary curriculum in January 2000 was the first significant secondary level curriculum reform since the introduction of the first post-colonial secondary curriculum in the late 1960s.

Thus local educational publishing was stultified for many years and local educational publishers tended to develop as marketing agents for the importation and sale of foreign textbooks, rather than as creative educational publishers focused on publishing for local needs. Foreign textbooks (largely British in the early days but now increasingly from the southern African region[38]) were (and still are) used as basic textbooks in many non-core secondary subjects and particularly at senior secondary level where pupil roll numbers traditionally were too low to support Malawi-specific local publishing.

The curriculum inertia in Malawi also had an adverse impact on the development of local authorship. There has been very little opportunity for local authors to develop school textbook writing skills over the past 25 years.

Changes in textbook financing policies

In the early 1970s the government decided to purchase bulk supplies of core textbooks for primary school students. Primary textbook publishers sold English, Maths and Chichewa textbooks to the MoE, which then delivered to schools via the MBS. Other textbooks (History, Geography, Civics, Agriculture and Science) were still purchased by parents via the local book trade. After almost twenty-five years it is difficult to ascertain precisely what level of primary textbook supply was actually achieved by government. By the mid-1970s, however, the financial burden of providing free primary school textbooks, even for just three subjects, was sufficiently tough that the GoM had to use World Bank project funding to maintain the supply.

At the secondary level, the government introduced a textbook fee of MK5 per student for the four forms of secondary school.[39] This was intended to provide secondary schools with purchasing power (supported and supplemented by annual government budget allocations for textbooks and library stock) to buy and maintain textbook stocks for loan by students. The textbook fee was a deposit, which was returnable to students at the end of four years if all loaned textbooks had been returned to the school in good condition. It is reported that the combination of user fees and regular financial subventions from government to the school 'textbook' budget line was sufficient to maintain adequate textbook supplies for secondary school students throughout the 1970s and for most of the 1980s.

It should be noted that throughout this period both primary and secondary roll numbers were small in comparison to the roll numbers that now have to be provided for at the turn of the millennium.

---

38   It is interesting to note that the World Bank funded Secondary Education Project (SEP) that procured secondary school textbooks and library books in 1999 purchased 55% of the total titles from Southern Africa and 45% from the UK.

39   In the mid-1970s, MK5 was approximately equivalent to US$5. The Ministry of Education maintained the original, secondary textbook deposit fee of MK5 per student for over 25 years without any increase. By 1999 the fee was virtually worthless. The new secondary textbook fee of MK180 per student per year, which was introduced in January 2000, is equivalent to US$4 – or 20% less than the dollar value of the original textbook fee in 1975. It is evident that US$1 in 1975 would have purchased far more than US$1 in 2000.

The emergence and role of Dzuka

The first significant change in the pattern of local publishing development occurred in 1975 when a group of senior staff members of Longman Malawi resigned to form their own 100% locally-owned company. This was the Dzuka Publishing Company. With the majority of their local senior staff involved in the new company, and no other obvious local alternatives, Longman was forced to reach an accommodation with Dzuka. It was agreed that Dzuka would take over the representation of the Longman UK list in Malawi and that local publishing rights for the Longman Malawi primary and secondary school textbook lists would be licensed to Dzuka for local reprinting. Within a short period Dzuka became the dominant school textbook publisher in Malawi and other overseas companies with interests in Malawi (Macmillan, Evans Brothers, Nelson, etc) also signed representation agreements with Dzuka.

Eventually, a majority of the Dzuka equity passed into the ownership of the Blantyre Print and Publishing Company. This, in turn, was owned by Press Holdings which in turn was owned by the then Life President of Malawi, Dr Hastings Banda. The government then established Dzuka as the virtual monopoly publisher in Malawi of school textbooks for both primary and secondary schools. Blantyre Print and Publishing Company printed Dzuka's textbooks. Via its representation agreements with foreign publishers, Dzuka quickly established a position of overwhelming dominance in school textbook publishing and printing at both primary and secondary levels. This dominance was not only in the supply of locally published, Malawi-specific textbooks (many reprinted under licence from Longman). It also extended to the supply of foreign textbooks, which were recommended for use in Malawi (largely at secondary level) in subjects where local textbooks had not been published and were not available.[40] From 1979 onwards (after the effective Dzuka take-over of the Longman list in Malawi), the original Longman primary and secondary school textbook lists were further adapted, not always with the permission of the original license holders, to reduce or obviate the licence fee payments to the original copyright holders.

In the thirty year period from the mid-1960s until the mid-1990s, government policies supported by agency funding created state or parastatal monopoly educational publishing, printing and distribution systems for school textbooks in a majority of African countries. Malawi is unique because, for a twenty-year period from the middle of the 1970s to the mid-1990s, a privately-owned publishing company exercised the state textbook publishing monopoly at

---

40 The Inspectorate Division of the MoESC, now the Educational Methods and Advisory Service – EMAS, established this recommended list of secondary school textbooks. The original list of approved secondary textbooks was first produced in 1976. It remained virtually unchanged (including some titles which had been out of print for many years) until it was revised and updated in 1998 by the MoESC/DSE DEC Pilot Project and later in the same year for the MoESC/WB SEP. It is now MoESC policy to review and update the approved textbook list annually as an encouragement for local publishing development, and also to make certain that the best of new textbooks are always available for Malawi schools.

primary level and also supplied most of the secondary requirement as well. The combination of a standstill in curriculum development activity combined with the Dzuka textbook publishing monopoly was extremely effective in inhibiting almost any investment in new textbook development in Malawi for approximately 20 years at the primary level and for approximately 25 years at the secondary level. New textbook development requires long-term investment finance[41] and this in turn reduces profitability in a system where there is no competition and thus no need to invest in new books. The absence of curriculum development activity, and the lack of any new book investment requirements, enabled Dzuka to maximise its profits during the period of its textbook publishing monopoly.

The rise and fall of Malawi Book Services

The Blantyre Print and Publishing Group owned a book wholesaling and retailing operation (The Times Bookshops), which also included hotel bookshops and airport kiosks. However, this was not considered to be an appropriate outlet for textbook and other educational book distribution activities. In 1974 the GoM established Malawi Book Services (MBS) out of the previous African Book Centre as a state-owned book wholesaling and retailing organisation specialising in educational book supply for all levels. All the primary school textbooks continued to be published by Dzuka and sold to the GoM, but Dzuka now delivered the stock to MBS, which was responsible for onward distribution to schools. The MBS charged a basic 20% commission on retail prices for this service.[42]

MBS received low cost, government investment funds to develop national and regional warehousing facilities and to establish a national network of retail bookshops to serve educational needs. Inevitably, MBS also stocked a wide range of other books including tertiary textbooks, children's' books, readers, local language books and general and trade books.[43] All government-funded schools were required to buy from MBS and MBS was also granted the lucrative primary textbook distribution monopoly. All other educational book wholesaling and retailing operations in Malawi withered under the pressure of this intense, state-subsidised competition.

---

41 One of the critical characteristics of new textbook publishing is that it requires a long cash cycle investment profile. It is rare that set-up and origination costs are covered within the first year of the life of a new textbook. For this reason, publisher investment in new textbooks requires a stable textbook provision and financing policy. Constant changes in policy and direction and chronic unreliability in financing are inimical to the development and establishment of adequate textbook provision. Good publishing can occur in very small markets, but they *must* be stable and predictable.

42 A recent calculation based on the actual costs of delivering Danida funded textbook procurements to 495 Community Day Secondary Schools suggests that 5–7,5% of retail price is a more realistic charge for in-country storage and distribution of textbooks to schools in Malawi. It is evident that the state owned and monopolistic MBS had very high textbook distribution charges.

43 MBS also supplied stationery, chalk, chemicals and a wide range of other educational consumables.

MBS always had a good reputation for the speed and efficiency of its textbook delivery services. The extensive chain of retail bookshops throughout the country provided sales outlets for other local, regional and international publishers of local language, children's and trade books, which have not existed to the same degree since MBS closed in 1994. The MBS retail shops also provided a genuine service to rural and provincial communities and supported the growth and maintenance of local language publishing, reading and basic literacy.

The decision of the World Bank funded primary textbook project in 1992 not to use MBS as the distribution organisation for the new MIE primary textbooks removed a significant market sector and a major source of income from MBS. In 1990/91 Dzuka, still a dominant force in secondary textbook publishing decided that the discounts levied by MBS for textbook sales to secondary schools were too great. Dzuka established its own retail outlets to enable it to supply direct to schools without going through the MBS network. 1992 to 1994 were bad years for book funding in Malawi because of the decline of funding as a result of the pressures for change on the Banda government. General secondary school textbook funding also declined sharply because in 1994 the new government announced the introduction of a policy of free primary education. Primary roll numbers increased dramatically. Government budgets were diverted away from secondary consumables toward support for the rising costs of the primary sector.

By 1994, MBS was suffering financially from these serious setbacks. All of the above factors, plus a bureaucratic structure characterised by high overheads, proved to be too much for MBS and it was forced to close in 1994.

Despite the disadvantages inherent in its dominant, virtually monopolistic, market position, the closure of MBS left a huge gap in book distribution in Malawi, which still remains in 2000. The network of warehouses and retail outlets, which provided genuinely national coverage, disappeared overnight and has not yet been replaced. The steady decline in the financial strength of MBS from 1990 to 1994 also removed the investment finance, which had been used for many years to support stock purchases and thus to guarantee the availability of all types of book stock throughout the country.

In the past few years no new supplier has emerged with either the national coverage or the investment finance to achieve the level of national availability previously provided by MBS. All book distribution and local publishing in Malawi have suffered significantly as a result. Unfortunately, when MBS closed as a result of severe financial problems and the shortage of government budgets, it had effectively eliminated any successor organisation with the experience, national facilities and financing to take over its critical role. National book distribution has been a major problem in Malawi ever since.

The emergence of the Malawi College of Distance Education publishing monopoly

At the same time as the Dzuka primary textbook monopoly was being undermined by donors and the MIE, there also emerged a parallel form of *de facto* state publishing learning materials monopoly at secondary level. Historically, access to state secondary education in Malawi has been very limited. As a result, parents increasingly turned to the Malawi College of Distance Education (MCDE) and the network of Distance Education Centres (DECs) as a means to achieve secondary education for those students who had failed to gain entry to conventional state-funded secondary schools.

Originally, the MCDE had been established to provide access to secondary education for adult students who learned from specially designed correspondence courses. Over the years, as demand for secondary education grew and the DEC system expanded, the concept of distance education for adults disappeared and the DECs became simply second division secondary schools providing lower level face-to-face teaching for those students who had failed to get into the conventional system. In 1994, when the barriers to the growth of secondary education were effectively dismantled, enrollments into DECs began to increase sharply and by 1999 it was estimated that there were 180,000 students in over 500 institutions taking secondary examinations via the DEC system. This represented approximately 70–80% of all secondary students in the country.

There was a significant difference between conventional secondary schools (CSSs) and DECs in the types of learning materials used. CSSs used conventional textbooks published by private sector publishers, but students in DECs were required to use the learning materials sets, originally developed for a distance education audience, which were published and provided by MCDE. Until 1995 the tuition fees paid by DEC students included the free provision of all required learning sets in all subjects to every student. Unfortunately MCDE never received sufficient budget from government to come anywhere near providing the needs of all students for learning materials and in 1995 the system was changed so that MCDE only had a responsibility to provide sets of materials to DECs for loan to students. Even this more limited objective was considerably beyond the budget allocated to MCDE and it is estimated that most DECs never received more than 10% of their required learning sets. Although MCDE could not supply sufficient learning sets to satisfy demand, the MoESC prohibited the sale of learning sets to students.

There were also severe quality problems with many of the learning sets produced and published by MCDE. These included:

- Factual errors as well as poor editing with many misprints, spelling and grammatical mistakes.
- Poor design including inconsistent typefaces and type sizes within the same book, self study symbols provided without explanations.

- Wide variations in the clarity and level of writing and in the difficulty of content.
- Questions and work assignments were often not related to information in the text.
- Maps were not related to the text.
- Poor and confusing pagination, including contents lists without page numbers.
- Poor quality printing and insufficient books printed due to ageing and badly maintained printing equipment, budget problems and constant machine break-downs.
- High costs of production (not competitive with a comparable private sector printer).

The learning set supply policy, which was applied to DECs, effectively removed all choice of materials from the students. The tuition fees charged to students were paid solely for materials published by a monopoly parastatal publishing institution (MCDE). The DEC market, which by 1998 was 70–80% of secondary student roll numbers, thus was completely closed to private sector publishers.

By 1995 private sector publishers and book distributors in Malawi had no access to any part of the primary school textbook market or to at least 70% of the state secondary school market. The remaining 30% of the secondary school market, which was available, and the relatively small tertiary and general trade markets suffered from seriously inadequate funding for textbooks and school libraries and a lack of significant purchasing power for trade books. The combination of state dominance of the sector with inadequate funding had brought the Malawi book trade to the edge of extinction. It cannot be claimed that monopolistic state publishing and distribution provided cheaper prices, cheaper operating costs, better books, higher quality, faster distribution or better service to schools.

In December 1998 all DECs were re-designated as Community Day Secondary Schools (CDSSs) by the MoESC. The significance of this move was that the MoESC accepted that there was no distance education taking place in DECs and that henceforth they should be treated as parts of the mainstream secondary education system. The act of re-designation also removed the MCDE publishing monopoly over these secondary schools and gave them the right to select their own textbooks from the list of approved books recently developed by EMAS and MIE. At a stroke, 75% of the secondary education textbook market was once again made accessible to private sector publishers and booksellers in Malawi.

Book distribution in Malawi

The primary textbook requirements are still supplied entirely by the School Supplies Unit operating out of Blantyre. There is no private sector involvement in the distribution operation apart from the sub-contracting of approximately 80% of the required transportation services to private sector trucking companies.

Recent surveys of the efficiency of the SSU textbook supply operation to primary schools demonstrate continuing problems:

- The operation is entirely supply-oriented. Stock is allocated to regions and to individual schools on the basis of out-of-date enrollment information. There is no attempt to identify priority school needs and to fulfill these needs.
- The supply is unpredictable and irregular and depends largely upon the availability of budget funds. Schools have no idea what stock will be delivered or when it will arrive, although the SSU is now attempting to get stock to schools in December every year before the start of the new school year. The first information on textbook deliveries provided to districts, however, is usually the arrival of the trucks en route to zones and schools.
- Available stock is not distributed evenly to every school. Mission schools with their own transport, for example, are often able to get better stocks than remote rural schools.
- Remote schools are still generally expected to collect stock from zonal centres but have no transport or budget to do so.
- The supply is generally insufficient.
- Most schools have unplanned textbook stocks which may be good in one subject at one grade level but are rarely continuously adequate through several grades. Most schools suffer from a serious shortage of textbooks in the upper grades and in the non-core subjects.
- The main SSU warehouse is too small to clear the huge textbook consignments provided by CIDA, which in turn creates a pile-up of stock and enhanced storage and demurrage charges, which the SSU cannot always meet.
- Stock management systems are inadequate and warehouse facilities require upgrading and the provision of basic equipment.
- Free textbook stock is leaking out of the system and is being sold to private schools and to the more affluent parents.

All of the above problems are widely recognised but there is still little movement to change the system. In early 2000 à DFID/MoESC study was set up to examine alternative primary textbook publishing and distribution strategies. At the time of writing no proposal had emerged.

At the secondary level, the conventional, state schools' textbook budget lines were removed in 1995/96 and re-allocated to the SSU. Schools were required to order their textbooks directly from the SSU. Unfortunately the SSU received almost no budget allocations for textbooks and therefore was not in a position to meet the secondary school orders. Nevertheless, until 1999, all conventional secondary schools were theoretically supposed to be supplied through the SSU. Distance Education Centres (now Community Day Secondary Schools) continued to receive very few learning set stocks from MCDE, but once again the official supply channel until 1999 was via the state-funded,

MCDE central warehouse in Blantyre and regional stores in Lilongwe and Mzuzu.[44]

In 1999, two agency-funded projects, the World Bank Secondary Education Project and the Danida Community Day Secondary Schools Project, decided that neither the SSU nor the MCDE distribution systems could cope with the quantities of secondary textbooks and library books that were scheduled for procurement. The MoESC created updated lists of approved and recommended books. Purchasing power budgets (not cash) were provided to the schools. The schools selected the books that they wanted and sent order forms in to a central point where they were consolidated using a specially selected software programme. Competitive tenders were issued to professional, experienced, book consolidators working in partnership with local trucking companies. The local trucking companies then delivered books to the value of US$5 million to over 625 secondary institutions throughout Malawi. There were only eleven cases of wrong supply (most due to faulty enrollment information) and in all cases the wrong supplies were corrected quickly and to the satisfaction of the schools concerned. Schools received the books that they wanted, accurately and in good condition.

It should be noted that book distribution to primary and secondary schools generally has to take place in the middle of the rainy season if supplies are to be in schools for the beginning of the school year. This adds considerably to the transport and storage problems.

As has been mentioned already, the local book trade has little or no involvement in tertiary level book supply.

Although the BAM has over thirty registered members, the national retailer coverage is still very poor after years of being dominated by state-funded monopolistic suppliers. CLAIM has the largest number of book outlets, but many of these are very small and carry very little stock. Only in Blantyre, Lilongwe, Mzuzu and perhaps Zomba is there a possibility of finding a reasonable stock of books. For bookshops to order a specific title, which is not in stock, is still rare. Local booksellers suffer from the following problems:

- Turnover is generally low. Most booksellers do not have the financial resources to buy the stock required to fulfill basic educational requirements.
- Most booksellers have poor credit records and most publishers do not wish to supply them on open credit.
- Most publishers would rather supply textbooks direct to the schools than operate through the local book trade.
- Most book retailers have small and inadequate premises to hold the considerable stocks required for critical school needs.
- Most booksellers still have little or no experience and no operational systems to cope with large scale educational requirements.

---

44 The MCDE distribution system is a parallel supply system to the SSU. Both are run-down and seriously under-funded and it would be better if both were combined into one operation. So far, the logic of this suggestion has not been followed through.

Donor impact on book policy, financing, publishing, printing and distribution

By the mid-1970s, government financing to support education was already coming under pressure. From 1979 to 1987 the costs of primary school textbook provision for the three core subjects, English, Maths and Chichewa, published by Dzuka, were funded by a World Bank project. The World Bank also funded the printing and the MBS distribution costs. Thus agency funding was used to support both private sector and state publishing and distribution monopolies. By the late 1980s it was obvious to development partners and the MoESC that the primary school curriculum and the primary school textbooks published by Dzuka had become very dated.[45] The MoESC/World Bank Primary Education Project had, as one of its principal objectives, the creation of a new primary school curriculum and the development of a new generation of primary school textbooks. By 1987, the World Bank was unwilling to fund or support a monopoly private sector company in the task of new materials development and publication. Thus, the available agency funding for new textbooks was channeled not into Dzuka, but into the Malawi Institute of Education as a combined primary curriculum development and teaching and learning materials development centre.

From 1989 until 1994 the World Bank funded MIE to develop a new primary school curriculum, to write and publish the new primary textbooks and teacher's guides. The World Bank (and more recently CIDA) has funded the printing and the free distribution of the new textbooks for the new curriculum since 1992. Indeed, it is probable that funding agencies have financed virtually all of the primary textbook publishing, production and distribution costs for at least the past twenty years. In 2000 there is still no primary textbook budget in MoESC financial allocations.

From 1995, CIDA took over the funding of primary textbook production on the basis of manufacturing in Canada and shipping into Malawi for free distribution to primary schools. This project has not been problem free. Initial production specifications were too low and the book life actually achieved was less than expected. There were many delays in warehousing and distribution and a proportion of the stock is reported to have 'leaked' from government warehouses. In 1999 many of the 'free' textbooks manufactured in Canada were being sold widely and openly to parents and to private schools throughout the country from 'pavement' booksellers and also from legitimate bookshops. The CIDA funded textbook manufacturing support in Canada is scheduled to continue until at least 2002.[46]

---

45 The same conclusion would also have been true of the secondary curriculum and textbooks, but at that time there was no funded secondary education project which could focus attention upon these issues.

46 Twelve years after the initiation of the primary, curriculum development reform, approximately one third of the titles developed by MIE with agency funding have not been published or provided to primary schools. Most of the missing titles are in the upper standards of primary schools.

The MoESC/WB/CIDA textbook projects provided a new primary curriculum, textbooks and teacher's guides. These were supplied free of charge to primary students throughout Malawi and thus supported the policy drive toward UPE. It is difficult to estimate precisely how effective the projects were in terms of providing acceptable book to pupil ratios, but delays in achieving the planned publication programme, shorter than expected book life and ongoing problems with distribution obviously had an adverse impact on the educational effectiveness of the projects.

The projects generated a substantial investment into MIE from a number of funding agencies. Publishing training (editorial, design, lay-out and DTP, etc), pre-press equipment, printing facilities and the upgrading of premises and equipment plus VSO professional attachments have all been provided over the past ten years. As a result, MIE in 1999 is probably the best-equipped educational publisher in Malawi. However, MIE was never set up to be a marketing and sales organisation and it had (and has) no mandate or capacity to operate as a self-financing, cash generating, risk-taking, sustainable, educational publisher. Thus, without on-going, front-end financial support from funders, its role as a core educational publisher for Malawi is extremely limited.

While the WB and CIDA funded projects provided much needed textbooks free-of-charge to schools and students, the projects contributed nothing to the development of sustainable educational publishing and book distribution in Malawi. No commercial, private sector, local publisher benefited from the donor investments in any way. No private distribution company was allowed to develop skills, capacity and profit. The previous private sector, textbook publishing monopoly was replaced by a state sector monopoly. The very substantial agency investment in publishing skills and equipment upgrading in MIE has not been sustainable without continued agency funding.[47]

It is important to note that when the state distribution company collapsed, all of the agency investment accrued by MBS through its distribution commissions was also lost. By putting all of the eggs in one basket there was no alternative organisation available to take over the role of MBS. Indeed, alternative organisations had been consciously weakened by donor and government policy. Bearing in mind the high level of MBS commissions it cannot even be claimed that state monopoly distribution was cheaper than private sector distribution services.

The role of multinationals and regional publishers

All multinational and regional publishers with an interest in Malawi are strongly focused on the educational markets. Almost all of the multinational companies listed in Table 6 on p. 64 have recently made significant investments in the

---

47   MIE probably recognised the truth of this assertion earlier than any other organisation in Malawi. It was MIE, which first proposed the termination of state textbook publishing in favour of the private sector publishing industry in a paper presented to a book development workshop held in Malawi in September 1997.

development or adaptation of new course materials for the new junior secondary curriculum via a competitive evaluation and approval process. In the recently published, approved list of secondary schoolbooks, titles were approved or recommended for use in Malawi secondary schools not just from Malawi and the UK, but also from South Africa, Namibia, Botswana, Zambia, Zimbabwe, Kenya and Nigeria. Of the total order value of secondary school books procured by funders during 1999, 55% by value were published in Malawi or in the Southern Africa region. Small local publishers (Dzuka, CLAIM, Chanco and Popular) have demonstrated their competitiveness by winning approved textbook awards in head to head competition with multinationals and large regional publishers.

The MoESC requires all publishers, who wish to submit books for approval, to be either locally incorporated in Malawi or to have a current legally registered representation agreement with a local company. This is to ensure that all approved and recommended book sales bring some financial benefit to Malawi. Similarly BPAM requires all members to be locally incorporated in Malawi. There is, at present, little or no division or tension between local, regional and multinational publishers in Malawi and good working relationships are being developed between publishers via the trade association.

It is noteworthy, however, that regional publishers that are *not* part of a multinational group have taken little interest in the recent secondary book developments in Malawi, despite the provision of information via the African Publishers Network (APNET).

It is obvious that the multinational publishers tend to dominate the critical textbook markets in Malawi because they have the investment finance, the backlists and the editorial, design and production skills to compete quickly and effectively when new course materials are required, often at short notice. In many cases, however, the multinational companies work in partnership with local companies. This can create an injection of skills, knowledge, cash flow and profits for the local partner companies, which in turn enable them to grow and develop both professionally and financially.

In the recent junior secondary textbook submissions some local companies achieved significant success because they were in partnership with a multinational. Without this partnership arrangement it is doubtful if the companies concerned could have competed as well. It is also significant that entirely indigenous publishers such as Dzuka, Chanco, CLAIM and Popular also achieved successful textbook evaluations and approvals in competition with the multinationals and the partnerships. An important reason for this is that the MoESC and the development partners (particularly Danida) have worked very closely with the total local book trade. This has involved discussing problems, identifying key issues, working out mutually acceptable solutions and generally keeping all of the local book trade fully up to date and informed. Local publishers are thus given time and space to make their concerns known and to organise themselves to compete successfully. Danida, in particular, holds regular informal briefing meetings with all interested BPAM and BAM members. These meetings provide opportunities to discuss and resolve outstanding problems, to monitor progress and to plan next steps.

The textbook competitions were organised so that the requirements of local publishers were accommodated as much as possible. Similarly, the marketing arrangements concentrated on regional book fairs, and financial support for a comprehensive approved book list distributed nation-wide, which gave small publishers a chance to show and promote their books and meet schools at an acceptable cost. Without the book list and the book fairs, small publishers would have found it too expensive to send sales representatives around the country. Perhaps the key to achieving a sensible balance between the interests of local companies and the financial and professional weight of the multinationals is for government and development partners always to see the total book trade (local and multinational) as an essential partner in both policy and implementation and thus to be in a position to take early note of all concerns.

Regional trade in books

There is a significant regional trade in educational materials as evidenced by the high proportion of textbooks and library books published in other countries in the region, which were included in the recent secondary approved book list. The number of Chichewa language books imported from Zambia also bears testimony to this fact. There are no legal or financial barriers to the trade in regionally published books and Malawi is a signatory of the Florence Agreement and Nairobi Protocols on the free flow of books and information.

Perhaps the biggest problem inhibiting the regional book trade is the postal system. Sending books by post has become unreliable and very slow over the past decade and most importers now either use airfreight or containerised shipments if quantities are large enough. It is the small quantities, often the basis of regional trade, which are penalised by the ineffective postal system.

Recent policy initiatives

There have been dramatic changes in policy on textbook provision since 1995, which have led to the re-emergence of a Malawi-based educational publishing industry. Most of the critical changes have taken place at secondary level where the partnership between the MoESC and donors such as Danida on specific projects have provided opportunities for new approaches to textbook provision. Progress on policy development has been reinforced by the requirement to finalise the MoESCs Project Investment Framework during 1999.

As explained in the history of publishing in Malawi above, the first breakthrough occurred in 1995 and related specifically to commercial publisher access to the primary textbook market. In spite of the problems associated with the publishers' reprint contracts there were two tangible outcomes. Firstly, the MoESC negotiations demonstrated that the private sector publishing industry might achieve access to the key primary school textbook market, from which they had been excluded for many years. Secondly, in preparation for the possibility of licensing contracts, a number of private sector publishers re-established themselves in Malawi and began to take a serious interest in the Malawi textbook market, again for the first time in many years.

The preparatory phase of the Danish Support to Education (DSE) programme in September 1997 initiated a period of intense policy debate on the evolution of a national textbook policy. This policy debate was strongly focused on the secondary sector because of two donor projects (the WB SEP and the DSE DEC Pilot Project), which intended to provide significant finance for textbook and library supply to conventional secondary schools and to the then Distance Education Centres. A National Book Development Conference also took place in September 1997 at which MIE produced a key paper, which recommended the ending of state textbook publishing and the full participation of the private sector.

The formation of a National Book Development Council Steering Committee provided an opportunity for local publishers and booksellers to enter into dialogue with the MoESC and with funders. As a result of ongoing discussions between MoESC, development partners (strongly led by Danida) and the local book trade associations *plus* the availability of donor finance to support secondary school textbook finance, a number of critical agency policy decisions were taken and implemented. These are:

- State textbook publishing, printing and distribution for core school textbooks was terminated. MoESC policy has now established the private sector as the prime mechanism for the creation, publication and delivery of textbooks and other teaching and learning materials. Local private sector publishers will now be actively encouraged to develop and publish new textbooks for the new secondary curricula (and, perhaps, even for an emerging competitive primary sector as well).
- Textbook choice is now the prerogative of each individual secondary school and there is a range of textbooks available for each subject and each form. Transparent mechanisms for the submission, evaluation and approval of textbooks and for the annual publication of a list of approved secondary school textbooks have been created and successfully implemented.
- After the initial provision of textbook and library supplies by funders, secondary schools will become responsible for financing their own textbook and library stocks out of annual textbook rental fees charged to each parent. New, realistic textbook fees of MK180 per student were introduced in January 2000 for the first time in over twenty years. Danida will provide matching funds for five years to establish school-based purchasing and selection.
- Schools will retain all collected textbook rental fees and will be responsible and accountable to parents and to the Divisional Education Departments (DEDs) for their use and for the adequacy of levels of textbook provision in schools.

81

- Textbook policy in CCSs and CDSSs will be unified for the first time in over thirty years. The same system will now apply to all state supported secondary schools. There is already some evidence that a number of private schools wish to adopt the same or similar strategies for textbook financing and supply. Private schools are now active members alongside state-funded schools of a national network of self-help 'clusters' of 5–10 secondary schools organised according to geographical proximity. Private schools are now automatically included in all national secondary school training initiatives.
- The creation of minimum physical production specifications and the achievement of long book life are now established key textbook policies in an attempt to reduce the high annual textbook loss and damage rates and to create an affordable system for textbook provision in secondary schools. There is early evidence that the DEC Pilot project has significantly reduced book loss and damage rates so far.
- Intensive training has been provided to design and implement effective library and resource based management systems to increase student access to books and to reduce loss and damage.
- The establishment of an operational school library in every secondary institution is also now a key secondary education policy.
- Over the next few years there will be a steady shift at secondary level from procurement through professional suppliers/consolidators selected as a result of competitive tenders to supply via purchase from local booksellers. Each year, increased numbers of schools will be selected to buy locally thus providing business, experience and profitability to local book retailers without crushing them with a supply burden that they do not yet have the facilities, finance or experience to handle.

In September 1999, a workshop on primary school teaching and learning materials policy was held in Lilongwe. The workshop recommended the development and implementation of a primary policy, which would end monopoly state textbook publishing and distribution and would introduce competitive textbook supply, school-based choice and consumer based financing via a per capita purchasing power budget for every school. At the time of writing the UK government's Department for International Development (DFID) is financing the development of a detailed MoESC policy and implementation proposal along the lines specified above.

Suggestions and recommendations
- All textbook funding from development partners should be channelled to the consumers so that genuine markets can be created.
- Sensible cost sharing between government and parents for educational books is recommended to create annual budgets, which would enable schools to increase their stock and replace losses.
- Parental book fees need to be reviewed annually so that the fees are never

allowed to decay to the point where they are worth nothing as has happened previously in Malawi.
- Additional agency funding should be directed to developing librarianship training in schools and tertiary institutions.
- More support is needed for the National Library.
- All educational institutions should be encouraged to purchase at least some of their stock requirements from local booksellers so that local book retailing develops.
- Funding agencies' distribution tenders should always require local partnerships so that local companies can participate in, and benefit from, these tenders.
- Technical and Vocational Colleges and Teacher Training Colleges are also in urgent need of library and textbook funding.
- Senior secondary curriculum reform is urgently needed to re-orient requirements away from a purely academic approach.
- Funding for tertiary level book, journal and information supply is urgently needed.

Postscript

At the end of July 2000 the first phase of local bookseller involvement in textbook and library supply to secondary schools has almost been completed. Of the 216 secondary schools allocated for supply from 10 nationally approved local textbook suppliers, 96% have contracted with one of the ten local booksellers and have provided their pre-financing cheques in advance. A high proportion of these orders have been successfully supplied already and spot-checking by the MoESC suggests high levels of school satisfaction with local bookseller performance.

The 96% order submission rate for commercial bookseller supply can be contrasted with a 65% order submission rate achieved from those schools scheduled for supply from the divisions. Obviously, commercial bookseller motivation to go out into the country and chase orders was rather higher than the motivation (and the access to transport and allowances) of education staff in divisional offices.

One of the two wholesalers (BSAD) opened for business in March 2000 and provided essential cash flow, stockholding and back-up support to a number of the local booksellers. Two of the local booksellers (TBS and Dzuka) have nevertheless managed to finance all supplies out of their own financial resources. To date there have been no reports of unpaid bills to publishers, probably because the publishers have been extremely tough on credit terms and limits.

Of the ten nationally approved textbook suppliers, seven have been active and five have shared the great majority of the school contracts. This has provided a completely new bookseller turnover of around US$350,000 in the first year. As an example of the impact, the CLAIM bookshop in Mulanje achieved a turnover from its first secondary school contract, which was considerably in excess of its total retail bookshop sales in the whole of the previous year. From the point of view of the schools, the official textbook suppliers have competed on discounts (discounts of up to 12% have been recorded) and have delivered direct to all schools free of charge. The booksellers also have replaced any inaccurate and mis-supplied orders quickly and efficiently and have dealt with the whole issue of substitutions by discussing replacements direct with the schools concerned. Most of the nationally approved textbook suppliers are now very aware that their level of service will determine whether or not they maintain a school contract next year.

Other side effects have included a very rapid understanding of the need for good record and filing systems, plus a realisation that giving away high levels of discount just to win contracts is not necessarily very sensible. Finally, most of the involved booksellers now understand, through practical exposure to the realities of school supply, that repeated visits to distant schools with small supplies (or re-supplies) is expensive and erodes profitability.

The funder and the MoESC are generally happy with bookseller performance and there is a real possibility of an expansion of the market in 2001 to enable booksellers to supply far more schools. It should be noted that the close and very detailed working relationships between booksellers, publishers, MoESC and funding agencies have been largely responsible for the success achieved so far. There is now a real hope that effective bookseller coverage of school requirements on a national scale can be re-established in Malawi within the life of the MoESC/DSPS.

Case study C: Kenya

By David Muita, Chairperson of the Kenya Book Publishers' Association & MD, Macmillan Kenya Ltd, Nairobi

---

Basic facts
- Located between Latitudes 5° N and 5° S and Longitudes 33–43° E.
- Bordered by Sudan and Ethiopia to the north, Somalia and the Indian Ocean to the east, Tanzania to the south and Uganda to the west.
- Population: 28,7 million (1999 census).
- Area: 583,000 square kilometres.
- Population density of 51 per square kilometre.
- 31% of the population is classified as urban.
- Per capita GNP was US$330 in 1998.
- The capital city is Nairobi with a population of 2,1 million (1999 census).
- 70% of the population are Christian (40% Catholic and 30% Protestant), 6% are Muslim, 10% adhere to traditional religions and a further 14% have other religions.
- Life expectancy is 52 years with a female life expectancy of 53 years and a male life expectancy of 51 years.
- A former British colony, independence was attained in 1963.
- English is the official language. Kiswahili is the national language. There are numerous other local languages of which Kikuyu and Luo are the most widely spoken.
- According to the World Development Report (1999) 80% of Kenyans were functionally literate. Of these, 87% of men and 72% of women were functionally literate.
- Main economic activities are agriculture (coffee, tea, maize, wheat, sugar cane, dairy products, beef, pork, poultry, fruit and vegetables), service and consumer industries and tourism.
- Kenya is administered via eight provinces and 72 districts and municipalities.
- The unit of currency is the Kenya shilling (KSh). In January 2000, KSh70 = US$1.

The education market

Enrolment

Table 7   Education enrollments 1994–97   *Source: Kenya Education Directory*

Educational Institutions	1994		1995		1996		1997	
Pre-primary	19,083		20,186		21,261		23,344	
Primary	15,906		16,155		16,552		17,080	
Secondary	2,834		2,878		3,004		3,028	
Tertiary			686					
Pre-primary school enrollment					Male	Female		
					527,017	506,350		
Grand total					1 033,367			
Primary school enrollment (thousands)	Male	Female	Male	Female	Male	Female	Male	Female
Standard 1	491	463	492	460	494	464	498	468
Standard 2	425	400	427	406	437	415	443	421
Standard 3	388	379	392	373	397	374	402	370
Standard 4	379	375	368	366	373	364	380	372
Standard 5	330	337	329	334	331	331	332	335
Standard 6	294	297	292	300	298	307	304	312
Standard 7	296	301	290	1	296	300	301	311
Standard 8	213	190	212	194	217	199	221	207
Total	2 816	2 742	2 802	2 434	2 843	2 754	2 881	2 796
Grand total	5 558		5 236		5 597		5 677	
Secondary school enrollment (thousands)	Male	Female	Male	Female	Male	Female	Male	Female
Form 1	91	78	96	84	97	86	98	89
Form 2	88	77	89	76	94	81	96	87
Form 3	79	66	83	66	84	72	89	79
Form 4	79	62	74	61	78	66	80	69
Total	337	283	342	287	353	305	363	324
Grand total	620		629		658		687	

The majority of Kenya's population are the youth. About 60% of the population are below 18 years of age. Hence, the school population should be very large. The actual enrolment figures however tell a different story: from the above figures, it is evident that less than half of the school-going population (about 26% of the population) actually attend school. Factors limiting enrolment are mostly economic, although social and political factors are also significant. An overloaded curriculum with a large and expensive textbook requirement has been cited as a disincentive to children and parents, and it is because of this that the government has stated its willingness to streamline the primary and secondary education curriculum from 2002 or 2003.

Public and private education

At independence, the government set out to fight poverty, ignorance and illiteracy. The government thus initiated and developed many primary and secondary schools in a bid to provide education for all. Education in Kenya has, as a result, traditionally been public. However, the last two decades have seen the establishment of many private institutions throughout the various education levels. These have been started by enterprising individuals and by companies for their employees' children. Some are local branches of international institutions. It is estimated that about 60% of pre-primary schools are private. However only 5% of primary schools are private while 20% of secondary schools are private. The private schools nearly always perform much better than the public schools and they offer a range of different international curricula and examinations. Most tertiary institutions are private, that is, twelve out of seventeen universities in Kenya are privately owned.

From the above it is clear that a significant proportion of the education sector is gradually moving towards private ownership, as are many other sectors of Kenyan economic and social life. Spurred on by the World Bank and other funding agencies, the government is gradually disengaging from a direct role in many aspects of education, including textbook publishing, and is becoming solely a policy, monitoring, evaluation and quality assurance body.

The evolution of book distribution in Kenya

The publishing and distribution of books in Kenya dates back to the early twentieth century during the colonial period; at that time, missionaries set up schools in various parts of the country to provide Kenyans with the rudimentary skills of reading, writing and arithmetic. Apart from distributing booklets from Britain, the missionaries set up printing presses, the first one at the Coast, and another one at Kijabe in the central highlands. Books from these presses were mostly translations (into local languages) of English books, including the Bible. A spate of nationalism and Pan-Africanism ushered in independence for the country in 1963, and with it many new government institutions were established. The Kenya Institute of Education (KIE) together with the Curriculum Development Centre, was started in 1964. They were entrusted with the development of curricula and syllabi for Kenya's newly independent education system.

The new government opened many schools to fight illiteracy and the book market became very vibrant. The East African Literature Bureau (EALB), a government publishing firm, which had been founded in 1948, received a new lease of life after independence (EALB later became the Kenya Literature Bureau (KLB) after the break-up of the East African Community in the late 1970s). The Kenyan agents of Longman (established in 1950) and Oxford University Press (established in 1954) locally registered their firms to become local private sector publishers. Other international publishers also started Kenyan companies, most notably Macmillan and Heinemann. Several publishing houses owned by Kenyan nationals also came into being. These included East Africa Publishing House (EAPH) and Equatorial Publishers. The government also launched the Jomo Kenyatta Foundation (JKF), a parastatal publishing trust. The creation of state-owned educational publishers set the stage for, sometimes bitter, disagreements between private publishers, state publishers and the Ministry of Education as the Kenyan book market evolved.

The Ministry of Education was inevitably embroiled in these disagreements because textbook publishing was, and still remains, the most viable and financially rewarding form of publishing in Kenya. Unfortunately, the Ministry of Education did not join the textbook publishing game as a referee, but rather as a player, worsening an already volatile situation. For reasons that could not exclude financial gains, the Ministry discredited teaching and learning materials produced by private sector publishers as expensive and irrelevant to the education situation in Kenya. Instead, it used KIE to develop textbook manuscripts, which were allocated to either KLB or JKF (the two parastatal publishers) for publication. The JKF/KLB textbooks were classified as the compulsory textbooks. All the textbooks published by the private sector publishers were classified only as supplementary books. Inevitably, this benefited the parastatal publishers at the expense of the private sector.

A centralised supply of textbooks via the Kenya School Equipment Scheme (KSES) was started in 1970. Working in conjunction with the KIE – whose mandate now included the vetting and recommendation of private sector textbooks[48] – KSES generated order lists that it distributed to schools via District Education Boards. Schools then selected titles from the list, which KSES procured with government funding and supplied. Inevitably, any compulsory title on the list generated huge orders and hence huge print runs and much lower published prices. This fueled the government claim that private sector publishers were expensive and exploitative. Unfortunately, corruption began to creep in as publishers clamoured to get their books on the compulsory and supplementary list.

The high costs of the KSES operation plus a number of other inhibiting factors led to the system becoming effectively moribund in 1984. From 1984 onwards, parents increasingly funded textbook provision as KSES failed to deliver textbook supplies. This situation provided a new foothold in the textbook

---

48   There appeared to be a clear conflict of interest in this situation. At this time the KIE was vetting private publishers' textbooks while also being the 'author' of the compulsory textbooks published by JKF and KLB.

market for both publishers and booksellers.[49]

The introduction of cost sharing as a government policy for primary education in 1988 formally established parental contributions as the main funding mechanism for textbooks. Parental demand for books in turn stimulated the growth of local bookselling. Private sector publishing growth was still inhibited however by the continued use of an approved list in which only the titles published by the parastatals were categorised as compulsory core textbooks. All other private sector published textbooks for primary schools were categorised as supplementary. Inevitably, the parastatal books were favoured in purchasing by parents. In addition, government and agency funded projects to provide free textbooks in poor areas as part of the Education Sector Adjustment Credit (EdSAC) purchased parastatal textbooks only.

This situation continued until 1997 when the Kenyan government and the Royal Netherlands Embassy launched the pilot primary textbook project. This project introduced school-based purchasing power for the first time in Kenya. Schools could choose books from an approved list of competitive textbooks from which the 'core, compulsory' status was removed completely and no specific advantage was conferred on the textbooks published by the parastatals. The playing field between parastatal and private sector publishers was levelled for the first time.[50] School based purchasing power and school based choice were all confirmed in 1998 as the central components of a new Ministry of Education, Science and Technology (MoEST) textbook policy document.

The development of bookshops

In spite of the Kenya School Equipment Scheme (KSES), a few bookshops did survive in the early years after independence. These stocked a few of the school titles, especially from publishers not favoured by the government's *modus operandi*. The bookshops also stocked academic, professional and general publications, most of which were from international publishers. Wanyee Bookshop was one of the famous bookshops at the time and Equatorial Publishers also had a few bookshops along with a printing press.

The ending of the KSES era coincided with the change of the education structure to eight years in primary, four years at secondary and four years at university (8-4-4). These two events marked a turning point insofar as book publishing and distribution in Kenya are concerned. The number of bookshops increased from 205 in 1980 to about 400 in 1985. There are reported to be over 1,100 bookshops in Kenya today but this figure may not be entirely accurate considering:

---

49   The basic philosophy was that the Ministry of Education could only demand compliance with the use of compulsory books if it paid the bills. If parents paid for the books they could exercise some freedom of choice.

50   It is perhaps significant that on the first occasion in which parents and teachers were given a free choice of textbooks (in the 1997 RNE pilot project) 65% of all textbooks ordered were from private sector publishers.

- The current mortality rate of businesses in Kenya. Many booksellers will come alive during the main bookselling season, and then hibernate for the rest of the year.
- Some small bookshops operate as stationery stores and only deal in books against firm orders.
- Many bookshops are not registered; thus the statistics are not official.

The main players in book distribution

Many companies and organisations in Kenya sell and distribute books nationally and internationally. These include publishers, booksellers, the government, United Nations bodies, Kenya's bilateral and multilateral partners, non-governmental organisations, and even street vendors, not to mention the courier companies. Regardless of the fact that the main market is for textbooks, there is a wide range of all types of books available in Kenya. The book distributors, the types of books they distribute and the areas they cover are discussed below.

Publishers

There are over a hundred book publishers selling and distributing books in Kenya. These can be categorised into international publishing companies, indigenous publishers, state-owned publishers, university presses, author-publishers, agency-funded publishers and religious publishing groups. Most, if not all, of these publishers have attempted to publish and distribute educational books and materials, with varying success. This is because over 70% of the book business in Kenya is school oriented. The state-owned and the international publishing houses tend to dominate textbook publishing. These include, JKF and KLB as already mentioned, Oxford University Press, Macmillan Kenya, East African Educational Publishers (EAEP) and Longhorn. The last two companies are now locally owned companies formed respectively from the previous Heinemann and Longman companies in Kenya. All of the publishers listed above have a substantial share of the school textbook market.

Apart from textbooks, another favourite area for Kenyan publishers is literature, both for children and adults. Companies that have excelled in this area are EAEP, Macmillan Kenya, Phoenix and Focus Publishers. Some publishers moved into this area of publishing because of the past unfavourable government textbook policy (EAEP and Macmillan) and others because of a love for literature (Phoenix and Focus).

Book publishing outside the categories of textbooks and literature constitutes only about 10% of the book trade in Kenya and it is the international publishers that usually venture into publishing for areas outside these market sectors. The future of tertiary publishing looked bright sometime back when the government had in place a policy encouraging the buying of books in the higher institutions of learning. A certain amount of money was deposited in the respective university bookshop for every student at the public universities. Every student could then buy books up to the value of the cash deposited.

Citing irregularities, the government eventually scraped this system, to the detriment of the students and to academic and scholarly publishing. Another factor currently affecting tertiary level book distribution is the mass unauthorised photocopying of tertiary titles, which inhibits local publishing and local stocking of tertiary titles.

It is noteworthy that Kenya is the second largest exporter of books in Africa, after South Africa. With the partial opening up of country boundaries in the region, Kenyan publishers now sell many books to the neighbouring countries of Uganda, Tanzania, Rwanda, Malawi and Zambia, etc.

Some big companies are also reconstituting themselves in Kenya after a period when they withdrew from the market. Thus Pearson now operates under the auspices of Metameta and Heinemann under Jacaranda Designs. Thomas Nelson and Cambridge University Press are also increasing their profiles in Kenya. Books from these publishers are finding a niche in the market mostly at secondary level with some tertiary publications and readers, especially from the Longman stable.

Publishers in Kenya are working closely together for their mutual benefit. The Kenya Publishers' Association (KPA) is very active. The Nairobi International Book Fair, which is a relatively new event organised by the KPA, is now an annual event in the country's book calendar. This forum brings together all those with a stake in the book business in Kenya and the region at large.

Bookshops

Apart from the permanent versus seasonal categorisation of the 1,100 bookshops operating in Kenya (see above), bookshops can also be categorised into privately owned and institutional bookshops. Privately owned bookshops are businesses run as sole proprietorships, partnerships or private companies. Privately owned bookshops are the majority and seem to be the most successful in Kenya. The biggest, the Text Book Centre (TBC), which is a family concern, spans two generations. Privately owned bookshops sell all kinds of books according to market demands.

Institutional bookshops include university, research and even religious bookshops. These usually cater for a specific clientele, be it university community, research centres or religious groups. Institutional bookshops support the objectives of the parent organisation, which include catering for the organisation's entire community.

Religious bookshops do also stock school textbooks and a few general books. In Kenya, these include Catholic bookshops and Bethany bookshops. It must be said here that the Catholic Church in Kenya has started and supported many successful schools in the country. Other religious bookshops include Keswick, SU Christian Bookshop, St Paul's Theological College Bookshop and Daystar University bookshop.

Bookshops are found throughout the country, with most towns, large and small, being adequately served.

Distributors/wholesalers

There are not many wholesale book distributors in Kenya. Some are simply bookshops that have excelled in bookselling, and have ventured into selling to other bookshops. Other distributors are registered agents of local and international publishers. For example, the proprietors of EAEP have set up a distribution arm, which caters for their group of companies. Metameta is a distribution agent for the Pearson group of companies. The other main book wholesalers are TBC, Savannis and Laxmi. TBC and Savannis now publish, market and distribute their own books in addition to wholesaling the titles of other publishers. All these wholesalers stock locally published as well as imported stock.

These wholesalers, who are all located in Nairobi, mainly deal in school textbooks. However, they also stock all other publications, including children's books; scientific, technical and medical books; academic/professional books; stationery, etc.

Government

Since the demise of the KSES (as discussed earlier), the government has become less involved in book distribution. However, its policies still affect the book business, including book distribution, in a big way. The government is also involved in several projects concerned with book provision to various parts of the country. Some of the book projects target the seemingly less developed areas, namely Arid and Semi-Arid Lands (ASALs) and Pockets of Poverty (PoP). In conjunction with certain partners (who are discussed below), the government buys and distributes books for these disadvantaged areas.

Funding agencies

There are a number of agency-funded education projects in Kenya, which have been important catalysts for educational change in the country. Agency-funded projects not only target specific districts, but in some cases operate on a national scale.

Table 8, on p. 93, is a summary of bilateral and multilateral partners involved in education projects (especially in book provision), with notes on their areas of operation, and the type of support provided.

Table 8 Funding agency investment in education

Partner	Areas of operation	Type of co-operation
World Bank	The national education system	• Implementation of the 8-4-4 system of education • Acquisition of learning materials for public universities, e.g. KIUP I, II & III • Provision of basic learning material* • Support for curriculum reform • Support for consumer based textbook funding (STEPS)
Department for International Development (DFID)	• 600 Teachers' Advisory Centres in 47 districts • Moi University • 72 Districts • All primary schools in 27 districts	• Supplementary reading materials in English at primary level (SPRED1) • Construction of and book supply to schools • Margaret Thatcher Library • Primary School Management (PRISM) • Support for consumer based textbook funding (SPRED 3)
Japanese International Co-operation Agency (JICA)	Jomo Kenyatta University of Agriculture & Technology – nine districts in pilot project, and entire country later	• Procurement of books and other learning materials, research, construction, staff training, etc • Strengthening Mathematics and Sciences in Secondary Education (SMASSE), this includes teacher training and book supply
German Technical Co-operation	• Primary Education throughout Kenya • Meru Technical Institute & Rift Valley Technical Institute	• Practical Subjects in Primary Education (PraSuPe), training including provision of teaching and learning materials* • Machinery support and book procurement
European Union (EU)	Eldoret Polytechnic University and Strathmore College	• Building of physical facilities and procurement of library books
Dutch Development Agency (DGIS)	Arid and semi-arid areas (14 districts)	• Provision of primary school textbooks (currently suspended)
Canadian International Development Agency (CIDA)	135 schools in Coast Province*	• Readers for primary school libraries*

* not yet implemented

Non-governmental organisations

Bilateral and multilateral agreements with the Kenyan government fund several NGOs which have projects that address themselves to a wide range of development activities in the East African region. Several NGOs are involved in book buying and provision in the region. These include Plan International, which has provided books to many parts of the country and is currently supplying books to Coast Province as well as Thika, Kiambu, Embu and Kisumu districts. In the recent past, World Vision has distributed books to Elgeyo, Marakwet, Laikipia and Makeuni districts.

Religious groups

As mentioned earlier, missionaries introduced formal schooling and books to East Africa. As borne out by the role of the Catholic Church in the provision of education, religious groups continue to be in the forefront of the book sector. Other churches that are important in book provision are the Methodist Church in Eastern Province, the Presbyterian Church in Central Province, the Anglican Church in the Rift Valley, and Maranatha in Nyanza Province. Muslims run Madrassa schools in most major towns throughout the country. The curriculum of the Madrassa schools is tailored to Islamic doctrines, and hence promotes the buying of Islamic books. The Aga Khan Foundation also runs several schools in Kenya. A Hindu organisation, the Visa Oshwal, runs schools in Nairobi, Mombasa and Kisumu.

Book distribution today

Learning materials distribution in Kenya is now an intricate network that involves the government and its partners, publishers, courier companies, bookshops and many other organisations. But what types of learning materials are distributed and who distributes them? In answering these questions, this section will, among other issues, look at the operation and effectiveness of the distribution of learning materials. The materials to be focused on are textbooks, general and reference materials, children's books, tertiary materials and religious books.

School textbooks

Continued demand for education will ensure that textbooks remain big business. Table 9, on p. 95, provides enrollment projections up to 2001.

Table 9 Projected demand for education, 1997–2001 (millions)
Source: National Development Plan 1997–2001

Primary	Age of students	1997	1999	2000	2001	% increase
Primary school	6–13	6,03	6,25	6,36	6,46	7,0
Secondary school	14–17	2,72	2,82	2,85	2,89	5,9
Tertiary school	18–22	2,95	3,16	3,25	3,34	13,1
Total	6–22	11,71	12,24	12,47	12,68	8,3

Bookshops. According to the government's Sessional Paper No 6 of 1988, education and training were henceforth to be financed through the principle of cost-sharing – by the government on the one hand, and parents and communities on the other. Funding agency projects have in the past (and will in the future) attempt to provide additional support[51] and parents' actual contributions to the costs of education vary from district to district and between public and private schools. The parents may also consolidate funds by paying an agreed fee for book purchases to the school or schools and parents may fund raise (*harambee*) to get money for buying books. Generally, though, parents buy books from the nearest bookshop and most bookshops in Kenya mainly sell schoolbooks.

Appendix 2 gives a list of the main bookshops, which are located in major urban areas. There are many other bookshops scattered throughout the country and in smaller urban centres. The existence of a large and widely spread bookseller network throughout the country results from the simple fact that since 1984 parents have had to purchase most of the textbooks used in schools and have thus required the services of local bookshops.

The schoolbooks are sourced directly from local publishers and/or from wholesalers such as TBC and Savannis. Courier companies are used to link the publisher and the bookseller. The bookshops dotted throughout the country provide a very wide network for textbook distribution, a network that offers the crucial link between the publisher and the consumer. Increasingly, the publishers and booksellers are employing the sale or return method, and this ensures that reliable bookshops are well stocked.

---

51 While there can be little doubt that the introduction of the cost sharing policy provided a lifeline to publishers and booksellers in Kenya, it also had a serious and adverse impact on many aspects of the education system. For example, roll numbers have declined alarmingly since the introduction of cost sharing, largely because a significant proportion of parents cannot afford to send their children to school, and, in particular, to buy books. MoEST and funding agency policy is now aimed at reducing the costs of education and providing targeted assistance to the very poor. Fortunately funder assistance is now provided for textbooks in the form of consumer-linked funding, which simultaneously supports the poor while allowing private sector publishing and bookselling to survive and contribute to educational development.

However, it is not all smooth sailing for the bookshops. The obstacles that they face include poor infrastructure, a situation quite pronounced in the northern parts of the country. This inhibits contact with suppliers and customers. Finances, including lack of credit facilities from bankers and publishers, especially for newly established booksellers, are another drawback. Textbook buying also tends to be seasonal in Kenya, with the booming months being between September and March. This promotes the phenomenon of 'briefcase' booksellers. Suffice it to say that there is a dearth of professionalism in the sector. Apart from Moi University, which offers a course in the book trade, bookselling is not very professional in Kenya. That said, there are a few booksellers who have laid down impressive bookselling practices in their places, prime among them being the Text Book Centre in Nairobi.

The book to pupil ratio. The government aims to achieve a ratio of one book between three pupils per subject in Stds 1–5 and one book between two pupils per subject in Stds 6–8 within the next couple of years, according to the National Policy on Textbook Publication, Procurement and Supply for Primary Schools. This target book to pupil ratio is far from being widely realised, especially in districts that have not received any partner/donor assistance. A random survey shows an average ratio of one book to five pupils. Nonetheless, the ratio is already as high as 1:1 in certain private schools. Eventually, the government aims to have a ratio of one book per pupil per subject per grade in all schools. The number of required subjects is currently uncertain because the government aims to reduce the number of examinable subjects taught in primary and secondary schools with the introduction of a new curriculum in 2002 or 2003.

Choice. In the past, as discussed above, the Ministry of Education, via the KIE, recommended which book had to be used in which subject. Often the state publishers were often unable to cope with the demand for some of the titles. This is all changing because KIE can now recommend a maximum of six books per subject per year for use in schools and all of the books on the approved list have equal status. This situation definitely gives schools more choice on what textbooks to use. It is also a shot in the arm for the booksellers in the country, as they are now not bound to just one publisher's ability to supply.

Publishers. Kenya Literature Bureau (KLB), Jomo Kenyatta Foundation (JKF)[52], Oxford University Press, Macmillan Kenya (Publishers), East African Educational Publishers (EAEP), Longhorn and Dhillon Publishers are the major primary and secondary textbook publishers in Kenya. All these have their main offices in Nairobi, but they also have distribution outlets and/or sales

---

52 It is interesting that in Kenya, unlike in many other liberalised book trades in Africa, the two parastatal publishing houses are continuing to publish and compete with the private sector in the core textbook markets. Both JKF and KLB are now full members of the KPA. Private sector publishers in Kenya have no fears or worries about competing with state owned publishing trusts now that they are certain that the two publishing houses receive no hidden subsidies and are no longer favoured with the 'compulsory' textbook status.

representatives scattered around the country. The above publishers have courses in almost all the subjects taught at both primary and secondary school levels. It is noteworthy that over 95% of the books used in Kenyan schools are locally published. The majority of school textbook publishing companies are also Kenyan owned. It is important here to note that many small publishers are limited by a lack of sufficient funds not to mention their inability to successfully access and use the distribution network.

Publishers have become quite professional in production, marketing and distribution of their publications in a bid to capture an increasing share of the huge school market. Their offices and sales representatives now work even more closely with booksellers, schools and other stakeholders to increase their market share. The competition has become even stiffer since the recent liberalisation of the textbook sector, which has attracted many international companies into the market, especially from South Africa and Europe.

Government policies on books. Government attitudes and policies are crucial to the operation of effective book distribution. As mentioned above, the Kenyan government is working with bilateral and multilateral partners to develop the education system in Kenya. The government's role includes identifying areas of investment priority for particular projects.

The government also makes budgetary allocations for school textbook purchases every year. This budget goes into buying textbooks for schools throughout the country. Through the Ministry of Education, the government has published the 'National Policy on Textbooks Publication, Procurement and Supply for Primary Schools'. The document contains new policy guidelines on textbook development, publishing and distribution; methods of procurement; future policy on textbook financing; and textbook management.

Rather than authoring, the KIE will now concentrate on its mandate of curriculum development as well as the evaluation, vetting and approval of books for use in schools. The books to be approved are a minimum of six textbooks per subject for each class at any given time. All publishing firms can publish textbooks, but have to submit these to KIE, with a fee, if they want the books to be approved for use in schools. Each school will make its choice from the list of approved textbooks and will buy from a bookshop of their choice, except in areas with poor distribution networks where procurement will be by the district education officers through a competitive tender for consolidation and distribution services.

The government has also restated its commitment 'to maintaining its own budget line for primary school textbooks and will gradually increase this budget line year by year up to a target of 50% of the required national textbook financing costs'. In the recent past, this budget line has been concentrated in remote regions, especially the Arid and Semi-Arid Lands (ASALs) and the districts said to be Pockets of Poverty (PoPs). It must be said here that the current government is not averse to misrepresentation of its own policy papers with a view to ensuring political survival.

97

Table 10 below shows the government's actual primary textbook expenditure versus the total primary education recurrent expenditure in the last twenty years. The figures are in millions of Kenya shillings.

Table 10 Actual government spending on primary textbooks, 1979–1997
Source: Government of Kenya: 'Appropriate accounts and estimates',
various years

	79/80	75/86	83/84	87/88	89/90	92/93	93/94	94/95	95/96	96/97
Spent on textbooks	5,9	4,8	2,2	1,3	0,002	1,6	0,1	0,9	0,8	1,0
Total spent on schooling	74,7	181,2	127,4	246,2	247,0	413,5	551,2	675,3	769,2	858,9

From the above, it is obvious that whereas the total government expenditure on primary school education has been increasing, textbook expenditure has been decreasing.[53] This was especially so after 1988 when 'Sessional Paper No. 6' announcing the Cost Sharing Policy was launched.

The primary textbook policy document has provided for management of textbooks. Head teachers, school management committees, teachers, parents and pupils will now be trained on selection, procurement, storage, handling, use and conservation of textbooks. To enable this, the MoE has published handbooks on 'Primary School Management and An Approved List of Primary School Textbooks'. The government has also developed 'A Manual for Trainers in Textbook Management'. It is hoped that these publications will boost the handling of textbooks in schools, and thus increase durability of book life.

Development partners. As mentioned above, the Dutch, through DGIS, Britain's Department for International Development (DFID), the Japanese International Co-operation Agency, the World Bank and other funding organisations are active in education and book support. Nonetheless, most funded projects have been short lived. Most of the projects have satisfied the immediate need for learning materials, but hardly any are self-sustaining. If anything, such projects can be accused of creating a dependency syndrome, which upsets the usual booktrade. The haphazard distribution methods used in some of the projects do not support the growth and development of any particular distribution system. If these shortcomings can be redressed, the funder/state partnership remains one of the most viable mechanisms to ensure that pupil to book ratios improve, in the short to medium terms at least.

NGOs and churches. That these groups operate as charities/humanitarian bodies means that they can buy learning materials direct from the publishers and distribute them to schools without raising eyebrows. Some of these bodies

---

53 In 2000 the Kenyan government has released KSh260 million (US$3,7 million) for consumer funding support for textbook provision, the highest textbook allocation for very many years.

even co-publish materials with established publishers and distribute the materials to relevant audiences. A case in point is the joint publishing and distribution of Kiswahili Aids Awareness Readers for Tanzania between Plan International and Macmillan. Overall, the importance of NGOs and churches cannot be underestimated.

Tertiary books

Research shows that over 95% of books and almost 100% of the journals used at tertiary level are imported. The underdevelopment of tertiary publishing in Kenya can be traced to a few factors, the most important of which is the small market size. Other factors are poor government policy regarding tertiary book funding as well as book piracy at the universities. The few tertiary books that have been published locally are mainly by university presses, particularly the Nairobi University Press and OUP (EA). Local publishers such as EAEP, Macmillan, Longhorn, Focus and JKF also have small local tertiary lists.

Tertiary learning materials in Kenya are mostly distributed through university bookshops and libraries. Apart from books, the materials distributed in this way include journals, research findings, seminar and conference papers, and CD-ROMs, etc. The introduction of parallel degree programmes in local public universities is expected to boost sales of tertiary publications. In addition, a few major bookshops in Nairobi and other urban centres cater for the many colleges offering certificate and diploma courses.

Table 11, below, is a breakdown of tertiary institutions in Kenya as of 1995, and the respective enrollment figures.

Table 11 University enrollments		
Type of institutions	Number of institutions	Enrollment
Youth polytechnics	600	31,000
Institutes of technology	17	6,244
Technical training institutes	20	7,945
National polytechnics	3	7,927
Technical teacher training colleges	1	510
Primary teacher training colleges	25	16,878
Diploma teacher training colleges	3	1,362
Public universities	5	43,038
Private universities	12	4,845
Total	686	119,749

Direct importers and overseas suppliers. In liaison with the tertiary market in Kenya, a number of local companies specialise in direct importation of tertiary publications, mostly sourced from Britain, India and North America. These materials mostly go to university and college libraries. Registered companies importing materials into the country include Metameta Creative Services, Suba Books & Periodicals, Approtex, Book Distributors Limited and Jacaranda Designs. These companies account for about a quarter of the book distribution into Kenya's tertiary market.

There are also overseas suppliers who distribute directly into Kenya's tertiary market. Apart from supplying through agency-funded projects, these companies get orders from college and university libraries and bookshops. The main overseas distributors include Blackwell's, Regent, Bookazine, SWETS and SMI.
Development partners. The main government partner insofar as tertiary book distribution is concerned has been the World Bank, which has facilitated book procurement in all the five public universities over the last four years. Other bilateral partners – including DFID, GTZ, and the European Union – have played a big part in providing learning materials to Kenya's tertiary education system. Learning materials here include books, information technology, citation indexes, journals and science and engineering laboratory equipment.

General and reference books

General and reference books in Kenya include adult fiction, atlases, dictionaries, wall maps and wall charts, encyclopaedias, books on tourism and cookery, as well as biographies. A significant proportion of these materials have been published locally. Established companies in this sector are EAEP, Macmillan Kenya, and OUP (EA). There are also many general publications that are imported into the country, especially adult fiction, dictionaries, wall charts and encyclopaedias. Distribution of general reference materials is mainly through major bookshops. Most bookshops will stock reference materials, but specific bookshops, mostly located in Nairobi, usually stock other general books. These include Prestige Bookshop, Bookpoint, Westlands Sundries, Legacy Bookshop and Hidden Treasures. Libraries will also have good quantities and varieties of reference materials, including atlases, dictionaries and encyclopaedias. Supermarkets will also stock dictionaries, wall maps, adult fiction and other general books. Some of these materials are also hawked on the streets.

Children's books

Besides textbooks, children's literature is the other seemingly most viable area of publishing in Kenya. Almost every publisher in the country has a children's list and many Kenyan publishers have been quite active in this area, notably Macmillan Kenya, EAEP, KLB, and Longhorn. Other publishers, including Phoenix, Focus and Acacia Stantex, are now publishing children's books in a big way. This area of publishing has also attracted a large number of imported children's books. The most notable imported children's books are from Longman and HarperCollins.

The children's readers are usually distributed alongside school textbooks and are therefore available in most bookshops across the country. Primary school libraries as well as the national library service also buy children's books. Other distribution channels for children's books include supermarkets and street hawkers.

Religious books

Over the years, religious literature has had wide readership across the country. It remains one of the most widely published areas after school textbooks. These religious publications include the Bible, translations and children's Bible stories, the Koran and its translations, hymn books, prayer books, guidance and counselling books and other related literature. About 60% of these publications are published in Kenya, and the rest is imported.

The major publishers of religious materials include Evangel Publishing House, Uzima Press, Pauline Publications, Baptist Mission, Muslim Foundation, AIC Kijabe, Kesho Publications, National Council of Churches of Kenya, Christian Learning Materials Centre, the Catholic Secretariat, the Gaba (AMECEA) Publications in Eldoret.

These materials are mainly distributed through the church network. This is a network with a very expansive reach, which ensures that these materials are very well distributed in the country. These materials are also distributed through bookshops, especially religious and institutional bookshops.

Regional book trade

The governments of Kenya, Uganda and Tanzania have laid the groundwork for establishing a common market for the region. This includes the drafting of a treaty addressing transport and communications, fiscal and monetary policies including tariffs, and the harmonisation of curricula and the certification of education, encompassing co-ordinated human resources development. The discussions and writing of the draft culminated in the signing of an East African Co-operation Treaty (EACT) at the end of November 1999. As a result, a potential market of 80 million people for goods and services has been created.

The book fraternity has been involved in deliberations towards the common market. Suffice it to say the Kenyan education curriculum is changing to be in line with curricula in the rest of the world (if not the region), according to President Daniel arap Moi. The respective book fraternities have been organising annual national book weeks, with each country's festival drawing participation from the other countries.

Another regional economic forum still at the formative stages is the Common Market for Eastern and Southern Africa (COMESA). Regional market integration will foster the book trade in the region, as indeed it will foster other businesses targeting the integrated markets.

Proposals and suggestions

The deliberations in this paper have so far centred on analysing and evaluating the book industry in general, and book publishing and distribution in particular. This section lists proposals that would help to further develop an effective and efficient book distribution system in Kenya.

- Publishers should encourage the growth, development and sustenance of bookshops in every region. Their sales and marketing activities should create awareness as to the importance of bookshops in the book chain by (re)directing buyers to the bookshops. In so doing, publishers will not only create goodwill with booksellers, but will also reduce their distribution overheads. The growth of bookshops will undoubtedly increase the availability of books throughout the country.
- Publishers should support the wholesaling of books. The wholesalers would in turn serve bookshops in their respective regions. Such support can be by way of longer credit periods, higher discounts for wholesaling purposes only, referring other bookshops in the region to their appointed wholesalers and including the wholesalers' names in their promotional materials. Wholesalers would thereby be encouraged to desist from retailing in order to rather sustain the bookshops operating in their areas. For regions with no well-developed book distribution system, District Education Offices could forward consolidated orders from schools to wholesalers in their respective regions.
- There is a need to inject more professionalism into book distribution practices. More college courses equipping publishers' sales reps and marketers, and other book trade practitioners – including bookshop staff – with sharper book-selling skills would be a boon to the industry.
- Besides setting up book provision projects, funding agencies working with the government should put in place longer-term and self-sustaining mechanisms of textbook financing and distribution. It must be acknowledged that one-off projects tend to disrupt the book distribution system. One way of doing this is to spread out support over a period, with evaluation at different levels. The other way would be to support the income-generating arms of educational institutions, for example grants to university presses would enable mass, subsidised publishing of tertiary material.
- Development of the existing transportation and communication infrastructure would go a long way in ensuring that books, and indeed other goods, reach the target audience effectively and efficiently. As it is, some parts of the country are hardly accessible.
- The government should de-regulate the telecommunication and postal services to a greater extent. This would propel the country into the information age and avenues as publishing and distribution of e-books become a reality in this country.

Conclusion

From the foregoing study, it is evident that book publishing and distribution in Kenya has come a long way since the days when missionaries were translating the Bible for distribution. Publishers now produce textbooks, children's literature, general and reference material as well as religious books. There is also the umbrella organisation, the Kenya Publishers' Association, which coordinates and regulates activities in the publishing industry. In ensuring that books are available to as much of an audience as possible, publishers have started the Nairobi International Book Fair, the National Book Week, and are also working with the government and publishers in other countries to develop a regional market. The one area local publishers need to seriously address though, is tertiary publishing.

Through the National Policy on Textbooks Publication, Procurement and Supply for Primary Schools, the government is committed to supporting book provision in Kenya. The government will also ensure that only the good quality books reach the market, via the Kenya Institute of Education's syllabi writing and book vetting arm. Foreign agencies will remain a major support to the government for book provision especially in the less endowed regions of the country. This funding is likely to be pronounced at primary and tertiary levels of education since at secondary school level, the cost-sharing policy is better entrenched.

It is evident that bookshops will remain the most important channels of book distribution in Kenya in the near future. Bookshops are the most effective means of making books available to the target audience. Towards this end, school and institutional libraries require more support from all concerned to be better channels of book distribution. Efforts by supermarkets and street vendors towards the provision of learning materials are commendable.

Generally, great strides have been made in the provision of books and other learning materials in Kenya and in the development of a genuinely national book distribution capacity. Few other countries in Africa are as well endowed with bookshops as Kenya and these bookshops have provided essential support for the growth and diversification of Kenyan publishing into other, non-textbook, market sectors. After many very difficult years, government and donor policies are now very supportive of private sector involvement in the critical textbook market. The eradication of compulsory textbooks and the introduction of school-based purchasing power and school-based choice of the books and the bookshops that they wish to use are significant policy breakthroughs. Parental contributions to textbook purchase remain crucial. Kenya has learned that funders and projects come and go and that government funding is unreliable and that in these circumstances it is the parents (or at least some of them) who maintain some level of textbook supply to support education during the bad times.

Despite the recent progress, much remains to be done. At the dawn of a new millennium, technology should become the catchword in taking the book industry to new heights.

Case study D: Uganda

By Fred Matovu, Chairperson of the Uganda Publishers' Association and MD of Kamalu Ltd, Kampala and
Tony Read, MD, International Book Development Ltd, London

Basic facts
- Located between Latitudes 5° N and 3° S and Longitudes 28–35° E.
- Bordered by Sudan to the north, Kenya to the east, Tanzania, Rwanda and Lake Victoria to the south and the Democratic Republic of the Congo to the west.
- Population: 21 million (1998 estimate).
- Area: 241,000 square kilometres and a population density of 105 per square kilometre. 14% of the population is classified as urban.
- GNP per capita was US$320 in 1998.
- The capital city is Kampala with a population of approximately 1 million (1995 estimate).
- 66% of the population are Christian (33% Catholic and 33% Protestant), 16% are Muslim and 18% adhere to traditional religions.
- Life expectancy is 43 years and is the same for both females and males.
- Independence was attained from Britain in 1963.
- English is the official language. There are approximately ten significant other languages, of which Luganda and Kiswahili are the most widely spoken.
- 62% of Ugandans were functionally literate in 1995. Of these, 74% of men and 50% of women were functionally literate.
- The main economic activities are agriculture (coffee, tea, cotton, tobacco, maize and livestock), mining (copper, cobalt, limestone, salt), consumer industries, food processing and tourism.
- Uganda is administered via 45 districts.
- The unit of currency is the Uganda shilling (USh). In January 2000, USh1375 = US$1.

The education market in Uganda

Pre-schools

The official enrollment age for primary education is six years. In rural areas many children start their primary schooling much later than the official age and in urban areas there is considerable pressure from more affluent parents to start education at a much earlier age. However, to date there has been no official provision of pre-primary facilities, although with the introduction of Universal Primary Education (UPE), the National Curriculum Development Centre (NCDC) has recently developed and published a pre-school curriculum with the emphasis on activity and manipulative skills rather than on reading. Throughout Uganda there is a steady growth in the provision of private nursery schools and daycare centres to cater for working parents with no access to home help. Children in daycare are occupied almost entirely in play and play-related activities. Most centres charge moderate fees intended to cover the costs of staff and stationery only and very few of the pre-schools can afford to buy learning materials. Those more 'elite' pre-schools that do buy books are located in Kampala and so purchase through the larger booksellers.

Some private primary schools in Kampala have introduced pre-primary classes for the specific purpose of preparing young children for Grade 1. These schools are for children from affluent families who value 'headstart' programmes. They tend to invest in wall charts and picture books, but the market is tiny.

Primary schools

Enrollments in state and private primary schools are provided in Tables 12 and 13. In the state and private system combined there are approximately 7,5 million students. Between 1995 and 1997, with the introduction of free primary education and the drive to achieve UPE, student numbers in primary schools more than doubled, creating a huge potential expansion in the market for primary school textbooks and huge additional costs for the state.

Table 12 Primary school enrollments in government schools in 1999 *Source: Uganda Provisional Head Count Data, 1999*		
Grade	**Number of enrolled students**	**Number of teachers**
1	1 700,851	15,462
2	1 199,105	10,901
3	1 171,923	21,308
4	840,083	15,274
5	673,981	12,254
6	533,791	9,705
7	366,796	6,669
Totals	**6 486,530**	**91,573**

Table 13	Enrollment in private primary schools in 1999
Source: MoES Annual Statistics, 1997	
Grade	**Number of enrolled students**
1	376,000
2	214,000
3	154,000
4	120,000
5	101,000
6	71,000
7	54,000
Total	**1 090,000**

For 1999, the total number of primary schools in Uganda is estimated to be 11,211, of which perhaps 800 are private schools, leaving around 10,400 government and government-aided primary schools.

Funding for the primary school book market comes from two main sources. These are:

- The textbook procurement budgets of the Instructional Materials Unit (IMU) of the Ministry of Education and Sport (MoES).
- UPE funds provided directly to schools for school-based spending on 'other teaching and learning materials'.

Between 1995 and 1999 the IMU has undertaken five major materials procurements on behalf of the MoES. Four of these were concerned solely with core textbooks from the MoES approved textbook list. One of the procurements (in September 1996) also included supplementary reading materials and teaching aids (mostly wall maps and wall charts). The five procurements have purchased a total stock of 6 325,081 textbooks and teacher's guides (not including the supplementary readers and the teaching aids). All of these books were selected by individual schools on the basis of allocated school budgets (based on roll numbers) from IMU printed order forms which listed all titles (with current prices) approved by the MoES for use in Ugandan primary schools. The cost of the procurements to date has been approximately US$30 million. On this basis, the average unit cost of textbook procurement for primary schools in Uganda over the past five years has been approximately US$4,74 per book and the size of the basic state funded textbook market has averaged around US$6 million per year. Sales to private schools and direct to parents are additional to this figure.

The projected future funding allocated specifically to textbook and teacher's guide procurement is significant, amounting to a total of approximately

US$47,5 million at current exchange rates over the next four years if all projected budgets are spent as indicated. On the basis of the unit textbook procurement cost calculated above of US$4,75 per book, this budget is sufficient to procure around ten million textbooks over the next four years at current textbook prices and constant currency values. This in turn would provide access to approximately 4,5 textbooks per enrolled primary student (assuming 6,5 million enrolled primary students, zero starting stock, a 1:3 book to pupil ratio, a four year book life and zero loss and damage).

However, if the projected budgets are consistently under allocated by one third over the next four years (as happened in 1999/2000) only around 6,5 million textbooks will be procured amounting to three textbooks per primary student on the basis of the assumptions listed above. It should be noted also that the projected financial allocations for centralised textbook procurement vary considerably year on year.

In addition to the budget line allocated to IMU centralised textbook procurement, the government also makes capitation grants (UPE Funds) available direct to schools. The forward budgets for the school capitation grants allocated to teaching and learning materials amount to over US$60 million for the period 2000–2003.[54] Unfortunately, although the sums of finance allocated to direct book purchase by schools appear to be very large there are considerable practical problems involved in accessing the funds successfully:

- Diversion of funds by schools to other purposes and misappropriation of funds is reported to be quite widespread.
- Schools, particularly in rural and remote areas, often have great difficulties in spending their textbook budgets because there is usually no conveniently located and well-stocked retail sales outlet close by from which to buy these materials.
- Most publishers will only supply most district booksellers on C.W.O[55] or C.O.D[56] terms because of the risks of non-payment. Booksellers in the districts are unwilling to buy on these terms in case they fail to achieve sales and are left with the stock.
- Most principals are unwilling to supply cash with orders because they fear that they won't see the cash again, and won't receive the books.

The combined impact of these factors is that it seems likely that only a small proportion of the UPE funds allocated to teaching and learning materials (either core textbooks or 'other' teaching and learning materials) will actually be spent on these materials – informed guesses suggest no more than 10–20%.[57] The lack of an adequate distribution infrastructure and the difficult credit problems,

---

54 Since the introduction of decentralised capitation grants the GoU has maintained its financial allocations for this purpose.
55 C.W.O = Cash with Order.
56 C.O.D = Cash on Delivery.
57 20% is very much a 'high side' estimate. Most guesses suggested a general level of spending on teaching and learning materials of closer to 10%. In many cases it depends on precisely how 'teaching and learning materials' are defined.

which prevent adequate stockholding, are major obstacles preventing the Ugandan book trade from accessing the UPE funds. This is a problem that publishers and booksellers need to solve urgently. Both are failing to exploit a very rich potential market and the schools are missing out as a result.

Secondary schools

The textbook market at secondary level is still relatively small in comparison to primary schools. It is expected, however, that it will expand considerably over the next three years as the introduction of UPE in 1996/97 has a progressive impact on future levels of enrollment in the secondary school system. Estimated current secondary roll numbers are provided in Table 14 on p. 110.

There are approximately 550 government-aided secondary schools and around 100 private secondary schools. A majority of secondary schools are concentrated in and around Kampala and in districts such as Mpigi and Mbarara, which makes it difficult to estimate the secondary school coverage through all of the 45 districts. It does, however, reduce the costs and difficulty of marketing and supply to the secondary schools. Schools of English, and a small but very significant International Schools sector with high purchasing power, supplement the secondary market.

No statistics exist to estimate the size of the market in cash terms and book prices vary considerably across the country from subject to subject and even between individual titles. However, the government has recently started to provide some financial assistance for secondary textbook purchase in maths and science and in 1999 it is estimated that the Instructional Materials Unit (IMU) purchased secondary school textbooks to the value of around US$2 million. A similar government budget allocation has been made for 2000 and there is some hope in the book trade that government purchasing of secondary school books will become established as a regular budget item.

A recent DFID funded teacher-training project has purchased books for 37 new secondary teachers' resource centres. The British Council has provided support also for 'A' level textbooks and secondary school library books. However, these titles were procured in the UK using John Smith & Son (a UK based library supplier) as the purchaser and consolidator and no direct benefit accrued to local booksellers. UNESCO has assisted with English and science texts and Rotary International and other charities and sponsors also support secondary school textbooks to some degree.

All of these inputs, combined with the direct sales from publishers and booksellers to schools and parents, probably put the current value of the secondary school book market at somewhere between US$2,5–3,5 million per year. This market size is, however, heavily dependent upon government and foreign financing and thus it is neither stable nor completely secure and predictable.

There are seven compulsory subjects at 'O' level out of a total of thirteen. The most popular subjects (and therefore the biggest selling) are English

Language, English Literature, Mathematics, Chemistry, Physics, Biology, History, Geography, Religious Education and Business Education. The publishers that dominate the primary school market also tend to have strong secondary school lists. Kamalu/Longman, Rorash/Heinemann, Macmillan and OUP are the market leaders but John Murray, CUP and Nelson all do well at secondary level. It is obvious from this list that British publishers, usually working with local partners, are still the most important source of secondary school books.

Table 14	Estimated secondary school enrollment, 1999
Year[58]	**Enrollment**
1	100,000
2	90,000
3	90,000
4	60,000
5	15,000
6	15,000
Total	**370,000**

With the exception of the funder inputs described above, most textbooks are purchased either by parents or by schools, or, very occasionally by districts. The commonest source of purchase is through the major bookshops in Kampala such as Aristoc, Mukono Bookshop and Gustro. Parents and schools in rural areas will often travel considerable distances to purchase their books in Kampala. District level bookshops and retailers are less significant because of limited stock levels and choice, but there are some very good book retailers in districts. Schools often provide book lists to pupils and collect cash prior to placing their orders. Bookshops in Kampala do deliver to the districts, particularly where orders can be consolidated. Alternatively, schools come to Kampala to collect their books. Publishers rarely distribute directly to schools.

Curriculum development for secondary schools is the responsibility of the National Curriculum Development Centre (NCDC) in conjunction with the Uganda Examinations Board (UEB), Macmillan have recently co-published an English course for secondary schools with NCDC. Kamalu/Longman are currently working with NCDC on the development of new, locally authored and published courses for Physics, Chemistry, Biology and History. There is no formal approved list of secondary school textbooks and schools make their own decisions on selection and purchasing.

---

58 Forms 1–4 prepare for the Uganda Certificate of Education (UCE) 'O' Level examination. Forms 5–6 prepare for the UCE 'A' Level examination.

Tertiary books and journals

The higher education sector is small but has grown recently by evening class students who have demonstrated their willingness to purchase core textbooks. Textbook provision in higher education is notable for its use of 'book banks'. Universities organise their own book banks, which are supported by government funding. Makerere University introduced the concept, originally developed in India and Pakistan, into Uganda. It has now spread to other institutions (Ndejje, Uganda Martyrs University, Bugema University, Mbarara University, Mbale Islamic University and Nkumbe University).

Under the book bank scheme, each department has its own book bank manager who is also usually a lecturer. The universities collect textbook orders from the departments and faculties and then channel them via the university library. Orders are based on reading lists and order quantities are aimed at achieving a 1:2 book student ratio for the core textbooks. The schemes are now sufficiently well established that major investment is no longer required and annual budgets are now aimed at topping-up and maintenance. Much of the stock is procured overseas and Blackwells (a UK based library supplier and journal subscription agent) has a supply contract to procure and consolidate on behalf of some of the universities.

A small number of students purchase textbooks and supplementary books locally through Makerere University Bookshop, which is now owned and managed by Fountain, a local Ugandan publishing house.

Thus much of the book and journal stock is procured outside Uganda with specialist library suppliers and journal subscription agents and it is impossible to estimate the size of the higher education market. It is small in comparison with the current and future prospects for primary and secondary textbook supply, but the market is developing and is becoming more interesting.

Trade books

The size of the 'reading population' is small in Uganda and is concentrated in Kampala, Entebbe and a few of the larger urban areas. Most book sales are connected in some way to education. The larger booksellers in Kampala maintain a limited stock of trade books consisting of mass market paperbacks, children's books, reference books, African literature and works on Ugandan, regional and African political and economic themes. Tourist guides and coffee table books on African themes also do well. The trade market in Uganda is, however, small.

Key players in the sales and distribution of books

The Instructional Materials Unit (IMU) of the MoES

The Instructional Materials Unit (IMU) was established within the MoES in 1993 as a specialist procurement agency to procure and distribute textbooks, supplementary reading materials and teaching aids to all primary schools in

Uganda.[59] The funding came from the World Bank and USAID and the project is known as SUPER (Support for Ugandan Primary Education Reform).

Its founding principles, negotiated between government and funding agencies in the project appraisal documents, introduced a new era for book publishers in Uganda. The IMU was required to support and develop a fully competitive, market-oriented, textbook system in Uganda based on the provision of school-based purchasing power (consumer funding) to every primary school in the country and the introduction of school responsibility for the selection of their textbooks. The rapid development of private sector involvement was considered to be fundamental.

From 1993 up to the present, the IMU has purchased approximately US$30 million textbooks from locally established publishers for supply to primary schools throughout the country. The IMU is by far the largest single source of book purchase funding in the country and has been very largely responsible for the renaissance in Ugandan educational publishing over the past decade.

The IMU initially established a textbook evaluation and approval system to enable publishers to submit textbooks for MoES approval as suitable for use in Ugandan primary schools.[60] It created school-based book budgets and annually sends up-to-date order forms to schools, which include details of all titles approved for use in schools, plus their current prices. Schools order the books that they want via the official order forms up to the limits of their allocated per capita budgets and return the order forms to the IMU for order consolidation and procurement. The IMU negotiates with publishers on the prices for the quantities of textbooks ordered by the schools.[61] Publishers promote to schools in support of their own titles and supply the quantities ordered direct to the IMU.

Until recently, the IMU has very successfully handled the consolidation and delivery of textbook stock to schools. In 1999, for the first time, it sub-contracted the textbook consolidation element to a local supplier as part of wider government policies of decentralisation and the contracting-out of specialist services; but the delivery component still requires districts to collect from the consolidator in Kampala. The final delivery stage from districts to schools is still via school collection from the district stores or district funded deliveries to schools.

---

59 It also occasionally assists in the procurement of some secondary school textbooks.

60 The approval system currently in use is a 'threshold' system, in which any textbook course that achieves the established minimum standards can be approved for use in Ugandan primary schools. There is a perception within the MoES that this has led to too many approved books, too much choice and the reduction in annual print runs, which in turn has led to higher unit costs and higher than desirable prices. The alternative is a 'competitive' system in which the best three (or two or four) textbooks that meet minimum standards are the only ones approved. The reduction in choice is expected to increase order quantities and thus print runs and to reduce unit costs and thus annual budgetary requirements.

61 One of the current problems in the system is that price is not a factor in the evaluation and approval process. Thus, when IMU comes to negotiate prices with publishers for the quantities ordered by schools, it has little real bargaining power. A revised evaluation system in which a mandatory price formula is used as one of the evaluation criteria is currently under consideration.

This system has been of considerable benefit to the smaller local Ugandan publishers because the up-front payments for bulk quantities and the IMU role in organising consolidation and supply to schools has removed the element of risk and has significantly reduced the costs and problems of financing. For small local publishers who don't have easy access to the lower cost investment finance available to multinationals, the IMU system from 1993 up to the present has positively supported their growth and competitiveness. As an example of the steadily growing impact of local textbook publishing in Uganda, in 1993 the SUPER ONE procurement purchased 7,5% of the total book requirement from local publishers. In SUPER TWO, 8,6% of the books procured came from local publishers. In SUPER THREE the local component had risen to 10.4% and had increased again to 17,5% in SUPER FOUR.[62] The new system has not yet provided similar growth opportunities for either booksellers or local printers.

Publishers

Competitive private sector educational publishing recovered rapidly from the state-dominated structures and the poor market prospects of the 1970s and the early 1980s and there is now a wide variety of national, regional and multinational publishers operating competitively in the Ugandan school market. These publishers include Fountain, Rorash/Heinemann, Kamalu/Longman, Macmillan, OUP, CUP, EAEP (Kenya), Evans, MK and Crane, etc. All of these publishers have established local offices and now offer a full range of educational publishing services including author development, editorial, design, DTP, marketing, promotion, warehousing and distribution.

The income and profits from the primary school textbook business has also encouraged other types of publishing including children's books, fiction (in English, Kiswahili and other local languages), history, politics and books of general trade interest. It is very significant that the spectacular growth over the past seven years in the number, professionalism and profitability of locally-based publishers was created by the simple expedient of creating a market and enabling publishers to have access to it.

Booksellers

There has been much slower progress on the re-construction of an effective national network of retail bookshops. The UBA has a list of member booksellers, which indicates that retail outlets are available in more than half of the current districts. But most publishers are very wary of supplying most of these booksellers on open credit. There are a number of excellent booksellers in Kampala and in some other towns in Uganda (notably in Mbarara, Mukono, Iganga, Mityana, Masaka, Luwero, Kitgum, Kabale, Arua and Jinja). However, most booksellers outside Kampala are under-financed, often have inappropriate

---

62   Ikoja-Odongo J. R. 1999 'Publishing in Uganda: Trends and Developments 1989–1999', unpublished paper.

premises and lack the experience and the management systems to handle large-scale textbook business, which is still overwhelmingly the 'core' of the book trade in Uganda.

The only bookshop 'chain' is The Uganda Bookshop group which has a number of operational outlets in different parts of the country, many of which stock small quantities of primary and secondary textbooks, but this is also perceived to be seriously under-funded and under-stocked. An analysis suggests that, in 1999, more than 30 out of 45 districts do not have a reliable, creditworthy bookshop capable of holding good stocks of educational materials in sufficient quantities to serve school requirements. This is an important consideration in the development of any decentralised system of book procurement.

Most booksellers in Uganda feel that their major market for textbook sales lies with the growth of private schools and with parent purchases for children at state primary schools who do not want their children to share textbooks. Despite the textbook liberalisation policy, which has revitalised educational publishing in Uganda in the 1990s, there has been little bookseller or printer access to the new agency funded educational markets. Booksellers seem to accept that the government and agency-funded textbook markets in the state school system are closed to them.

From the late 1960s, when Uganda School Supplies was first established, textbook supplies for the primary school system have been dominated by parastatals or by state-financed and organised supply systems. Thus, the decline of USS during the Idi Amin regime did not see a reversion to private sector book supply. It saw instead the creation of a MoE textbook warehouse. When the second Obote government was overthrown, textbook supplies to the school system once again did not revert to the local private sector (which was not, in any case, in any condition to handle the task). School textbook supply was instead tendered by agency-funded procurement procedures to international suppliers. Even the advent of the USAID SUPER Project created a system that initially consolidated and distributed the procured textbooks within the MoES. Thus none of the supply and distribution systems created in Uganda since the late 1960s have allowed anything other than the temporary involvement of educational textbook wholesalers and suppliers in the state school primary market. As a result, there are only a few adequate textbook and educational book outlets in Uganda outside Kampala. Even the developing private sector and parental purchase markets for primary and secondary textbooks are not without problems. There has been a recent court case involving the piracy of a well-known secondary school textbook. There is evidence that some of the primary textbooks supplied to schools via the IMU are being stolen and sold to private schools either direct or through 'pavement' bookshops.

Table 15 Reputable local booksellers in Uganda	
Name of Bookseller	**Location**
Pauline's Book & Media Centre	Kampala
Atistoc Booklex	Kampala
Alphamat Bookworld	Kampala
Mukono Bookshop	Kampala
Fountain Bookpoint	Kampala
University Bookshop, Makerere	Kampala
Gustro Bookshop	Kampala
New Kampala Styles Bookshop	Kampala
Ibuza Bookshop	Kampala
Kasanda Stationery and Book Supply	Kampala
Adit Bookshop	Mbarara
Standard Afro Bookshop	Mukono
New Iganga Bookshop	Iganga
New Mityana Bookshop	Mityana
Sendikwanawa Bookshop	Masaka
Luwereo General Merchandise	Luwero
Padibe Friendship Stores	Kitgum
Heani Enterprises	Kabale
Kem Students' Centre	Masaka
Arua Religious Educational Centre	Arua
Buzimba Bookshop	Jinja

In 1998/99 the IMU procured and supplied quantities of secondary science textbooks for government secondary schools from the MoES science budget. It is planned that the IMU will procure more secondary science textbooks in 1999/2000. Although it is recognised that the IMU secondary procurements are 'new' money, many booksellers and suppliers still feel that they are once again excluded from the benefits of agency support and that piracy and stolen and second-hand books could begin to undermine even the private school market.

Table 15 above, provides a list of well-regarded local booksellers and their locations. Outside of Kampala there are only eleven significant booksellers listed, covering just ten out of the 45 districts.

Districts

There are a limited number of districts in Uganda (probably no more than eight or ten) that give sufficient priority to education and textbooks to allocate some of their district level budgets to increasing levels of provision. This is generally organised via small scale District Development Projects (DDPs) supported by a limited number of funding agencies and NGOs working at the district level. It is extremely difficult to get an idea of the scale of district level

115

book procurement, which appear to cover both primary and secondary school-books but it is likely that the majority of district level funding is spent on textbooks rather than on other teaching and learning materials. An experienced local observer has recently estimated that DDP and NGO funding of teaching and learning materials amounts to no more than US$300,000 per year. DDP expenditure on textbooks is often on the basis of district level textbook selection and supply to the schools rather than via school-based selection. To this extent, district level book purchasing sometimes runs contrary to national policy.

Parents and private schools
Despite the government policy of free primary education, there is evidence that the private school market is growing and that even at state primary schools there are some parents who are prepared to buy textbooks to avoid their children having to share books. It is difficult to estimate the size of parental and private school book purchase but it seems unlikely that turnover amounts to more than US$600,000 per year. Once again expenditure is reported to be mainly on textbooks rather than on supplementary books, reference materials or teaching aids. Private schools are perceived to make up most of this market with direct purchases by parents of children in state schools being relatively small.

The evolution of educational book publishing and distribution[63]
Up to independence most textbooks used in Uganda were British. They were supplied for sale to parents via local bookshops and wholesalers. The most significant textbook wholesalers and retailers in the pre-independence period were ESA (a UK based bookselling company with a branch in Uganda), DL Patel Bookshop, The Uganda Bookshop chain (owned by the Church of Uganda and still in existence) and the Catholic Secretariat bookshop.

The Milton Obote Foundation
Shortly after independence the Milton Obote Foundation (MOF) was established. This consisted of a number of subsidiary parastatal organisations including the Uganda Publishing House (UPH), Uganda School Supplies (USS – a textbook distributor), Ugationer (a specialist stationery manufacturer based in Mbale) and the Uganda Press Trust (UPT – an embryonic state print shop). These parastatal enterprises did not operate as legal monopolies but they had such significant operational advantages in terms of easy and almost unrestricted access to low cost investment finance and active government support that they soon dominated the market.

---

63 Material in this section has been derived from previously unpublished work by Fred Matovu and Tony Read undertaken for the MoES.

Early developments in school textbook publishing

Uganda, in common with all other newly independent countries, wanted its own, nationally developed textbooks to reflect national aspirations and priorities. The prevalent political philosophies of the period considered that the development and provision of a new generation of locally authored and originated textbooks was definitely a state responsibility.

UPH initiated its textbook publishing programme between 1964 and 1965 with the publication of the 'Okello Maths Course' for primary Grades 1–3. At the same time UNICEF was providing support to strengthen the teaching of language in Uganda and was instrumental in the establishment of the Buloba Language Unit within the MoE, which eventually produced the 'Nile English Course' for primary schools. The Milton Obote Foundation first published this in the early 1970s. The publication rights were subsequently transferred to UPH. Other core textbooks in use in Uganda at this time were the 'Oxford Progressive English Course' (OPEC) published by OUP in Kenya and 'This is Science' published by Longman Uganda.

At this stage Uganda School Supplies (USS) was still not a monopoly textbook supplier and continued to compete for school sales with the established private sector book suppliers. However, USS with strong financial support from the Ministry of Education, established a major book warehouse in Kampala[64] with a national network of bookshops and depots and invested heavily in stock from publishers. This investment programme provided USS with a clear competitive advantage over its private sector rivals.

In the late 1960s the National Institute of Education (NIE) was established at Makerere University. It started development work on 'Essential Maths' (a primary maths course designed to link up with the secondary level 'Entebbe Maths' Course). The NIE published 'Essential Maths' as the core primary maths textbooks for Grades 6 and 7 but then, after disputes with the authors, the publication of the Grade 4 and 5 titles was undertaken directly by the Ministry of Education. UPH continued with the publication of the 'Okello Maths Course' for Grades 1–3.

By 1970, the MoE, UPH or NIE were the publishers of all of the core English and maths primary textbooks. State, parastatal or institutional publishers thus dominated primary textbook publishing. USS, with strong state support had achieved a dominant position in textbook supply and distribution, which amounted to an effective monopoly. DL Patel and the ESA bookshop had closed and the Uganda Bookshop chain had been forced out of the profitable textbook market and had become a stationery, religious, general and children's book supplier.

---

64   This warehouse is now owned by the MoES and is rented out to UNEB. The warehouse has been used in the recent past by the IMU in consolidating primary textbook stocks.

The Idi Amin era

In 1971 the advent of the Idi Amin government saw the closure of both the Milton Obote Foundation and UPH and a rapid decline in the fortunes of USS. Under the Amin government the UPH primary textbook titles were taken over by the Education Ministry. The Ministry also established a small textbook warehouse and bought small quantities of textbooks from commercial publishers for free distribution to secondary schools. During this period, the government funded only small quantities of textbooks for free supply. The basic supply methodology was still direct sales to parents.

The National Curriculum Development Centre

In 1973 the National Curriculum Development Centre (NCDC) was formed as an autonomous organisation reporting to the Ministry of Education under the auspices of Presidential Decree No 7. This decree, never repealed, is still the legal basis under which NCDC operates in 2000. NCDC was given the task of streamlining the curriculum reform process and immediately set about reviewing and unifying the primary maths and English curricula. It also developed new curricula in social studies and science. The social studies curriculum was heavily based on the African Social Studies Programme (ASSP). By 1977 a new primary maths curriculum had been developed to combine the perceived strengths of both 'traditional' and 'new' maths.

NCDC saw itself not just as a curriculum development organisation but also as an originator of core textbook manuscripts and other teaching and learning materials. By 1978, NCDC had written and developed both a primary maths course and a primary English course for the new curriculum. With the closure of UPH and with no other state enterprise either professionally qualified or sufficiently well-funded to underwrite the publishing costs, Longman (which had established an office in Uganda in 1964) signed contracts with the NCDC for the publication rights of both of these courses. The contracts provided for a royalty for both the authors and for NCDC. These courses, written and developed by NCDC and published, sold and distributed by Longman Uganda were 'Primary Maths for Uganda' and 'Uganda Primary English Course'. The publication of these courses initiated a new phase in textbook provision policy in Uganda. Textbooks originated by the state now were published and distributed on an exclusive basis by a private sector, commercial publisher.

The second Milton Obote government

Before the NCDC developed courses could be published by Longman, the Idi Amin administration was overthrown and the second Milton Obote government returned to power. The Milton Obote Foundation (MOF) was re-established along with Uganda Publishing House and Uganda School Supplies Ltd. The Longman publication contracts for the NCDC courses were eventually confirmed by the MOF and UPH but only on the condition that an additional royalty was paid by Longman to UPH. All distribution and school supply once again became the monopoly of USS. The ongoing war and upheaval in Uganda from 1979 through to 1984 caused huge disruption to education and the book trade and it was not until 1983 that the NCDC/Longman primary courses were eventually published. At about the same time Macmillan signed contracts with NCDC for the publication of a primary social studies course and a Uganda primary school atlas. Longman signed additional publication contracts with NCDC for primary science textbooks. Macmillan reached agreement with UPH to revise and publish the 'Nile English Course' as a competitor to the NCDC 'Uganda Primary English Course'. Macmillan also took over the publication rights for a revised 'Essential Maths' which was re-titled 'Uganda Primary Maths Course' to compete with the NCDC/Longman 'Primary Maths for Uganda'.

Up to the present

By 1986 there was a somewhat competitive, school textbook publishing industry in Uganda with private sector publishers offering competing state developed courses. There was also sufficient stability and optimism in the Ugandan book trade to support the creation of the Uganda Publishers and Booksellers Association (UPABA). Unfortunately, over the next ten years, the differences between the booksellers and the publishers became so acute that UPABA was dismantled in 1997. Two separate successor trade associations, the Uganda Publishers' Association (UPA) and the Uganda Booksellers' Association (UBA) were formed.

The reasons for the break-up of UPABA probably stemmed from the growing tension between an increasingly successful educational publishing sector and a struggling bookselling sector. The booksellers felt that they had been effectively excluded from the financial benefits deriving from donor investments in textbook provision for Ugandan primary schools. The booksellers perceived UPABA to be an association that concentrated too much on publishing issues. To rectify this perceived imbalance, the booksellers wanted their own association. To understand the background to this situation it is necessary to consider the role of the funding agencies in the development of textbook provision and the Uganda book-trade over the past twenty years.

Donor impact on book-trade development in Uganda

Throughout the 1970s, the government funded textbook supplies to primary schools had been very irregular and small in scale. Only the richer schools and richer students could afford to buy textbooks. This led to significant reductions in the volumes of textbooks in the classroom, which in turn had a negative impact on pupils' educational performance. This situation was exacerbated by the destruction and unrest of the early 1980s, which included the burning and looting of schools and the wholesale destruction of book stocks.

From 1983 onwards, funding agencies have provided most of the funds for teaching and learning materials for primary schools in Uganda. The two major agencies during this period have been the World Bank through four IDA projects (Education III, IV, V and the Northern Uganda Reconstruction Project) and USAID via the SUPER Project. Since 1998 six agencies[65] have combined, via the Education Strategy Investment Plan (ESIP), to provide budgetary support for education, which also includes financial support for materials provision.

In the mid-1980s, the World Bank's IDA Education III Project provided the first major funding for materials provision in Uganda. It was essentially a large, one-off emergency supply of textbooks designed to fill the immediate and very serious shortfall in textbook availability in all Ugandan schools. Because this was an emergency project, there was little or no concern with wider and longer-term policy issues such as the development of local publishing, bookselling or printing. Nor was there any consideration of strategies such as competitive textbook supply, the creation of a choice of approved textbooks, the development of local private sector capacity for educational publishing, bookselling and printing, or school-based budgets and decision-making on which books were to be used in schools. Not surprisingly, therefore, little or no benefit accrued to the Ugandan book trade, apart from the publishers of the key primary school textbooks whose materials were purchased in large quantities – and these were mostly the local subsidiaries of multinational publishing companies. The textbook procurement, consolidation and distribution contract under IDA Education III was put out to an international tender because the World Bank and the Ministry of Education PIU could not identify a Ugandan textbook distributor with the experience, facilities or funding to handle the very large quantity of books required. The logistical problems in achieving the supply of books to thousands of primary schools throughout Uganda were also very difficult. The international supply tender was won by a UK company – JMLS. It was at this time that Uganda School Supplies, in debt, seriously under-financed, lacking active government support and with little immediate prospect of any significant textbook business once the textbook supply contract had been awarded outside Uganda, finally closed down. UPH suffered from similar problems and also closed down at about the same time.

In the late 1980s a second World Bank project, Education IV, became concerned with the wider issues of long-term teaching and learning materials provision and sustainability as well as with the proper use of the textbooks in the classroom. This project was also concerned (among many other issues) with initiating curriculum review and reform and with the development of a coherent national education strategy. On the specific issue of teaching and learning materials provision, the project provided additional supplies of core textbooks to fill identified gaps in provision. Once again, the textbooks were purchased direct from the main educational publisher. Supply and distribution was organised by the state and did not provide benefit to the private sector booksellers and distributors in Uganda.

---

65   The six funding agencies are the World Bank, the European Union, DFID, USAID, DGIS and the Irish government.

The Ministry of Education also initiated an experimental attempt at sustainable textbook provision through the Textbook Pilot Project (TPP) which aimed at providing books for schools via a rental scheme and revolving fund using both parental and government contributions on a 50/50 matching fund contribution basis. The experiment, although flawed in some respects in both design and implementation, achieved over 60% of the targeted cash return from parents in the first year of operation and thus indicated considerable potential. This high level of initial return, despite significant implementation problems, clearly demonstrated parental willingness, even amongst the poorer parents, to contribute something to the costs of their children's textbooks. This finding was presumably the basis of the Government White Paper recommendation for cost sharing as a funding policy in the procurement of primary teaching and learning materials.

Education IV was followed by a successor World Bank project, Education V and by the USAID funded SUPER Project. The SUPER Project funded textbook procurement and free supply to primary schools and the World Bank project funded only the procurement of supplementary reading materials for primary school libraries. These two projects, working in tandem, established a new national textbook policy in 1993 based on the principles of competition, full private sector involvement, MoES approval of textbooks, multiple textbook choice, school-based selection and school-based purchasing power.

It is these principles on which the current textbook provision system is based. The current policies aim to create an accessible educational book market, school-based responsibility for textbook selection and developed book industries in Uganda as the basis for all future textbook provision developments. This policy, which reflects and incorporates wider economic policy in Uganda, has already led to the publication of a wide variety of new textbooks in a very short period and at no cost to government. It has also led to significant investments in local, regional and multinational school book publishing specifically for Uganda. A major government initiative to achieve universal primary education (UPE) was instituted in 1997. Within two years primary enrollments had more than doubled. Much of the enrollment growth was concentrated in the first two or three years of primary schooling. This development has self-evidently had a significant impact on the projected textbook budgets for primary schools in Uganda. But, simultaneously, it has also more than doubled the potential size of the primary school textbook market and has thus created an even more attractive investment market for commercial textbook publishers. Competitive private sector educational publishing has recovered rapidly from the state dominated structures and the poor market prospects of the 1970s and the early 1980s and there is now a wide variety of national, regional and multinational publishers operating competitively in the Ugandan school market. In the past two or three years, government and funding agencies have become concerned about a number of unexpected outcomes resulting from current government textbook policy. These include:

- The perceived inability of many schools to order textbooks effectively.
- The perceived high prices of textbooks.
- The low print quantities (and thus higher unit costs) resulting from too much choice.
- The lower than expected book life.
- Evidence of poor or non-usage of textbooks in schools.

It is in the context of these issues that the MoES at the beginning of 2000 is engaged in a review of progress to date and then planning the next phase in the development of book policy in Uganda in association with funding agencies. Further decentralisation of book procurement is likely and there are signs that there is increased interest in finding ways to achieve greater involvement for local book distributors.

Book distribution in Uganda

The core of the book market in Uganda is the provision of primary school textbooks and teacher's guides to both the state and the private systems. The basic textbook market is supported by the sales of supplementary materials (including readers, wall maps, dictionaries, atlases, etc) also to the schools.

In good funding years when there are agency and government funds available for both the secondary and tertiary markets, the primary sector probably accounts for over 70% of the total book market in Uganda. In bad years, when agency and government funds are scarce outside the primary sector, the primary school market is probably worth over 90% of total market value. From this it is clear that primary school purchases are not only far larger than any other market sector, but they are also more reliable and predictable as well.

The development of the IMU as the key co-ordinator of the primary school book market has considerably eased the distribution burden for primary school publishers. Book procurement contracts between publishers and IMU require only that the publishers' books are delivered in bulk to a nominated MoES warehouse and consolidation point in Kampala. The books are consolidated and packed into school consignments, which are then organised by districts. The fundamental problem of distribution to each one of the 10,400 primary schools throughout the country is currently accepted as a government rather than a private sector responsibility.

From 1993 until 1998 the process of order consolidation into individually packed and labelled school consignments was undertaken by the IMU. Districts came into Kampala with their own transport and at their own cost to collect the consignments for their districts. Where local district storage wasn't available or was inadequate or unsuitable the book consignments were often stored in the offices and corridors of the District Education Office (DEO).

At the district level a variety of strategies was adopted to move the stock on to the schools. In some cases districts delivered to schools; in others the districts delivered only to remote schools and local schools collected their books. In some cases all schools came to the DEO to collect the books. Overall, monitoring checks have indicated that this system has worked pretty well and that most consignments have reached most schools in reasonably good condition and without unacceptable delays. If there was a flaw in the system, it was simply that there was no place and no role for local private sector booksellers and distributors and thus no opportunity for local booksellers to benefit from the newly liberalised book policies.

In 1999, and once again in pursuit of general government policies to outsource services that are better performed by the private sector, IMU put the textbook consolidation exercise out to local tender. The consolidation contract was awarded not to a local bookseller, but to a local publisher (Kamalu). All the indications so far are that the private sector contractor has performed well and that the established primary textbook distribution system will continue to function effectively.

For booksellers and distributors, with the primary textbook market still effectively closed to them, the market possibilities are limited. The majority of secondary sales are also centrally procured and distributed by IMU and the majority of the tertiary market is contracted to highly specialised international suppliers. The only market sectors currently available are therefore the rapidly growing private school market, some tertiary level student purchases, the general trade, tourist and paperback markets and the huge potential of the UPE capitation funds, which are spent directly by every one of the 10,400 state primary schools in the country.

The first three of these market sectors are heavily concentrated in and around Kampala and are relatively easily serviced by a dozen of the good to excellent bookshops in Kampala City. Even where private schools exist in remote locations, they are still sufficiently well-organised to travel to Kampala for their book supplies.

The most fundamental book distribution problem lies in the current inability of the local book trade to access the school UPE funds. Both publishers and booksellers are losing out. There are simply too few good, well-stocked, professional and creditworthy booksellers in the districts. As a result, 75% of the schools in the country do not have a local bookshop that can fulfil their needs, even when they have the money to buy materials. This is the most pressing problem facing the book trade at present and it is a purely distribution issue compounded by the twin, recurrent African book trade problems of poor credit ratings and thus insufficient stock on the ground.

Uganda does not have enough creditworthy bookshops outside Kampala, and particularly in the up-country districts. For many years the scarcity of bookshops in rural areas was the direct result of low-purchasing power and low book purchase priorities for the disposable incomes of the consumers. The provision of UPE funds direct to schools has dramatically changed this situation and there is now clear and significant book purchasing power in every district in the country. Unfortunately, the existing bookshops are under-capitalised and credit is a major problem. Publishers are wary of extending credit to very many of the district booksellers and the booksellers will not buy on firm sale because of the unpredictable nature of the market. Because schools cannot find the books that they want to buy in the district booksellers, they often divert the available budgets to other items.

The role of the multinational and regional publishers

The publishing industry in Uganda is still young, yet the current demand for books, and particularly educational books, is high and is increasing. Some Ugandan publishers have entered into joint ventures with multinational companies like Longman, Macmillan, Heinemann, etc. Others have negotiated agency and representation arrangements with multinational companies. Such arrangements have helped in the areas of personnel training (skills transfer) and in the capitalisation of the local companies to cope with the large pre-financing requirements of the agency-led market developments of the past decade.

Even publishing companies that on the surface appeared to be 100% locally financed sought access to training and other services from multinational companies. In 1990 there was not a single Ugandan publishing company that had the capacity to handle a big publishing project. In 2000 there are now Ugandan publishing companies who can handle and finance publishing projects to the value of US$1 million, or even more. It is important to note that Uganda has a national curriculum for both primary and secondary schools. Therefore, all books vetted and approved by the MoES follow the Ugandan curricula, irrespective of whom the publisher may be.

Multinationals and regional publishers that do not have local joint ventures can operate branch offices in Uganda or can sell direct to local booksellers. During the 1990s some Kenyan publishers attempted to penetrate the Ugandan school market. Due to differences in the school curricula between the two countries, and thus in the ability of schoolbooks to 'travel' between the two countries these attempts have not been as successful as originally envisaged. Overall, there are no major tensions between local, regional and multinational companies in the Ugandan book market at this time. All the managerial and professional staff are Ugandan nationals and the training and capitalisation roles of external companies are generally perceived to have been beneficial.

Regional trade in books

Before the break-up of the East African Community it made sense to think in terms of the development of an inter-regional trade in books for the countries of Uganda, Kenya and Tanzania. In those days the East African Examinations Council issued a common curriculum for the three countries. In 2000, each of the three countries has its own education system, which differs significantly both in structure and curriculum from the other two. Thus, Tanzania and Kenya have eight-year primary systems but Tanzania uses Kiswahili as the medium of instruction, whereas Kenya uses English. Uganda has a seven-year primary system with English as the medium of instruction but the new curriculum is proposing that locally dominant languages should in future be the media of instruction.

Despite these obvious differences the recent signing of the East African Cooperation Treaty signals the beginnings of an era of much greater cooperation and thus might well herald the opening up of a regional market and thus a much stronger regional trade in books and information. The formation of the East African Bookweek Association five years ago has helped the publishers and booksellers of the region to come together every year for book fairs and to conclude trade deals among themselves.

The book industry in Rwanda is still very small and is further fragmented into Anglophone, Francophone and Kinyarwanda sections. Nevertheless, the market is developing and with substantial funder assistance expected soon to support educational development and perhaps teaching and learning materials, Ugandan publishers and booksellers are hopeful that Rwanda could be a focus for inter-regional trade.

The school curriculum and culture of Southern African countries are quite different to those of East Africa and there have been relatively few educational titles that have been successfully traded between the two regions. The subject of the inter-regional trade in books has been discussed at the APNET General Council meetings. The fourth APNET General Council meeting was held in Kampala, Uganda, in 1999. The apparent problem with Uganda is that publishers appear to have few titles to sell to Southern African countries, whereas there may be many titles from Southern Africa that could find a market in Uganda and East Africa. There is perhaps a fear in some East African countries of a potential trade imbalance in any future inter-regional book trade developments with Southern Africa.

There is little or no inter-regional trade between Uganda and the countries of Central, West and North Africa. In some countries there are obvious language barriers. In a few instances there are countries that have not signed and ratified the Florence Agreement and therefore impose tariff barriers on book imports. Complex freight arrangements are another obvious obstacle to developing inter-regional book markets.

Recent policy developments

The two most significant policy issues currently facing the book trade in Uganda both relate to the primary textbook market. In late 1999 the MoES announced the proposed new primary curriculum recommendations. These recommendations suggested a significant number of additional primary school subjects for which additional textbooks would be required. They also proposed a shift toward local languages as the medium of instruction in the first three levels of primary school and the introduction of Kiswahili as an additional compulsory language from the first year of primary school.

It is not the purpose of this case study to comment on the educational issues involved in the new curriculum proposals. From a publishing standpoint, the proposals for additional subjects and additional textbooks and the proposals for new languages and languages of instruction immediately create new possibilities for publishing markets. From the point of view of government, the cost implications of a significant addition to the number of books required to teach the primary curriculum, combined with the doubling of the primary school population to achieve UPE, are very severe.

The Ugandan Government has already demonstrated its commitment to decentralisation. The IMU operation is no exception. Although the IMU manages to combine very effectively all of the benefits of decentralisation with the cost benefits of central purchasing (and everybody from funders and publishers to the Auditor General's office acknowledges this), the drive for further decentralisation is still very powerful. The MoES is therefore currently exploring the possibility of pilot experiments in textbook procurement at the district level. After considerable discussion, the following pilot proposal for decentralised procurement is now under consideration by the MoES:

- In a limited number of pilot districts (two or three), individual school textbook budgets should be moved from the IMU to the pilot districts.
- The pilot districts will create Local Purchase Orders (LPOs) on the basis of school roll numbers using the current per capita allocations used by the IMU. Each school will use the LPOs to purchase their textbooks and teacher's guides from local, district based suppliers of their choice.
- Local suppliers will have to apply to DEOs to be registered as 'official textbook suppliers' on the basis of nationally agreed criteria and standards.
- LPOs will only be redeemed at the 'official textbook suppliers'.
- The districts will evaluate, appoint and monitor their 'official suppliers'.
- The use of LPOs will guarantee that the IMU funds continue to be spent only on textbooks and nothing else.

The use of 'official suppliers' appointed on the basis of national criteria will provide an opportunity for local booksellers to be involved and will assist in improving standards. Publishers will be encouraged to work with local suppliers to access orders for textbooks. Information from the MoES at the time of writing suggests that any further experimentation in decentralised supply will be delayed until current national book to pupil targets have been achieved.

The Book Development Council of Uganda (BODECU) will soon publish a comprehensive national book policy. The book policy will stress links between all stakeholders in the book industry. One positive development is the existence of active associations of publishers, booksellers and printers. They will lobby the Ministries of Education and Commerce to address the cost and supply of printing materials, and especially paper, for educational purposes.

It is encouraging to note that the pace of reform in the context of privatisation, decentralisation and the development of consumer based financing and control still continues very strongly in Uganda.

Case study E: Guinea

By Mamadou Aliou Sow, MD, Editions Ganndal, Conakry and President of REPROLIG and Etienne Brunswic and Jean Valérien, both of Danaé-Sciences, Paris[66]

Basic facts
- Located between Latitudes 7–13° N and Longitudes 7–15° W.
- Bordered by Mali (Francophone) to the north-east, Côte d'Ivoire (Francophone) to the east, Sierra Leone and Liberia (Anglophone) to the south, Guinea-Bissau (Lusophone) to the north-west and the Atlantic Ocean to the south.
- A former French colony, independence was attained in 1958.
- Population: 7,2 million.
- Area: 245,800 square kilometres.
- Population density: 25 per square kilometre.
- 28% of the population is classified as urban.
- Life expectancy is 46 years.
- The capital city is Conakry, with a population of over one million; other main urban centres include Guéckédou (383,000) and Boké (294,000).
- 85% of the population are Muslim, 8% are Christian, and 7% adhere to traditional religions.
- French is the official language, and each ethnic group has its own language.
- 37,9% of Guineans are literate.
- Economic growth rate (1999): 2,8%.
- Main economic activities are mining (bauxite, gold, diamonds), aluminium and subsistence agriculture.
- The per capita GNP is US$550.
- The unit of currency is the Guinean Franc (FG). In March 2000, 1,666.67 FG = US$1.

The education market

Soon after independence in 1958, Guinea introduced a mass teaching system based on productive work and the use of eight national languages. As time went by, the situation deteriorated, and the country became more and more isolated. In 1984, after the death of Sekou Touré, international aid started to

---

66 John Hall's assistance with this study is acknowledged with thanks.

flow into the country again. It was also at this time that French regained its former status as the language of instruction.

Table 16 Basic education data for Guinea	
Gross enrollment rate	52,5% (arge discrepancies exist between enrollment of boys and girls, and urban and rural children)
Net enrollment rates	45,6% (primary), 14,6% (secondary)
Education budget	Approximately 25% of the State budget of which 39% is dedicated to primary schooling
Primary enrollment	674,632 (37% are girls, 12% of pupils are in private schools)
Secondary enrollment	153,661 (37% are girls, 5,6% of pupils are in private schools)
Tertiary enrollment	8,272 (10,5% are girls)
Percentage of students that repeat years	25% (Grade 1), 41% (Grade 6)
Percentage of pupils that proceed to secondary school	42% (of Grade 6 pupils)
Number of teachers	13,234 (there are 50 pupils per class on average)
Number of schools	3,543
Textbook to pupil ratio	the target is 1:1 in primary schools

Since 1990, the Government of Guinea has concentrated resources on textbook provision in order to upgrade the quality of teaching and to improve equity. Textbook publishing for primary and secondary education is undertaken by the state, whereas the provision of educational materials (mostly imported) for technical, vocational and tertiary education is the responsibility of the private sector and is based on demand.

Between 1989 and 1998, nearly four million textbooks with a value of more than US$10 million were provided for primary and secondary schools. Projects currently under way are planning the same level of output for the period 1999 and 2001.

The amount of money actually contributed for textbook provision by the Ministry of Education cannot be identified, because of the absence of a specific allocation for textbooks in the budget. The Ministry has devolved responsibility for textbooks and curricula to the *Institut National de Recherche et d'Action Pedagogique* (INRAP), a parastatal organisation. However, INRAP receives no financial allocations from the government and relies exclusively on foreign funding.[67]

A single title is used per subject, per grade in all schools. A teacher's guide supplements the pupil's book and an activity book is occasionally also provided. According to the number of titles and the quantity of books provided, the book to pupil ratio should have reached 3:1 in 1998. However, a survey conducted by USAID in 1998, based on a cross-section of 291 primary schools, concluded that there was on average one textbook per pupil. This suggests that the attrition rate for textbooks amounts to 67%, with an even higher figure for teacher's guides.

Key players in the sales and distribution of books

In spite of numerous recommendations (from the Book Summit in 1997[68] and the USAID survey in 1998), there is no such thing as a national book policy in Guinea.

INRAP holds the monopoly on textbook development. When put out to tender, local publishers and printers fail to win tenders. There have been a number of attempts to use Guinean companies to distribute textbooks funded by aid projects, but these attempts have failed and been abandoned.

The formal sector

The professional book trade sector consists of two publishers, four printers (including one state-owned printer), and three distributors.

Publishers
- SAEC (*Société Africaine d'Édition et de Communication*).
- *Éditions Ganndal.*

Each of these publishers have their own retail outlet in Conakry.

Printers
- IDEC (*Imprimerie de l'Éducation et de la Culture*), which is state-owned.
- NIK (*Nouvelle Imprimerie du Kaloun*).
- IPM (*Imprimerie Papeterie Moderne*).
- *Imprimerie Triomphe.*

Distributors
- SODIL (*Société de Distribution du Livre*), which is part of *Société Guinéenne de Distribution de la Presse* (SOGUIDIP). This distributor has one retail outlet in Conakry plus 20 stores in Coastal Guinea and in Upper Guinea.
- *Ma Bougie*, with eleven retail outlets in Mid Guinea and Forest Guinea.

---

67 A USAID led survey published in 1998 pointed out that no government funded financial support could be identified between 1991 and 1997. Grants or loans covered all textbook costs. Moreover, sums that should have been recovered from the 'Sale to the Families Plan' have never appeared in the accounts.

68 The Book Summit, organised in May 1997 under the aegis of INRAP, brought together representatives from several ministries, national book professionals, donors and NGOs operating in Guinea, publishers from the North East (Edicef, Hatier), and PTA representatives. The objective was to lay the foundation for a national book policy.

- SAEC (see p. 131), which has a few retail outlets in Conakry and in Coastal Guinea.

Following a recent initiative by the Ministry of Culture and APNET, the General Director of *Éditions Ganndae* now leads a Network for Book Professionals (REPROLIG) in Guinea.

The informal sector
There are a number of 'pavement bookshops', some of which sell books throughout the year, while others limit their activity to back-to-school periods only. Their market share is quite large. Many parents prefer to bargain for textbooks in one of the informal shops rather than in a conventional bookshop.

The evolution of book publishing and distribution in Guinea
Virtually every system of textbook financing, provision and distribution has been tried in Guinea since independence:

1958–84: 100% state control
After independence the state took on all responsibilities and costs for textbook development and provision. Unfortunately, the government was unable to afford the costs of supply. Spending declined to US$0,20 per pupil per year and the education system rapidly deteriorated. For schools where education was provided in one of the eight national languages, no books were available and teachers had to rely on notes made during their university days.

1984–90: massive imports and free distribution of textbooks
In 1984 and 1985, National Conferences on Education relinquished teaching in national languages and the international community stepped in again to provide Guinea with textbooks. There was a massive injection of imported textbooks, which were distributed via the state administration, but this didn't solve the main problems. The World Bank Education Project proposed the production of seventeen national titles, but by the end of 1998, only three manuscripts had been completed.

1990–93: distribution/sale by the private sector, then by government
In 1990, the three manuscripts that were ready were printed in Belgium, while four other titles were bought off the shelf from France. In December 1990, the Ministry of Education awarded the contract for distribution to the recently privatised company, *Libraport Nouvelle*. The contract specified that a 30% discount should be granted off the retail price, but the contract remained unclear on many other clauses. As a result, *Libraport* was never able to complete the contract.

To distribute the books remaining in store, the Ministry decided to organise a government-controlled 'distribution/sale'. Textbooks were delivered to district education offices and sold by headmasters to pupils at a discounted price. But headmasters never paid the money back to the government and the actual results of this experiment were never made available.

1994–96: distribution and sale of textbooks by the private sector

From 1994, the distribution of the numerous books provided by donors was entrusted to the private companies *Soguidip* and *Ma Bougie*, on the understanding that a 37% discount was granted. These distributors also imported alternative titles for sale on their own behalf. After some initial problems were ironed out, this system worked well.

1997–99: textbook rental scheme

At the end of 1997, the Ministry suddenly decided at short notice to put an end to commercial distribution via parental purchase and instituted a rental system managed by local committees.

The current situation in textbook distribution

From 1998 onwards, according to the rental policy, books have been delivered to the Ministry's warehouses where private contractors collect and dispatch them to urban schools and to the small rural towns (*sous-préfectures*).

Textbook Management Committees (TMCs) have been set up in primary and secondary schools. Each TMC has eight members. At *collège* level (junior secondary) the principal chairs the TMC while the deputy chairs the PTA). Parents take on the roles of treasurer and administrators. At primary level, the principal acts as the Committee's adviser and the TMC chairperson and treasurer are PTA members.

The annual rental fee has been set at FG1,000 (US$0,60) per pupil for a complete set of textbooks. In theory, every lost book has to be paid for, and the possibility of continued study depends on the return of all the loan books. All rental fees are paid into a fund aimed at contributing to the renewal of textbook stock.

This new approach unfortunately has proved to be difficult to implement as a result of errors and inaccuracies in the original circular sent out by the Ministry of Education. There is uncertainty on which titles are included; how many books are allocated to each school; who should take delivery of the books; the price of replacement copies, etc. There is also fear on the part of parents (some of them confiscate books borrowed by their children to make sure that they can return them without paying replacement costs). The system works best when PTAs are supported by an NGO.

The modest rental fees and difficulties with collections prevent the accumulation of sufficient funds in the Textbook Rental Fee (TRF) accounts to provide for sufficient stock replacement. Thus, there is a real concern that, when donor money dries up, textbooks won't be available to Guinean students any more.

The involvement of funding agencies

From 1989 to 1998, the main players in the funding community have been: the World Bank, the African Development Bank (AfDB), *Agence Internationale de la Francophonie (AIF)*, the European Union, *Coopération Française (CF)*, and USAID. Together, they managed to procure (taking into account both new editions and reprints) nearly four million textbooks for the six levels of primary school (comprising 30 titles) and the four levels of junior secondary (comprising 20 titles), for an estimated total expenditure of more than US$10 million.

Projects in progress funded by the World Bank and the AfDB will provide 2,4 and 2,2 million books respectively for junior secondary. USAID is funding 2,6 million books and more than 1,5 million brochures and AIF is funding 150,000 multidisciplinary activity books. All of the above should allow the provision of a basic 'teaching kit' of more than seven textbooks per pupil plus as many supporting teacher's guides.

The funding agency-led actions within the Structural Adjustment Programme are co-ordinated by the PASE *(Programme d'Ajustement Structurel Education)*, which relies on INRAP and acts under the supervision of the Ministry of Education's *Direction des Affaires Administratives et Financières (DAAF)*. The Director is a civil servant on secondment from the Ministry of Finance.

The USAID project uses the services of a private management company. AfDB's acquisitions are managed by the *Service des Infrastructures et Équipements scolaires* (SNIES). AIF's project is directly managed by INRAP.

In this complex situation, the only key partner remains INRAP. Their specialists and curriculum experts in different subjects work on all textbook publications. As far as co-ordination is concerned, this is certainly a positive input, but it also represents a potential delay factor, due to manpower and schedule constraints.

If import and production processes appear to be under control, funders and authorities seem to be less at ease when dealing with distribution issues. On one hand, funders demonstrate different approaches. Some seem to prefer short-term policies. To make sure that textbooks are available when students go back to school, it is necessary to purchase books off the shelf, either by tender or by directly negotiating with the procurement agencies (as AfBD does, for very large orders). Other development partners, including the World Bank, tend to prefer the in-country option (by relying on INRAP's experts) and to resort to international bids for publication services, which amounts to keeping local publishers out and giving preference to their counterparts in developed countries.

On the other hand, the debate on free distribution, sale or rental, creates a significant split among the agencies. AIF and *Coopération Française* are in favour of selling to the families, because this is the only way, according to them, to achieve long-term self-sufficiency and long book life (parents care for books if they pay for them). USAID, to obtain a wide and fast distribution, sticks to a policy of free supply. NGOs, in contact with schools and parents, would rather advocate a one-off rental fee or a lease system in collaboration with PTAs.

Other debates occur, even if they are not as open. For example, what kinds of production standards are appropriate? Should books be in full-colour as they are in the developed world while Guinea has 50 times less money to spend on educating a lower primary school pupil than is usual in Europe?[69] Alternatively, should basic production standards be established, which would be more in line with family purchasing power and the government's financial capacity?

So far, the MoE has not been able to impose a dual approach that would combine a short-term necessity (play safe in having required books available on back-to-school day by importing or bidding) with a medium-term local capacity development policy. Such a policy could lead on to self-sufficiency by African publishers in the publication of primary textbooks plus sustainability in textbook procurement based on parent purchase. The National Federation of PTAs has accepted the principle of parent purchase.

The moral and material interests at stake are considerable. Every government official is a supporter of (at least) one donor viewpoint. Most Guineans involved in textbook procurement still rule out the idea of turning a textbook into just another tradeable item. Ministry officials don't realise that 'free' textbooks do have a cost – which is, at the moment, paid for by grants and loans, which will disappear sooner or later. The current rental system, as already stated, does not set realistic loan fees and thus does not allow for the sustainability of replacement. Inevitably, replacement will have to be financed by new loans and/or grants.

Everything works as if there were a collusion of interests between the many different interest groups. Thus:

- The Ministry of Finance collects heavy taxes on import raw materials (27% customs duty and 18% VAT on paper and inks), whereas imported textbooks remain exempt from customs duties (in compliance with the Florence Agreement). Harbour taxes are appallingly high. Paper is purchased from France, Brazil and South Africa at an average price of US$650 per ton.
- It is in the interests of the informal distribution sector to buy books in Guinea at agency/state subsidised and discounted prices and to sell them at market prices in neighbouring countries. Thus, the *Horizon d'Afrique* textbook, donated in large quantities by AIF, should have been sold in Guinea at one third of its actual price (that is US$2). In a very short time

---

69 This cost per pupil is estimated at US$67 in Guinea, and US$4,134 in France (1998), that is a 1:60 discrepancy. This indicates the extent to which a standard 'Northern' textbook is an expensive luxury for a 'Southern' pupil.

it was no longer available in Guinea, but was widely available in the 'pavement bookshops' of neighbouring countries at US$6,50.

- Developed country publishers contend that their export sales (through books and services) are essential to their survival. Therefore, they have so far fought hard to maintain their direct sales income from Francophone African countries, rather than making significant investments in local publishing development.

The role of multinational publishers

Multinational publishers (particularly from France but also from Canada and Belgium) are very anxious to maintain their commercial positions in the Guinean market. The practice of international tenders for book publishing contracts suits them because the local publishing sector is usually not in a position to bid competitively. There is some cause for concern around this because current purchasing practices create high levels of competition between publishers and can lead to corrupt decision-making.

The regional trade in books

In spite of being located close to Côte d'Ivoire and Senegal (the only countries in Francophone Africa boasting reasonably well-developed publishing industries) imports from these countries are almost non-existent. The Guinean government's successive U-turns on educational policy are probably partly to be blamed for this situation, but other reasons include the facts that transport is difficult and that Guinea doesn't belong to the CFA Franc area.

The same obstacles inhibit any export development in books. The weak capitalisation of Guinean publishers and their inability to invest in developing new titles and the creation of export sales structures is also a problem. The initial capital of Guinean publishers only amounts to FG5–10 million (US$3,000–6,000) and is almost entirely derived from local sources.

Recent policy developments

Since 1998, AIF has been supporting an INRAP project aiming at the national production of exercise books for sale to parents and families. It is intended that the exercise books will be entirely produced and distributed by the private sector. The Ministry of Education has welcomed the AIF proposal to draft a framework agreement and this constitutes a significant breakthrough in the implementation of a national book policy.[70]

Obstacles to progress

With the government's goal of providing more than seven textbooks per student (in primary and junior secondary), it is not appropriate to speak about shortages

---

70 AIF's reshuffling in the course of 1999 has led to a break in the follow up of the project; the subsequent production delay has caused the exercise books to be available later than expected.

of books in Guinea. Unfortunately, this aim will be in vain as long as the books don't get to the students. And even if this goal is achieved, with a recorded attrition rate as high as 67%, the book supply will not remain abundant in schools for very long.

Lack of overall responsibility

At the moment, the responsibility for developing textbooks is shared between the various government ministries including the Ministry of Education, the Department of Finance and Administration etc, INRAP and various funders. (The inability of funding agencies to co-ordinate their approach has been noted above and there is no overall co-ordination of these groups as a whole.)

The assessment of the existing situation and the forecast of needs are highly inadequate. For example, there appears to be no understanding of the daily reality of a curriculum that requires a seven textbook set, with each title offering 100 pages, in terms of the number of pages of text that have to be absorbed every day. Similarly there is a lack of precision concerning the number of books that need to be delivered every year (bearing in mind that several years will be necessary to achieve the total delivery of a given textbook). Textbook production and distribution priorities (assuming that all subjects are equal) are also unclear. Annual loss, damage and replacement rates are not known and the costs of replacement have not been calculated. Nor is there any clear idea about future financing sources.

The logistics of distribution, storage, transport, etc. all need to be defined – the real costs of distribution are not known at this point, whatever operating level may be assumed. The fact that the inputs of NGOs' (*Aide et Action*, *Plan Guinée*, World Education, etc.) and PTA contributions are not included in cost breakdowns and that the government distribution costs are hidden, maintains the illusion of a low-cost distribution system. This makes the development of a professionally organised and managed distribution system all the more difficult because inevitably it will be perceived as costing more than the existing set up.

Lack of a national book policy

Textbook procurement is not included within a broader framework, which itself derives from a national book policy, the aim of which would be to strengthen and develop a professional book trade sector.

Lack of medium-term perspectives and financing strategies

Dependence on funders remains total and there is no funding transparency. Differing interests between the various government ministries involved (Finance, Culture, Industry, Education, etc.) make this divergence all the more acute because Education is not strong enough to arbitrate. The rapid alternations between free and paying procurement systems and between private and government-controlled distribution described above prevent officials from basing their future decisions on past experience.

A positive element

The fact that there is a potential publishing capacity, and it is ready to blossom, definitely adds a positive element to the current situation. The recent attempt to publish multidisciplinary activity books brought together, apart from the INRAP researchers, about 40 local authors with a previous writing and publishing experience, so far as authors are concerned, the capacity is obvious. As far as production and distribution are concerned sufficient resources do exist in Guinea, provided the above-mentioned obstacles are lifted. In fact, the Guinean publisher, Ganndal, have recently published a series of six multi diciplinary books and three teacher's guides. If national and international players could work harmoniously within a shared market giving local publishers preference for primary textbooks, publishing resources are strong enough to develop and distribute simply produced textbooks that are appropriate to local purchasing power. Such a system would make sure that self-sustainability prevailed in the provision of textbooks to schools.

Case study F: Niger

By Amadou Waziri, Publishing Manager, INDRAP, Niamey and Jean-Pierre Leguéré and Georges Stern, Danaé Sciences, Paris

---

Basic facts
- Located between Latitude 13–24° N and Longitude 0–16°E.
- Bordered by Algeria and Libya to the North, Chad to the east, Nigeria to the south, Bénin and Burkina Faso to the south west, and Mali to the west. All neighbouring countries are Francophone, except for Nigeria (Anglophone) and Libya (Arabic).
- A former French colony, independence was attained in 1960.
- Population: 10,1 million.
- The capital city is Niamey, with a population of 480,000; other main urban centres include Zinder (210,000) and Maradi (200,000).
- 80% of the population are Muslim, 20% are Christian or adhere to traditional religions.
- French is the official language, but Arabic and nine African languages are also spoken.
- 13% of the population are literate (men: 21%, women: 6%).
- Economic growth rate: 3,3% p.a.
- 48,6% of the population are under 15 years of age.
- Main economic activities are cement manufacture, mining (uranium), agriculture.
- Per capita GNP: US$210.
- The unit of currency is the CFA Franc (CFA). In July 2000, 100 CFA = US$0,147.

In terms of its geography and economy, Niger is, in many ways, typical of the Sahelian countries. It is a landlocked desert country and it has one of the lowest and weakest per capita GNPs on the planet. Moreover, Niger is politically unstable, a fact not positively perceived by donor nations.

The three main cities house less than 10% of the country's population, which is scattered and mainly rural. Almost half of the population is under fifteen years of age. Educational needs are thus very great in this deprived nation.

The education market

Table 17 Basic education data for Niger

Education budget	3% of GNP
Primary enrollment	482,065 (38% are girls, 4% are in private schools)
Secondary enrollment	98,878 (36% are girls, 16% are in private schools)
Tertiary enrollment	Around 5,000 (15% are girls)

Table 18 Synopsis of the education system

	Pre-school	Primary	Junior Secondary	Senior Secondary	Technical Vocational	Teacher training centres
Number of schools	123	3,175	171	21	2	4
Number of classes	430	11,304	1772	406	42	41
Enrollment girls	5,919	186,488	30,265	5,287	152	516
Enrollment boys	5,845	295,577	49,399	11,773	661	925
Total enrollment	11,764	482,065	79,664	17,060	813	1,441
GER%		30,35	13,22	3,76	3,76	3,76
Female teachers	490	3,651	539	141	10	8
Male teachers	4	7,874	1,844	868	102	109
Total number of teachers	494	11,525	2,383	1,009	112	117

Table 19 Primary schools by sector, area and type of teaching

Type of teaching	Public urban	Public rural	Private urban	Private rural	Overall urban	Overall rural	Total
Traditional	394	2,559	30	2	424	2,561	2,985
Medersa	57	48	33	6	90	54	144
Pilot	28	12	1		29	12	41
Specialised	5				5		5
Total	484	2,619	64	8	548	2,627	3,175

Key players in the sales and distribution of books

Publishers

Given the country's needs, Niger's publishers focus on textbook publishing. The government plays a major role through the *Institut de Recherche et d'Animation Pédagogique* (INDRAP), which is funded by the Ministry of Education. INDRAP designs and writes all primary school textbooks. Production is tendered out, but, even if a local company wins the tender, the printing is usually sub-contracted overseas.

The Publishers' Association of Niger (AFNIL) has two private company members. These are *Éditions Daouda* and *Éditions Alpha*.

For the secondary and tertiary education sectors, nearly all books are imported, mainly from France.

Booksellers

The capital city, Niamey, has two bookshops:
- *Librairie Daouda*, which belongs to the publishing company of the same name (see above). It is part of the primary textbook distribution network and is the main provider of secondary and tertiary textbooks, usually imported from France;
- *Librairie Mereda*, which is smaller and is not part of any other network.

Printers

There are five printing companies in Niger:
- *Nouvelle Imprimerie du Niger.*
- *Imprimerie Albarka.*
- *Grande Imprimerie IBS.*
- *Imprimerie des Arts Graphiques du Niger.*
- *Imprimerie Pivano.*

Some of the above companies bid for textbook printing tenders from INDRAP, but always on the basis that the work will be sub-contracted overseas rather than done in Niger. Overseas printing avoids the heavy taxes on imported raw materials and, more importantly, it makes it easier to adjust print-runs according to the available budget.

Distributors

The education ministry supplies government primary schools with books free of charge according to the system described. *Librairie Daouda* forms part of the distribution network for primary school books in Niamey and supplies textbooks to private schools as well as all imported secondary and tertiary texts. (ELT titles for junior secondary schools, are locally produced.)

The evolution of book publishing & distribution in Niger since independence

Because of the overwhelming dominance of the textbook market in Niger the history of the evolution of book distribution and the history of textbook development are identical.

From 1960 to 1974

The primary and secondary textbooks used in Niger were identical to those used in France. The Ministry of Education placed orders directly with French publishers, and paid for the books out of national budgets or with agency support.

From 1974 to 1988

Niger authors started to write local textbooks in co-operation with assistance from French volunteers (VSOs).

From 1988 to the present

Niger increasingly took responsibility for writing of all its own primary textbooks, largely supported by funding provided by the World Bank. Design, layout, illustrations and sometimes film preparation were locally provided by INDRAP.

Niger has thus partly reached its original objective of authoring and origination autonomy for primary school textbooks. This is very encouraging. If the Florence agreement were applied to local printing (that is if no customs duties were imposed on the paper and ink used to print textbooks), the whole production process, including printing, could be carried out in Niger. In addition, there are well-trained design, editorial and printing professionals available locally. The lack of distribution infrastructure is a stumbling block for the whole system.

The current situation in textbook distribution

The Ministry of Education is solely responsible for the distribution of textbooks. The current distribution system can be described as follows:

- At the end of each school year, local inspectors give the Ministry of Education the estimated textbook requirements for the next school year.
- These needs are compared with the funding available for textbooks from all sources – the national budget, bilateral grants, loans, etc.
- The purchase and/or production of textbooks is put out to tender. The selected bidder has to deliver the textbooks to the education ministry's warehouses in Niamey.
- Textbook deliveries are organised from the warehouse for schools in Niamey and books are delivered to the Inspectorates in the seven Regional Divisions of Agadez, Diffa, Dosso, Maradi, Tahoua, Tillaberi and Zinder.

(Each of the regional divisions has a truck, which travels to Niamey to collect the textbooks from the central warehouse and transports them back to the regions, where they are further dispatched to the Inspectorates.)

- Each inspector shares out the textbooks according to local quotas. After calling at the Inspectorates to take up their posting, head teachers take away the free books they need for their pupils.

The shortcomings of the current system

In theory, the system should be very economical and logical. Unfortunately, it doesn't work very well. For example, there may be a delay of several months between the textbooks reaching an Inspectorate and their delivery to schools and the number of allocated books is sometimes insufficient to meet basic needs. The main problems are not just the result of inadequate financing and difficult geographic and climatic conditions, although these factors do contribute to the problems. The most significant barrier to the establishment of an effective distribution process lies in mediocre organisation:

- Forward planning is inadequate and poorly performed. Orders are not placed in good time and they are often fragmented and incomplete when they are passed on to INDRAP. As a result, books are usually printed too late and in a disorganised and costly way. The number of copies printed frequently doesn't match the roll numbers and thus the actual need. In urban areas, the book to pupil ratio is 1:3, but it declines to 1:5 in the country. Local observers stress the fact that the lack of forward planning is the most significant problem and the one that is the most difficult to rectify, no matter where the funds come from.
- Textbook collection by the trucks from the Regional Divisions is often delayed because funding is not available to cover the cost of fuel and regular maintenance.
- Security in the stores and during transportation is poor and there are many thefts that reduce the number of books that actually make it to their final destination. Losses can be as high as 50–60% of the original printed stock.
- School buildings are often simple huts and frequently there are no secure storerooms or even lockable cupboards in which to store the books so losses continue to occur after the books arrive at the schools. The books that parents should have received free of charge through the official system are available from the informal markets for a price.
- Head teachers have almost no financial and practical means at their disposal to pay for the collection of the books from the Inspectorate and their delivery to their schools. Personal connections are becoming increasingly crucial to secure transportation and finding transport may take several months. It should be noted that the rainy season runs from June to October and coincides with the main distribution period. During the rains many roads and tracks are impassable.

- Many of the people involved in the distribution chain often don't get paid. Petrol vouchers handed over to officials for book collections may be used instead to visit family members or to fulfil any other activity that seems more urgent than collecting textbooks.
- Finally, the significance of book distribution often is not really appreciated by many of the decision-makers, including the funding agencies.

The involvement of funding agencies

Over the period 1996–1999, the main funding supporting primary textbooks was the World Bank, which is committed to continuing its support until December 2000. However, their support has been declining since 1996 and the Niger government has stopped funding anything related to textbooks.

It is doubtfull whether the World Bank or the publishers fully appreciate how poor the current distribution system is. The World Bank continues to finance textbooks which often do not reach schools and the publishers seem to be content to spend money on production without worrying about the delivery of stocks, to schools, on time. The fact that the government is responsible for textbook distribution hides the real costs of the exercise and makes distribution appear to be free. However, it is obvious that effective distribution requires transportation, storage, manpower and effective systems and management, which in turn represent considerable investments in human and material resources.

It is, of course, much easier and more visible for funders to estimate a figure for the development and production costs of textbooks than to assist in the establishment of a distribution structure where initial achievements may be uncertain and where discernible results may take time to become apparent.

The role of the multinational and regional publishers

Multinational publishers from developed countries show little motivation to distribute the textbooks they produce on behalf of African countries. These publishers appear to give priority to their short term interests and to cash in on the profits created by the situation, which is protected by the Florence Agreement (that is, that there are no customs duties for imported textbooks, but heavy taxes on the imported raw materials required for local book production such as paper and ink).[71] When multinational publishers do try to establish or maintain a sustainable intervention through an investment in a local African publishing company, they generally keep clear of investments in distribution in the Sahelian countries.

---

71 It should be noted that the Florence Agreement and the Nairobi Protocols require that signatory countries maintain the free flow of books and information unhampered by taxes, import duties or quotas. They do not require the imposition of heavy import duties on printing raw materials and printing machines and spare parts. In fact, the Nairobi Protocols specifically require that machinery and raw materials for book printing should be exempted from customs duties. Thus, where these duties occur they result from the decisions of national governments and not from the international agreements (editorial note).

Regional trade in books

Only a few years ago, the idea of a regional publishing industry in Francophone Africa would have seemed completely impracticable. Recently, however meetings between publishers, the training of local publishing and editorial staff – particularly by CAFED (*Centre Africain de Formation à l'Édition*) – and the changing nature of book production in Sahelian countries have contributed to a shift in regional thinking. The idea of co-publishing and co-producing within developing countries is now widely accepted. This creates a basis for these countries to move towards a better regional book distribution system.

Recent policy developments

Initially, the copyright of textbooks – now entirely written in Niger – was shared with French publishers. Now that textbook authorship and development are fully funded by the government (and funders) and performed within INDRAP, the government owns copyright to all locally published primary textbooks – nineteen titles in all. Reprinting is thus easier, even if, as mentioned above, the reprints still benefit overseas printers.

Suggestions and proposals

The ability to read newspapers, to read the instructions for the use of seeds or machines and to understand simple books on practical subjects should be a basic objective for the deprived and widely dispersed Sahelian populations – and particularly for Niger. Only significant increases in primary school enrollments will allow this goal to be achieved. In a difficult geographic and economic environment, there are many obstacles that stand in the way of this objective. Teachers are scarce and poorly trained. Parents sometimes would rather have their children working in the fields than studying in the classroom. The shortage of pupils' textbooks and teacher's guides only adds to the difficulties. Essentially the existing system must be strengthened to, create an environment where distribution will be part of a book chain, built and designed with the co-operation of both government and the private sector.

This study has demonstrated the inadequacies of the current distribution system. Nevertheless, it does exist. On analysis, it is clear that the distribution process is less hindered by economic or environmental difficulties than by a fundamental lack of organisation. It is recommended therefore that, to begin with, the current system could be strengthened as follows:

- Rigorous training and support of officials to help improve their planning capacity and their negotiations skills with funders.
- The inclusion of textbook distribution system reform within future agency investments in textbooks. In particular, this would require the need to address the critical issue of stock security during transportation, storage and in schools. In concrete terms this would require an investment in lockable school stores or cupboards. It is assumed that funding agencies

would be the first to want their investments protected against loss in the sands.

- The need to focus resources on the development of in-country printing. Here again, what is needed is improved organisation rather than a larger financial contribution. In addition, the Niger government (and other Sahelian countries) should be encouraged to become signatories to the Nairobi Protocols adopted by the UNESCO general conference in 1976 (which requires provision for the exemption from customs duties of materials and machines used for the production of books.

This first step, spread out over several years, would aim at ensuring better book distribution. It would also aim to create a new attitude toward book development among the key stakeholders. Moreover, it would favour the creation of local publishing structures. Niger would then be faced with a conjunction of positive development. The textbooks would be developed and produced by INDRAP, under the supervision of the government. Niger would be able to print and bind competitively and, finally, distribution would be improved compared to the current situation. Once this favourable environment is achieved, the basic conditions would be in place to move towards an integrated book chain where commercial companies would also have a role.

The creation of an integrated book chain

The creation of a favourable environment for co-ordination between government and the private sector is perceived by the authors of this study to be the only way to create a book industry capable of producing and distributing not only textbooks but also technical titles and trade books. In this co-ordinated approach, the Niger government would be responsible for the development of curricula and textbooks, while the private sector could take care of the production and distribution of the books. For example, a consortium of publishers could set up a distribution structure. This will only be possible if the principle of the free provision of textbooks is abandoned. Private distributors will only survive if textbook distribution becomes a source of profit for them. This doesn't necessarily mean that families should pay the full cost of the textbooks. Even in France, parents are granted an annual 'back-to-school allowance' for their children.

In 1995, under the auspices of the *Agence de la Francophonie*, the first steps were taken in this direction. At the time, it had the interest of local publishers, the World Bank and some local politicians. The education ministry was not entirely convinced but the proposed project had some chance of realisation. Unfortunately, the January 1996 military coup put an end to any further thinking on the proposal, but perhaps the time has come to reconsider these ideas once again.

Chapter Three

MINI CASE STUDIES ON DISTRIBUTION ISSUES

Case study G: Botswana

By Lesedi Seitei, Secretary, Botswana Publishers' Association and MD, Heinemann Botswana Ltd, Gaberone

---

Basic facts
- Located between Latitudes 18–27° S and Longitudes 20–30° E.
- Botswana is a landlocked country bordered by Namibia on the north and west, Zambia and Zimbabwe to the north-east and the Republic of South Africa on the south-east and south.
- Population: 2 million (1998 estimate).
- Area: 582,000 square kilometres.
- Population density: three people per square kilometre.
- 68% of the population is classified as urban (1998).
- Per capita GNP was US$3,600 in 1998.
- The capital city is Gaborone with a population of 150,000 (1995 estimate).
- 50% of the population is Christian; the other 50% adhere to traditional religions.
- Life expectancy is 47 years with a female life expectancy of 48 years and a male life expectancy of 46 years.
- A former British protectorate, independence was achieved in 1966.
- English is the official language and Setswana is the national language.
- According to the World Development Report (1999), 75% of the population is functionally literate. Of these, 85% of men and 65% of women are functionally literate.
- Main economic activities are mining (diamonds, copper, nickel, coal, salt, soda ash and potash) and cattle farming.
- Botswana is administered via nine districts.
- The unit of currency is the Pula. In January 2000, P4,50 = US$1.

The education market

Prior to independence a few missionary schools dominated the education system. Following independence there was an expansion in the size of the system and changes in its structure. Free education up to the final year of secondary school was introduced in the 1980s. The system has evolved in the following way.

- Up to 1985 there was a 7-3-3 system (seven years of primary, three years of junior secondary and three years of senior secondary).
- In 1986 there was a change to a 7-2-3 system (this was meant to be a transition towards a 6-3-3 system, but this was abandoned by the Revised Education Policy of 1993).
- In 1998 there was a reversion to the previous 7-3-3 system.

The official policy on the provision of teaching and learning materials is one textbook per student per subject and one book to five students for supplementary reading materials. The official provision rates have been achieved for textbooks but for supplementary materials the required ratio has not yet been achieved. The spending on supplementary books is cut whenever there is a shortfall in the allocated textbook budgets (and this happens every year). The supplementary book ratio is therefore never achieved and this is widely considered to be detrimental to the learning environment.

Primary education

In terms of curriculum design, implementation and monitoring, primary education is the responsibility of the Ministry of Education (MoE). Physical infrastructure and materials acquisition (including books) is the responsibility of the Ministry of Local Government and Lands. This division of responsibility creates conflicts, particularly in budgeting. The Curriculum Development Department (CDD) draws up the prescribed book list without reference to book prices. The Ministry of Local Government and Lands asks publishers to quote for books after they have already received their annual budget from the Ministry of Finance. Their estimates and budget allocations are always lower than the actual costs of procurement (see Tables 21 and 22 for basic statistics).

Primary education initially had a school leaving examination at the end of seven years. This has changed recently because basic education now includes junior secondary up to the end of Form 3 so there are ten years of basic education. Although there are sufficient student spaces available in schools, the government has not yet made basic education compulsory. This is the next anticipated education reform to be introduced by government. At the moment there are just over 700 primary schools.

Secondary education

Secondary education is the responsibility of the Ministry of Education. Until the mid-1980s there were only about ten secondary schools in the country. At present there are 205 government junior secondary schools and only 27 senior secondary schools. The next phase of educational expansion will be the construction of more senior secondary schools with a view to increasing the progression rate from junior secondary to 50% by 2003 (see Tables 20, 22 and 23). Secondary schools select their own book suppliers.

Table 20 Pupil enrollment and projected enrollment

	1996	1997	1998	1999	2000	2001	2002	2003	2004
Primary school	319,136	323,923	328,782	333,714	338,720	343,800	348,957	354,191	359,500
Junior secondary	75,957	77,138	115,830	117,528	118,528	120,306	122,110	123,941	125,800
Senior secondary	29,774	33,995	24,259	29,284	33,157	34,717	35,742	38,254	40,015
Total secondary enrollment	105,731	111,133	140,089	146,812	151,685	155,023	157,852	162,195	165,815

Table 21 Expenditure on primary school books (in Pula)

1994/5	1995/6	1996/7	1997/8	1998/9	1999/2000
16 760,724	18 090,258	14 790,942	20 982,768	22 896,602	25 086,142
Per capita	1996	1997	1998	1999	2000
allocations for books	57,00	46,00	63,00	68,00	74,00

Note 1: The portion out of P120,00 allocated to books

Table 22 Current and projected expenditure on secondary school books (in Pula)

	1996	1997	1998	1999	2000	2001	2002	2003	2004
Junior secondary	23m	23m	35m	35m	36m	36m	37m	37m	38m
Senior secondary	9m	10m	7m	9m	10m	10m	11m	11m	12m
Total	32m	33m	42m	44m	46m	46m	48m	48m	50m

Note 1: Because figures were calculated from per capita allocations there might be errors.
Note 2: In 1996 and 1997 junior secondary level consisted of two years of study. The increase in 1998 was when the system changed and Form 3 students also became part of junior secondary.

Table 23	Total expenditure on books for primary and secondary schools in Botswana (in Pula)				
1996	**1997**	**1998**	**1999**	**2000**	
50m	48m	63m	67m	71m	

Tertiary education

The tertiary sector is still small. It comprises the University of Botswana with an enrollment of 10,000 students, two Junior Secondary Teacher Training Colleges, four Primary Teacher Training Colleges, six Institutes of Health Sciences (which includes nursing training), about nine Vocational Training Institutes, one Auto-Trades Institute and some privately-owned professional studies colleges. The government offers bursaries and loans for tertiary education with good terms of repayment. The government colleges use a tender system to procure textbooks, library books and other learning materials. The University awards a portion of its procurement budget locally but the biggest portion is usually awarded to outside specialist suppliers and consolidators. See Table 24 for the enrollment profile in 1997 (the latest available).

Table 24	The number of students enrolled in tertiary education in 1997
Teacher training colleges (primary)	999
Colleges of education (secondary)	1,261
Automotive and mechanical trades	236
Vocational training institutes	2,866
Health institutes	1,300
Brigades	3,828
Colleges of agriculture	119
University of Botswana (1999 figure)	10,000
Total	20,609

Private schools

There are 31 private primary schools (International Schools), four of which also offer secondary education. Most of the private schools use UK textbooks, which are paid for by school fees. The private schools use a mixture of both internal and external booksellers and publishers for the procurement of their book requirements.

There are also four private international secondary schools, which operate more or less like the private primary schools described above in terms of procurement. Finally there are approximately twenty privately owned secondary schools specialising in coaching students who have to repeat classes. These students buy their own textbooks from local booksellers. In comparison to the size of the state school market, the total private school textbook market is insignificant.

The evolution of book distribution in Botswana

Before the abolition of school fees, part of these fees was used to purchase books. The schools ordered all textbooks from a prescribed list prepared by the MoE. There was no choice because only one course was prescribed per subject and per grade. The schools used the book fees to purchase their requirements from booksellers and distributed the books to students. This system ensured, at least, that all students received the same books and stationery. Once distributed, the books became the property of the students.

School fees were abolished in the early 1980s and students began to take the books on loan from schools. Free education increased enrollments and created a larger textbook market, which was essential for the development of a local educational publishing capacity. The major complaint from the book trade is that payments are now very slow. It is partly for this reason that the Botswana Book Centre has dominated book distribution in the country – it is financially stronger than its rivals and copes better with long payment delays. The system of centralised payment for books still operates for senior secondary schools.

The next phase in the development of the book market and the book distribution system was the separation of junior secondary schools from senior secondary schools. The Junior Certificate was also reduced to two years. In terms of the book market this change had the following impact:

- New syllabi and subjects came into being and this created a big opportunity for new publishing development.
- About 205 new junior secondary schools were built and the number of senior secondary schools increased to 27, each with a student enrollment of several thousand. As a result student enrollments multiplied and the secondary textbook market expanded dramatically.
- Junior secondary schools were able to open their own accounts with funds provided by government and thus to order and pay booksellers direct.
- The increased market size attracted more people into the book trade – a trend that has continued up to the present.

The last phase in market development was the re-instatement of a three-year junior secondary curriculum in 1998. This had the following effects:

- The extra year increased total roll numbers as well as the size of the market and thus book sales.
- The reversion to a three-year junior secondary system again required new syllabi and new subjects, which provided more opportunities for book development and stimulated local publishing.
- The additional year and the new publishing opportunities increased book purchases from a zero base. Prior to the new three-year JC syllabi, schools would just buy replacements for damaged or lost books, but as the syllabuses were new, each school had to buy new class sets of completely new textbooks. Thus the required quantities were much larger.
- Book selection procedures are described in more detail on p. 154.

149

The main stakeholders in the book system

The government

The government provides funding for both the infrastructure and the acquisition of instructional materials. This entrenches government control over book distribution, particularly for primary textbooks where the MoE selects, orders, pays for and distributes the books that may be used in schools.

The Curriculum Development Department (CDD) within the MoE writes the textbooks at primary and junior secondary level. (Senior secondary textbooks are still largely imported.)

The MoE awards publishing contracts to the private sector publishing industry and confers of an 'official stamp' on the publishers of CDD course materials. The first contract awarded to the private sector covered all publishing projects generated by the MoE and was awarded to Macmillan. Later other publishers were able to negotiate individual subject contracts but these were only for revisions of textbooks that existed before the award of the overall contract.

At primary level it is not possible for a publisher to compete against a MoE course because all book procurement funds are held and disbursed centrally by the Ministry of Local Government and Lands as mentioned earlier, who will not purchase titles other than the approved course book. At secondary level there was potential for competition because schools were provided with a school-based budget for textbook procurement. However, competing books could only be supplementary because every school *had* to purchase the one MoE prescribed book. During the 1980s and early 1990s this practice limited the growth of the local publishing industry and stifled competition.

The 1977 National Policy on Education and the 1993 Policy Revision determines the way the educational system works. These policies also set the framework for all book trade activity, including educational publishing and educational book distribution. Each year, the MoE organises the annual tender for teaching and learning materials and the direct supply of primary books from publishers to government as well as the centralised payment system for senior secondary school books (see below). This prescription system inhibits the exposure of students and teachers to other published material, which is not on the prescribed list.

Booksellers

The Botswana Book Centre (BBC) enjoyed a virtual monopoly of book distribution in Botswana until the opening of Via Africka in the early 1980s. This was quickly followed in 1982 by the opening of Botsalo Books. BBC is a trust of the United Congregational Church of Southern Africa – formerly the London Missionary Society. It was the first bookshop in the country and remains the largest with four branches. Via Afrika was originally a part of a Southern African bookshop chain but the Botswana shop was subsequently sold to two local directors. Botsalo Books also is a locally-owned bookshop.

In the mid-1990s there was a proliferation of small booksellers. The Botswana Publishing Industry Association now lists 45 bookseller members. While The Botswana Book Centre continues to have the major market share it has lost considerable ground to Via Afrika and Botsalo Books and to the wave of new small booksellers. Many of the small-scale booksellers do not have permanent bookshop premises. Those who have, it is said, sell anything that they can, other than books, during off-peak periods. Few of these more informal booksellers have any credit facilities either with suppliers or with the banks. A good number of them are locally-owned and headmasters often direct business to them for this reason. The government's small business scheme could be helpful to this group.

Booksellers use their own transport to supply schools; very few use freight companies. They therefore depend on bulk orders to justify the costs of supply. This means that during the off-peak season don't get books delivered because the orders are usually small and do not justify the costs of transportation. The peak season runs from September to December, but for secondary schools it often spills over into January and February.

The normal discounts from publishers to booksellers range from 25–30% with some enjoying additional settlement (payment) discounts of 2%. Due to the cut throat competition between the booksellers for school supply contracts, the booksellers' margins are very low with some making only 4% or less on their transactions and depending on bulk supplies to reduce costs and achieve profitability.

At primary level the core subjects of Maths, Social Studies, Agriculture, Science and Setswana all have locally published courses prescribed. For English, the prescribed course is imported. English language readers are imported but Setswana language readers are published locally. All the core texts for junior secondary are published locally but supplementary books, literature and readers are imported. Imported books still dominate at senior secondary level and make up almost 100% of the tertiary market.

Publishers

The first publisher to establish an office in Botswana was Longman in 1979, followed by Macmillan in 1980. Heinemann followed only in 1987 and Hodder and Stoughton opened an office in 1996. The establishment of Tasalls, a locally-owned publishing company, is very recent. Multinational publishing companies dominate textbook publishing in Botswana. There are three local publishers but none are significant in the educational field at present.

Macmillan was the traditional market leader, partly due to the contract that they had with the Ministry of Education, which *inter-alia*, gave them the sole right to publish Ministry initiated textbook projects. This contract expired in about 1993 and was not renewed. Since 1993 there has been relatively free competition with the result that Macmillan has lost some market share to both Longman and Heinemann, who are the second and third largest publishers in Botswana respectively.

Schoolbook procurement

Until the late 1980s the Botswana Book Centre (BBC) handled all primary school book distribution. At this time District Councils were responsible for procurement for primary books with all orders processed by the BBC. As there is no record of any inefficiency on behalf of the BBC it is not clear why this system was changed. The only assumption that can be made is that the change was intended to break the monopoly held by the BBC.

In the late 1980s, a company called International Professional Managers (IPM) was awarded the tender to administer the distribution of books. This contract was a disaster. IPM turned out to be dishonest and government lost millions. Many schools went without books, publishers had to write off huge debts because they were not paid. The whole fiasco was the subject of a government Commission of Inquiry, which reads like a James Hadley Chase novel. The details are documented in the infamous IPM Report, which is known locally as the IPM scandal. In the following year the tender was awarded to Coopers and Lybrand, who did a better job.

Subsequently government established a unit within the Ministry of Local Government and Lands to administer the tender. This unit has done a splendid job given the background described above. There are still issues to contend with, especially concerning training and the inexplicable cuts on the initial quantities quoted. The most important result of the establishment of the procurement and distribution unit in the Department of Local Government was the decision not to include local commercial booksellers as part of the primary schoolbook supply chain and to buy directly from publishers and publishers' representatives. Obviously the booksellers are not happy with this situation. However, there is little expectation that the primary book distribution will go back to the booksellers, because the current system is perceived to be successful and the government prefers the higher discounts achieved by buying direct from publishers.

Procurement of primary school textbooks: the current situation

The system is still in transition. Therefore the anticipated process suggested below is still subject to some guesswork. The current process based on the old system has an eighteen-month cycle, that is, from the time that books are submitted to the CDD to the time they are bought for schools.

- Deadline for publishers' submissions: 31st Dec
- Textbook evaluation and production of approved
  book list: Up to March
- Schools orders sent back to Ministry of Local
  Government and Lands: Up to Dec
- List released to publishers for tender: March
- Books collected by local councils: July to Sept

Textbooks for the system can come from any one of three sources, Ministry contracts, risk publishing and imports. Risk publishing exists only in theory because there was no effective competition against Ministry authored textbooks. The MoE courses do not have to be reviewed by subject panels because the subject panels are the authors of the MoE textbooks. If no suitable MoE course exists, then the MoE prescribes an imported book. The selection procedures described below therefore only apply to imported books:

- The CDD selects submitted books and generates a prescribed list. There is no feedback to publishers and the system lacks transparency.
- Schools enter the required quantities on the prescribed list and then the District Councils and ultimately the Ministry of Local Government and Lands consolidate the lists.
- Publishers are then asked to quote for the quantities ordered.
- The Ministry of Local Government and Lands issues government purchase orders to individual publishers and the books are delivered to the Ministry.
- The books are supplied to students on a loan basis.

The system would work efficiently except that Ministry of Local Government and Lands often does not respect the times for the award of the tenders. In some cases there is a drastic reduction in quantity between the time of tendering and the time of the award, especially for supplementary materials. Economies of scale are lost and government is often reluctant to review prices. Councils collect directly from the publishers and thus the booksellers are further marginalised. Payment to publishers is usually made two weeks from the date of collection – a welcome development indeed!

The per capita spend has remained at P120,00 (including stationery) per student for quite some time and this accounts for the cuts in the quantities every year. Primary publishing has remained static since 1993, as new syllabi have not been put into place. This has given an advantage to the publishers that have been in the market for some time.

Secondary school textbook procurement – the current situation

Senior secondary schools are given a book budget but the actual payments to booksellers are made centrally. Booksellers are provided with a government purchase order but the MoE makes the actual payments, which are sometimes very slow. It is common for booksellers to wait for payment for up to six months or even more at the senior secondary level.

Junior secondary schools are also provided with a book grant. The JC schools select the books that they want from the approved list and purchase directly from the bookseller of their choice. The school receives the books from the bookseller and distributes them to the students on a loan basis. Subject departments are also given a small vote with which to purchase teachers resources, which include supplementary books. The approximate schedule is as follows:

- Deadline for submissions: 31 Dec

- Textbook evaluation and production of
  approved list: 1 April
- Publishers give prices to booksellers   30 April
- Schools order: 30 June
- Publishers and booksellers supply   Sept to Dec

After the expiry of the overall publishing contract with Macmillan in 1993, textbook publishing became more open as a result of pressure exerted by publishers rather than as a result of government changing its policies. Syllabus changes meant that the 'contract books' were outdated and the MoE had no alternative but to accept commercially published titles as the basis for the new syllabi. There was an initial reluctance to accept more than one book on the prescribed list but pressure from publishers led them to approve more than one book in certain subjects. The following process now applies:

- Publishers present course books to the CDD. (Originally the only printed books were acceptable but the CDD now accepts docutech copies of books that are almost final.)
- Subject panels review the books and make recommendations to the CDD.
- The CDD generates a final list for approval by the Textbook Development and Evaluation Committee (TDEC).
- The list is sent to schools, publishers and booksellers.
- Publishers quote to the booksellers who in turn quote to the schools for supply.
- Schools select their books and suppliers.

The per capita spend on books at this level is about P330 per student, including stationery. This budget has been overtaken by the cost of books schools are under-spending. The basic problem is that prices are not taken into account during the evaluation and approval process. Schools are just given a book vote with an inflationary adjustment over the previous year. The increase in subjects is not met by a commensurate increase in the budget. By agreement publishers do not supply directly to schools, but use booksellers for distribution but the proliferation of small-scale booksellers has not helped the situation. There are problems of delays and incomplete supply. Most of the small booksellers do not have credit facilities with suppliers and financiers.

The Textbook Development and Evaluation Committee (TDEC)

This committee was set up in 1998 following the recommendation of the Revised National Policy Committee of 1993. Its role is to guide the policy on textbook development and evaluation. It is made up of the major stakeholders including government departments like the CDD, teacher training centres and the National Library Service. It also has two representatives from the Botswana Publishing Industry Association (BOPIA).

The TDEC has produced a set of draft guidelines on book development. What emerges from these draft guidelines is that government still wishes to control educational book publishing and has rejected most of the submissions from BOPIA. In particular, the TDEC rejected the suggestion by BOPIA that publishers should have access to the reasons leading to the prescription or rejection of their textbooks. BOPIA went further to propose that fees should be levied on publishers' submissions to offset the cost of evaluation and the production of such reports for publishers. But this too was rejected. The view of the Ministry is that they would be providing content reviews for publishers, a role that they are reluctant to play.[72]

The key policy submissions from BOPIA to TDEC have been as follows:
- The MoE should leave publishing to publishers.
- The role of the MoE should be to select a wide range of books and allow schools to select from this list.
- There should be feedback to publishers on the rationale behind selection decisions from either subject panels or the CDD.

The draft guidelines spell out three future options for educational publishing in Botswana.

MoE commissions the production of materials. In this option the MoE will provide a detailed specification of the material to be produced. They will then put the specification out to tender and the winner of the tender will enter into a publishing and supply contract with the Ministry.

Materials are written/produced by the ministry. The Ministry will write the manuscript and put it out to a publishing tender. The winner of the publishing tender will then enter into a publishing and supply contract with the Ministry.

Risk publishing. Publishers will continue to be free to develop materials at their own risk and submit them to the CDD for evaluation and approval as at present.

The TDEC has made a commitment to a multi-textbook approval system. Ideally therefore textbooks resulting from the 'risk' option will not be disadvantaged. In practice, it is likely that Ministry initiated projects always will be given a priority. Publishers feel strongly that it is not the role of government to be involved in moneymaking activities, particularly when they are in a position to influence the rules of the game. The publishers are therefore lobbying that the first two options listed above should be dispensed with.

Some suggestions
- There should be a multiple textbook approval system.
- Textbook contracts between government and private sector publishers should be abolished in favour of free and open competition in line with current government policy.
- The Ministry of Education should leave publishing to the private sector.
- The textbook evaluation process should be transparent.
- Book budgets need to be increased via an increase in the per capita allocations.

---

72 This is also an issue in Kenya where the KPA offered to pay for evaluations in return for content reports. In Kenya, the KIE has agreed to this request.

- School-based financing and payment should be introduced in all senior secondary schools immediately. Eventually school-based financing and payment should also be applied to primary schools.
- School textbook suppliers should be approved on the basis of an agreed set of criteria.
- To encourage the development of a good national bookseller network, a limited number of reputable booksellers should be permitted to participate in the primary tender.
- Publishing should be recognised as a manufacturing industry so that it has access to Financial Assistance Policy funds.
- Booksellers should be able to benefit from the Small, Medium and Micro Enterprises Fund.
- There is a case for a quota system for local booksellers. There is ongoing discussion on citizen empowerment and a paper is to be discussed in Parliament in the near future. The general view is that where citizen owned companies are able to perform adequately they should get support from government. This suggestion emerged against the backdrop of 'briefcase booksellers' from South Africa who do not generate any employment or pay taxes in Botswana.
- There is a need for a national book policy for Botswana.

Conclusion

Overall the education system and the book trade in Botswana has achieved a great deal. Education and textbooks are free and although there are financial problems the level of provision to students is high in comparison with most other African countries. Although Botswana is a small country in terms of population it has a flourishing and very competitive commercial publishing and bookselling sector. There is a level of choice and decision-making by individual schools and the commercial book trade is perceived as a partner in education and, as such, has access to the market. Inevitably, there are areas of disagreement between the book trade and government and areas that still need attention but at the very least there is an active policy dialogue between government and the private sector book trade that gives some hope of a successful resolution to outstanding issues.

Case study H: Tanzania

By Abdullah Saiwaad, Executive Secretary, Publishers' Association of Tanzania & MD, Readit Books, Dar-es-Salaam

---

Basic facts
- Located between Latitudes 1–12° S and Longitudes 29–40° E.
- Tanzania is bordered by Kenya and Uganda to the north, the Indian Ocean to the east, Mozambique, Malawi and Zambia to the south and Burundi, Rwanda and the Democratic Republic of the Congo to the west.
- Population: 32 million (1998 estimate).
- Area: 945,100 square kilometres.
- Population density: 36 per square kilometre.
- 26% of the population is classified as urban (1998).
- Per capita GNP was US$210 in 1998.
- The capital city is Dar-es-Salaam with a population of 1,7 million (1995 estimate).
- 45% of the population is Christian; 35% is Muslim and the other 20% are Hindu or adhere to traditional religions.
- Life expectancy is 48 years with a female life expectancy of 49 years and a male life expectancy of 47 years.
- Independence from Britain was attained in 1964.
- Swahili is the official language; and English is the official language for commerce, administration and higher education.
- According to the World Development Report (1999), 70% of the population is functionally literate. Of these, 80% of men and 57% of women are functionally literate.
- Main economic activities are Agriculture (cloves, coffee, cotton, tobacco, tea, sisal, coconuts, pyrethrum, etc.), mining (diamonds), food processing and consumer industries.
- Tanzania is administered via 20 regions and 113 districts.
- The unit of currency is the Tanzanian shilling (TSh). In January 2000, TSh795,725 = US$1.

The book market

Around 90% of the book trade in Tanzania revolves around school textbooks. Current annual school textbook turnover is estimated at around US$3,3 million. Turnover on general trade books is around US$0,3 million. Of the money spent on schoolbooks, about US$2,8 million (78%) is for primary textbooks.

For the past sixteen years the Swedish International Development Agency (SIDA) has been the major funding agency, contributing variously between 80–100% of the expenditure on primary school textbooks in any one year. It is clear, therefore, that the health of the Tanzanian publishing and distribution sectors depends on the primary school textbook market. The form and nature of Tanzanian publishing and distribution depend equally on the policies of government and funding agencies toward this market.

The evolution of textbook publishing and distribution policy

In 1981, the textbook publishing and production programme was organised by the Ministry of Education entirely in favour of state-owned enterprises. Government policy, widely known as The Confinement Policy limited school textbook publishing to three state owned publishers in the country, Tanzania Publishing House (TPH), East African Publishing House (EAPH) and Dar-es-Salaam University Press (DUP). Textbook printing was confined to two state-owned printers, and textbook distribution and sales were confined to one state-owned distributor, Tanzania Elimu Supplies (TES).

The mediocrity, delays and inflated costs that characterise most state-owned, monopolistic enterprises, coupled with civil service bureaucratic red tape, ensured that textbook publishing, production and distribution were completely ineffective in Tanzania for many years after the introduction of the Confinement Policy. This situation occurred and was perpetuated despite the very large sums of agency funding invested in textbook support in Tanzania. During the period 1981–1991 it was not unusual for a child to go through seven years of primary schooling without ever having access to a textbook. Where books were available, the publishing and production qualities were usually poor.

In 1992, when the government recognised that state centralism and the Confinement Policy had failed to deliver, a new textbook policy was introduced. This new policy aimed to liberalise and commercialise the school textbook market. The state opted for a gradual implementation of this new policy whereby the Ministry of Education would keep an eye on the content and quality of the books via a Textbook Approval Board while publishers would gradually be given more control in the publishing and production processes and individual schools and parents would have more say in the procurement process. A similar approach to the development of commercial bookselling outlets throughout the country does not appear to have been an option.

After four experimental phases of the Pilot Project for Publishing (PPP), from 1992–1999, the Ministry of Education and the lead agency (SIDA) believed that Publishers had proved that they could produce quality books at affordable prices and that they could deliver them to all districts in Tanzania (see below). The new Textbook Approval Board (TAB) was ready to assess new textbooks developed by commercial publishers. However neither the Ministry of Education nor the funding agency were at all certain that the funds allocated to the districts for the purchase of textbooks would actually be used to purchase textbooks when the funds were disbursed to the districts as planned. Nor did the Ministry of Education and SIDA seem to realise that a majority of the districts did not have reliable booksellers. So where would the districts and/or teachers go to buy their books? Presumably districts would buy direct from publishers, but this approach did not represent support to the re-creation of a commercial book wholesaling and retailing sector. At the time of writing, this situation remains unresolved.

The Confinement Policy of 1981 marginalised commercial booksellers just as it marginalised commercial publishers. From 1981 onwards, commercial booksellers handled only 5% of the total book trade in Tanzania while the state-owned TES monopolised the fundamental school textbook market. The tiny non-school textbook market was insufficient to maintain the previous network of private sector booksellers that had covered the country and most were forced to close.

Most of the booksellers who have survived into the new liberalised policy era are representatives of churches and missionary organisations. There are 68 registered booksellers currently operating in Tanzania to cover a country of 32 million people spread over a land area of almost one million square kilometres.[73] However, only around ten of the 68 booksellers are considered creditworthy and reliable and thus able to maintain an ongoing trading relationship with publishers. A significant proportion of the operational booksellers are located in (or close to) Dar-es-Salaam. Most districts in the country, therefore, do not have any bookseller that a publisher, operating under normal commercial considerations, would wish to supply on credit terms. Without credit terms none of the booksellers are in a position to raise the finance to maintain the kind of stock levels required by the schools if they are to purchase locally up to budget limits.

Under these circumstances it is difficult to see how booksellers and commercial book distribution can be involved to any great extent in the new liberalisation and commercialisation policy. Without specific new policy initiatives it seems inevitable that school orders will have to go via districts and that districts will have to undertake additional distribution responsibilities on behalf of schools – if the districts actually use the allocated funding to order textbooks. Table 25 provides a list of the most reliable and viable booksellers currently operating in Tanzania.

---

73 Compare this figure with the 1,100 registered booksellers in Kenya to cover a smaller population.

Table 25 Some of the most reliable booksellers in Tanzania

Booksellers name	Town of operation
General Booksellers Ltd	Dar-es-Salaam
Textbook Centre Ltd	Dar-es-Salaam
Seifi School Centre	Dar-es-Salaam
Seifi Bookshop	Dar-es-Salaam
Kase Book Store	Arusha
Church Bookshop	Bukoba

Tanzania Elimu Supplies

Tanzania Elimu Supplies (TES) was formed to distribute locally manufactured educational supplies (including books) and to import educational supplies that could not be manufactured in the country. Ultimately, TES did not do well at either task, but for different reasons. Firstly, there were the problems associated with all state-owned monopolies: lack of motivation and responsibility, bureaucratic inefficiency, delays, poor financial management, etc. Secondly there were the problems associated with the overwhelming and unrealistic set of tasks and duties with which TES was burdened. TES not only had to order all school requirements for stationery, pens, pencils, rulers, chalk, textbooks, wall charts, science equipment, chemicals, hockey sticks, shin guards, footballs, etc. In addition, it was also required to be a major manufacturer of many of the above items, including exercise books, stencils, duplicator inks to mention just a few. TES was also required to run and maintain a national transportation and warehousing network plus a chain of retail bookshops (selling everything from tungsten wire to plasticine in addition to the basic textbooks, reading books and stationery).

At the beginning TES was adequately capitalised and could afford to buy whatever it wanted on a cash basis from suppliers. It then supplied its retail outlets and educational (and other) customers on credit. For fifteen years after its formation in 1966, TES operated successfully and even in the early years of the Confinement Policy it appeared to continue to thrive. But this situation did not last for very long after 1981. By 1986 TES had serious financial problems. Its fleet of lorries was grounded for lack of maintenance and spare parts so that it could not deliver to its outlets without hiring from private sector trucking companies. Its capital base had been eroded by unpaid debts from the districts. It was no longer able to finance its supplies on a cash basis and its credit status with suppliers was poor. Even with supplies it had problems in financing delivery to its outlets. With supplies often cut-off, retail sales declining because of lack of stock to sell and its major customers (the District Administrations) not paying their bills, TES was no longer capable of fulfilling its required functions.

Despite its problems it continues to survive today as a parastatal company reporting to the MoE. In 1999 it has managed to cling on to its fixed assets, which include warehouses in Dar-es-Salaam and ten other regions with enough capacity to hold the country's total book requirements for a year. TES also still has at least one bookshop in each regional headquarters and one bookshop in the centre of Dar-es-Salaam. However, it is no longer considered to have a significant role to play in national book distribution because of its lack of credit capability. TES has for some time been on the list of public companies available for sale to potential investors, but this exercise is temporarily suspended because 2000 is election year. Also there has been no interest expressed in purchasing TES.

TES currently survives largely from leasing its godowns. The Ministry of Local Government leases a majority of the TES Dar-es-Salaam warehouses. The Arusha TES branch leases its warehouses to the local Cooperative Union, which stores agriculture produce there. In its current condition TES has no role in textbook distribution in Tanzania but if an investor could be found that would run TES efficiently then it has at least one strategically located bookshop in every region and ten regional warehouses. TES is not, at the time of writing, considered to be creditworthy.

Publishers and printers

There are around 30 publishers in Tanzania, defined as companies that spend at least 50% of their operational time on the publishing business. Of these, twelve have published at least one school textbook, even though one publisher (Ben & Co) to date has won around 48% of the total primary school textbook titles so far offered for bid. Another twelve publishers publish children's books and there are about six missionary presses. There are around five purely general publishers. There is considerable overlap in activities and a number of publishers occupy more than one market sector. Table 26 lists the main textbook publishers currently operating in Tanzania.

Table 26 Current textbook publishers in Tanzania	
Publisher	**Number of textbooks published**
Mture Publishers	3 textbooks & teacher's guides
DUP (1997) Ltd	1 textbook & teacher's guide
Educational Publisher	2 textbooks & teacher's guides
Oxford Education Books	2 textbooks & teacher's guides
Aidan Macmillan	3 textbooks & teacher's guides
Oxford University Press	2 textbooks & 1 teacher's guide
Ruvu Publishers	1 teacher's guide
E&D Ltd	3 textbooks and 3 teacher's guides
Ben & Co	17 textbooks and 17 teacher's guides

All of the above textbooks and teacher's guides were written by the TIE and tendered to publishers. So far, the system is still largely monopolistic with only two alternative titles published and approved by the Textbook Approval Board (TAB). A typical textbook publisher will normally reprint around 30% of their textbook list every year towards the end of the calendar year. All the publishers who have specialised in textbooks now have all of the necessary operational infrastructures and professional skills, including investment finance, 'print buying' capacity, warehousing, etc. plus trained personnel to carry out these tasks. In the Pilot Publishing Project, and especially since the second round, most textbook publishers have been printing outside the country. Two main reasons have caused this exodus. First, is the availability of credit facilities from South African printers, which are attractive to Tanzanian publishers because Tanzanian printers do not normally offer credit. Second is the Tanzanian government's reluctance to reduce and/or remove import duties and taxes from book printing inputs.

The Tanzanian printer is therefore faced with both of these problems. Due to the stringent lending policies imposed by the IMF, local printers are finding working capital very difficult to obtain. The local banks offer loans only upon presenting 130% collateral and the interest rate is around 24% pa. Thus printers cannot meet the challenges of rapidly changing printing technology nor can they upgrade or rehabilitate their plant and facilities. All the printing inputs carry an import duty (5%) and VAT (20%). The importation of finished books carries only a 5% import duty. Tanzania printers are not competitive in long-run printing of 50,000 copies and above. Due to the dilapidated state of most of their machines, many printers can only undertake one-colour, saddle-stitched work, which the Ministry of Education has already rejected as below the required production values for textbooks.

Textbook financing issues

Tanzania is divided into twenty administrative regions, which are further divided into 113 districts. It is intended that decision-making and financing will soon be devolved to the District Education Officers (DEOs) for the purchase of all educational materials for primary schools. At the moment, the Ministry of Education purchases primary school textbooks direct from the publishers and pays for them centrally. Publishers however have to deliver the books to the district centres.

From June 2000 it is expected that DEOs will order books as the next phase of the PPP. The initial stock to be received by each school will be calculated on the basis of the latest enrollment information and on the basis of one textbook per three students. The initial supply is therefore based on a very traditional, supply-oriented system. Replacement copies will be supplied on the basis of school demand. Schools will return questionnaires to the DEO so that DEOs will have information on the numbers of books in schools.

Once each district has established the required order quantities, it is intended that each of the 113 DEOs will float a tender for the supply of books from suppliers. The success of the proposed system will depend upon whether suppliers (booksellers or publishers?) can cope with 113 simultaneous tenders and whether districts will actually pay the suppliers for the delivered books. There are many past precedents of non-payment of suppliers by districts. If the system does succeed then DEOs will continue to order books until such a time that schools can manage book funds for themselves. This might take at least another five years according to current government and funding agency thinking because most rural schools and some urban schools do not have bank accounts.

Textbooks are currently not delivered by districts to primary schools. Schools usually collect textbooks from the DEO's office. On rare occasions books may be delivered by the DEO during an inspection visit. Remote schools suffer because teachers only visit the DEOs at the end of each month to collect salaries. If book quantities are large the teacher may only be able to carry a few books each month for the school, thus seriously delaying the arrival of book stock. This is perceived as a serious problem and in the new system it is hoped that DEOs will be given funds equivalent to the list price of the books required by remote schools. Discounts negotiated with publishers/suppliers should cover the cost of transportation to the schools.

Most secondary schools are in close proximity to district headquarters and are therefore relatively easy to access. Funds and authority to purchase school textbooks for secondary schools are vested in the head teacher of each school. The same is the case with tertiary institutions.

The new textbook approval system became operational in September 1999. The TAB has begun accepting new manuscripts and new books for approval. According to the MoE a new approved list of textbooks has been started and will be updated regularly. The only books on the current list are those written by the TIE. Logically, it would have been sensible to include all books on the approved list of books that are currently in use by secondary schools.

Private schools

Private secondary schools buy a few books of their own choice using their own funds but most schools encourage students to buy their own copies of textbooks from wherever they can find them. Publishers and booksellers visit private and state secondary schools at the end of the first month after school opening. All sales are usually in cash unless a known, trustworthy teacher is contracted and stocks the books on behalf of publishers and booksellers. Education Boards (especially missionary boards) also sometimes purchase books for their schools. NGOs buy similarly in support of schools.

Transportation issues

The rail networks

Two rail networks exist in Tanzania. The TAZARA Railway starts from Dar es Salaam and travels southwards to Kapiri Mposhi in Zambia via Mbeya. This line passes through four district headquarters. The TAZARA railway charges a freight rate of between US$2–3 per 20 kilograms of freight. The Tanzania Railway Corporation (TRC) has two main lines with branches. This network covers 14 district headquarters. TRC charges a freight rate of between US$1–3,5 per 20 kilograms of goods.

When goods arrive at their destination, none of the rail companies will undertake to notify the consignee. Therefore it is up to the sender of the goods to notify the recipient to check at the station for the goods. After appropriate identification the goods will be cleared for the recipient. Both rail companies charge demurrage for uncollected goods after the expiry of a week after arrival of the goods at the station. Telephone or telegram is the normal method of providing information to the consignee on delivery schedules. Fax facilities are not available in some districts.

The road networks

All roads leading to district HQs are usually passable for 95% of the year. Transporters can deliver goods to all but two districts in Tanzania. Most transporters charge between US$11–15 per 20 kilograms of freight. Most of the transport companies have small warehouses at their destinations. Almost all of them will immediately notify the recipient that their consignments have arrived. Transporters generally do not charge demurrage for delay in the collection of freight. Transporters apparently do not differentiate between the goods that they deliver. Thus a box of books can be thrown about like a box of soap.

Air freight

Freight can be delivered by air to six district headquarters. Information to the recipient is given immediately upon arrival of the goods. The airlines apply a minimum weight restriction for cargo of 60 kilograms. However, for the sake of conformity, the rates charged are US$4–5.5 per 20 kilograms of freight. The airlines have adequate storage space at their destinations and can even handle eggs.

Shipping companies

Two districts, Mafia and Ukerewe, are islands. The former lies in the Indian Ocean and the latter in Lake Victoria. There is no reliable communication with these two districts except by chartered planes and the coastal services ships and lake services vessels, which are unreliable. Most distributors leave this type of business to the post office, whose rates may be high but are cheaper than the astronomical costs of chartering.

Courier companies
This is the most expensive method of freighting. The rates are between US$25–30 per 20 kilograms. There is one strong courier company and many fledgling ones. The strongest courier company claims that it can deliver a package to any corner of Tanzania within 72 hours. This company has branches in every district.

Recently, publishers who won tenders negotiated with this company to deliver their book consignments to all 113 districts and to collect signed delivery notes from every DEO. The quantities were large and one publisher had to deliver 18 metric tonnes. The freight charges were around US$23,000, which was 13% of the invoiced value of the books.[74] The company managed to deliver 80% of the books within a period of five weeks from accepted receipt into their warehouse.

Postal services
The postal service is supposed to be the most reliable means of delivery of small articles of less than 20 kilograms. The rates are between US$3–5 per 20 kilograms. The postal service used to have a system of informing the sender of the safe receipt of goods by the consignee. Most publishers recently interviewed on this subject claimed that in the past two years the postal services have deteriorated. In 1997, it was possible to send goods by post to all district headquarters in Tanzania and to receive arrival confirmation within 60 days for 90% of the districts in Tanzania. In 1999 only 50% of districts can confirm safe arrival over the same period. Often, no information of receipt of goods is provided.

Achieving reliable book delivery
It is clear from the above that the only method of achieving a high level of delivery success for all districts in the country is by the use of courier services or, potentially, road freight. Both of these options are, however, relatively expensive. If government is prepared to pay the bills for courier and/or trucking services they become viable options, but if publishers are to operate commercially in a free market they will have to develop reliable delivery strategies at competitive costs. It should be noted also that the delivery services described above only achieve delivery down to district HQs. To complete the delivery chain books will either have to be collected by schools or sent on by the districts. In either case there is considerable potential for delay or non-delivery. Textbook distribution problems in Tanzania down to the level of individual schools therefore remain very problematic.

---

74   Compare this with the 5,0%–7,5% specified in the Malawi case study.

Warehousing and personnel

Most publishers have warehouses of some sort. Most booksellers at district level have spacious accommodation for stocking adequate supplies of books but do not have the financial strength to fill their storerooms. District Education Officers generally have plenty of government storage at their disposal. For a distributor, it is not difficult to find warehouse space in all districts at affordable prices ranging from US$0,5–1,5 per square metre per month with the exception of Dar-es-Salaam, where rentals are more expensive.

Distribution involves planning and logistics. There are enough people in the job market with the required credentials. However there is a need for training personnel in the technicalities of physical distribution of books. The current government accounting systems use a very lengthy receipt and verification procedure resulting from years of bureaucratic centralism. A system of accountability is in place but this has made it cumbersome even for the genuine deliverer of goods and services to the government.

Conclusion

- The Tanzanian book market remains heavily dependent on school textbooks. Although liberalisation of textbook supply was initiated formally with strong funding agency support in 1991, progress has been very slow. In the primary sector in 2000 textbook provision is still basically monopolistic, although the introduction of textbook evaluations via the TAB in 1999 promises a new competitive, multi-textbook approach in the future.
- In the efforts towards the market-oriented reforms of textbook provision in Tanzania the wholesale and retail book trades appear to have remained outside the policy loop. In 2000, there are still only a handful of effective, creditworthy bookshops to serve a country of 32 million people. This situation exists because booksellers are still not seen to be an integral part of the textbook chain in Tanzania.
- Although there are freighting services in Tanzania that publishers can use to get books to the districts, this remains problematic and relatively expensive. And distribution from districts to the individual schools continues to be a serious problem, which hasn't yet been resolved.
- Textbook distribution policies remain very supply-side oriented. There is a longer-term vision of school-based purchasing power and decision-making, but no date or strategy yet exists for its introduction. The current policy of 113 parallel textbook tenders from each district, which will be introduced in June 2000, might provide contract opportunities for the limited number of booksellers who are sufficiently well-financed to be able to compete. Alternatively, the sheer administrative weight of

responding to multiple simultaneous tenders might prove too much for a still fragile book trade.[75]

- The demise of book retail outlets throughout Tanzania (and particularly outside Dar-es-Salaam) was caused originally by the introduction of the Confinement Policy, which deliberately excluded bookshops from the textbook supply chain. The present weakness of book retailing results from the ongoing exclusion of bookshops from the textbook supply chain. The lack of a good bookshop network throughout the country is a major constraint on the development of general and children's book publishing and thus on the development of a reading culture.

---

[75] It is interesting to note that in Uganda the MoES, publishers and booksellers have all rejected annual, multiple, district-based textbook tendering as a viable form of decentralisation. In Uganda the MoES have opted for a pilot project in which district based booksellers will be consciously developed through directing government funding into a limited number of 'official' booksellers in each district using school based LPOs as a method of guaranteeing the bookshops a minimum annual turnover.

Case study I: Burkina Faso, Mali and Chad

By Amadou Waziri, Publishing Manager, INDRAP, Niamey Jean-Pierre Léguéré and Georges Stern, Danaé Sciences, Paris

If one rates all West African countries using the Gross National Product (GNP) or Human Development Index (HDI), there is a 25–30 point difference between Sahelian and other West African countries. The Sahelian states (Niger, Chad, Burkina Faso and Mali) are clearly in a much worse position than their neighbours. The extreme poverty of these countries obviously influences the provision of education and, of course, the nature of textbook production and distribution.

Burkina Faso

Basic facts
- Located between Latitudes 9–15° N and Longitudes 2°30´ E and 6° W.
- Bordered by Mali to the north and west, Niger to the east, Bénin, Togo, Côte d'Ivoire (all Francophone) and Ghana to the south (Anglophone).
- A former French colony, independence was attained in 1960.
- Population: 11 million.
- The capital city is Ouagadougou, with a population of 681,000; other main urban centres include Bobo-Dioulasso (270,000) and Ouahigouya.
- 50% of the population are Muslim, 10% are Christian, 40% have indigenous beliefs.
- French is the official language, the main local languages are Mori, Gulmancema, Dioula and Lobi.
- 29% of men and 9% of women are literate.
- The growth rate is 2,7%.
- Main economic activities are cotton, beverages and agriculture.
- Per capita GNP: US$350.
- The unit of currency is the CFA Franc (CFA). CFA 100 = US$0,147.
- School population: 767,000 for primary (39% girls), 139,328 for secondary (20% girls).

The first textbook authored by a Burkinabé was written in 1981. It was a *cours moyen* geography book published by Edicef. Then in 1989 the *Institut*

Pédagogique du Burkina (IPB) published a reading book for *Cours elementaires2* (Grade 2) classes. Nowadays, all primary school classes are taught with textbooks written by Burkinabé authors, and both pupil's books and teacher's guides exist for most subjects.

The quality and the scope of the programmes designed by the IPB and approved by the ministry of education are a credit to Burkina Faso. The main programmes are:

- Programme Training and Information for the Environment (*Programme Formation Information pour l'Environnement*, PFIE).
- Population Studies (*Education en Matière de Population*, EMP).
- The Rural Management Programme (*Programme national de Gestion des Terroirs*, PNGT).
- The Education Programme, in charge of funding. This project works very closely with the main funding agency, the World Bank.

Although local authors write all the textbooks, they are far from all being published in Burkina Faso. At the time of writing there were no local private sector publishers so textbooks were all published in the developed countries, on a tender basis.

The French publishers Edicef and Nathan are particularly active in Burkina Faso. The *Direction de la Production des Moyen pédagogiques* (DPMP), supplies some elements such as illustrations, statistics and maps and corrects proofs before they are passed for press.

Teacher's guides are however published by the IPB and printed in Burkina Faso. Local printing is done by the printing facility in the Department for the Production of Pedagogic Resources (DPMP), or in the *Grande Imprimerie du Burkina* or the *Imprimerie Nouvelle du Centre*.

One of the problems associated with the involvement of multinational publishers is that they are not interested or when in whether, the books get distributed to schools. They simply produce, deliver and take payment. Primary school textbooks are distributed free of charge by the Textbook Division of the Ministry of Education.

The ministry of education in Burkina Faso has set up a ten-year plan (2000–2009) for the development of education, and this should improve the current situation. The plan aims to improve learning conditions, train more teachers and improve textbook availability. The plan should also stimulate local publishing and reduce the dependency on textbooks printed and imported by foreign publishing companies.

Mali

Basic facts
- Located between Latitudes 10–25° N and Longitudes 4°E and 12°W.
- Bordered by Algeria to the north, Niger to the east, Burkina Faso and Côte d'Ivoire and Guinea to the south, Senegal and Mauritania to the west, all of which are Francophone.
- A former French colony, independence was attained in 1960.
- Population: 11 million.
- The capital city is Bamako, with a population of 880,000; other main urban centres include Segou (85,000) and Mopti.
- 90% of the population are Muslim, 1% are Christian, 9% have indigenous beliefs.
- French is the official language, Bambara being the most widely spoken language.
- 31% of the population are literate (men: 39%, women: 23%).
- The economic growth rate is 3,2%.
- The main economic activities are agriculture, food-processing, mining (gold, phosphate, uranium).
- Per capita GNP: US$260.
- There are eight regions and one district (Bamako).
- The unit of currency is the CFA Franc (CFA). CFA 100 = US$0,147.
- School population: 23,548 pre-pimary students, 862,875 primary students, 188,109 secondary students, 13,847 tertiary students (1997 figures).

At present, primary textbooks are written and developed by the National Curriculum Institute (*Institut Pédagogique National*, IPN), and published and produced by French publishers such as Hatier for maths, Edicef for French and Nathan for history. The government purchases the textbooks via a tendering system funded by the World Bank and the European Union. When textbooks are purchased by the state, they are distributed free of charge. However, the government is not able to supply schools with sufficient quantities of the required books. PTAs are active and group together to purchase books from private booksellers which order books from French publishers. Informal 'pavement bookshops' sometimes obtain books in unorthodox ways and sell them to parents in competition with the conventional book trade. Thus, there are three distribution channels:
- The government (which owns the copyright in the books) that distributes the books free of charge. There are about 35 inspectors who take part in the state organised distribution process.
- The conventional booksellers.
- The informal pavement booksellers that thrive, at least partly, on illegal dealings.

The main booksellers are: Jamana, Ipage, *La Librairie-papeterie du Soudan*, *Afrique Diffusion* and *La Librairie Traoré*. In general, these distributors don't operate much further than the main cities. At present the average book to pupil ratio appears to be 1:3. Government policy is to devolve publishing responsibility to the private publishing sector, provided that they:
• Accept state controlled retail prices.
• Are financially self-sufficient.
• Take responsibility for distribution.
Because of continuing problems with distribution, the government may retain responsibility for distribution to the most remote areas.

Chad

Basic facts
• Located between Latitudes 7–23° N and Longitudes 14–24° E.
• Bordered by Libya to the north, Sudan to the east, Burkina Faso and the Central African Republic to the south, Cameroon, Nigeria and Niger to the west, the whole making up a diverse community of official languages (French, English and Arabic).
• A former French colony, independence was attained in 1960.
• Population: 7,2 million.
• The capital city is N'Djamena, with a population of 613,000; other main urban centres include Sarh (130,000), Moundou (118,000) and Abéché (96,000).
• 50% of the population are Muslim, 25% are Christian, 25% adhere to traditional religions.
• French and Arabic are the official languages but about 100 languages are spoken, Sara and Sango are the most widely used.
• 48% of the population are literate (men: 62%, women: 35%).
• The economic growth rate is 2,5%.
• The main economic activities are cotton (growing and weaving), cattle farming and agriculture.
• Per capita GNP: US$210.
• The unit of currency is the CFA Franc (CFA). CFA 100 = US$0,147.
• School population: 786,600 primary students (35% are girls), 117,200 secondary students (20% are girls).

In Chad, there is no formal textbook distribution structure. Primary and secondary textbooks are purchased with both agency and/or national funds. Imported books are only distributed via a few private bookshops, such as: *Al-Akhbar*, *La Source*, Always and *Établissements Aubaine*.

The government distributes primary textbooks for free to schools. A research project in 1995 concluded that the state distribution system was very inefficient, with an attrition rate close to 50%. Local correspondents confirm that this situation has not changed. In secondary education, the free supply of textbooks is limited to teachers and librarians. It is thus up to parents to buy the books but only the affluent can afford to do so.

The Higher Institute of Education *(Institut Supérieur des Sciences de l'Éducation,* known before 1991 as the *Institut National des Sciences de l'Éducation)* is primary concerned with teacher training and used to produce Chad's textbooks but textbook production in Chad is now almost non-existent. No steps are being taken to train teams to develop and produce textbooks and all the existing textbooks have been developed and published by Nathan, Larousse, Hatier, Edicef, etc.

This situation is particularly unfortunate because there is a printing house that has the capacity to produce textbooks. It is worth noting that, the team working on the Environmental Training Programme has published some school booklets (using the printing house mentioned above) which are widely used in primary schools.

The last attempt to breathe new life into the area of textbook publishing was a project to create a National Committee for Curriculum and Teaching Materials *(Commission Nationale des Programmes de Livres et des Matériels Didactiques).* The creation of this Committee was put on the agenda in 1995, but it still hasn't been set up. The stumbling block seems to be a debate about whether this body should have voting rights or just play an advisory role in curriculum development. Since curriculum development is one of the first steps in the development of a textbook policy, no further progress can be made until this argument is resolved.

Of course, the scarce financial resources available in Chad do not encourage the emergence of private publishers: Chad is the only Sahelian country that does not have even an embryonic publishing industry. It is also the only country without any book trade professionals. It is significant that, throughout its ten years of existence, CAFED, the main Francophone African publishing training organisation, has received no trainee from Chad, with the exception of four people from the Ministry of Education and the Ministry of Civil Service who came to learn basic desktop publishing.

More than anywhere else, the situation in Chad demonstrates how interdependent the different players in the textbook chain are. In the absence of any government policy on textbooks, there is no teacher training, no curriculum, the necessary processes towards the creation of a local book development capacity are blocked, the few existing production resources are paralysed, and all private initiatives are discouraged.

To assist Chad in the development of a textbook policy the National Committee for Curriculum and Teaching Material should be established without delay and teams of curriculum developers should be trained. For several years now, the manager of the Higher Institute for Education Sciences has been requesting a budget for an information and training mission on curriculum development. This mission could take place in any neighbouring country.

173

Burkina Faso, which boasts good experience in this field, would be a good choice.

Conclusions on textbook distribution in the Sahelian countries

The Sahelian countries share certain common characteristics as far as school textbook publishing and distribution are concerned:

- National government institutes take an active part in the writing of primary school texts.
- Raw materials required for printing such as paper and ink are subject to import taxes which make local printing very expensive.
- Production and printing is widely sub-contracted, mostly to French publishers.
- Foreign aid is crucial to textbook production; the main players are the World Bank, the *Coopération Française*, *Agence de la Francophonie*, the European Union, etc.
- Most countries attempt to provide free textbooks to primary schools.
- Distribution is inefficient, delays are common and theft is rife.

Creating the conditions for an independent publishing industry

Publishing opportunities do exist in several Sahelian countries: the IPN in Niger and the IBP in Burkina Faso have shown that they can write, develop and publish textbooks. Printing houses, with competent, well-trained staff are also present but need access to tax-free raw materials in order to be able to compete with external printers. Imported books are exempt from these taxes, in accordance with the Florence Agreements. No Francophone Sub-Saharan African country has yet ratified the Nairobi Protocols, that remove all taxes on imported raw materials such as paper and ink. The first step should be for all the Sahelian countries to ratify the protocols so that locally printed books are not disadvantaged by imported titles.

A more rigorous forward planning system within the Ministries is also badly needed. Local printing houses are not always adequately equipped in terms of material and human resources to produce large quantities of well-produced textbooks, at very short notice. This situation forces them to sub-contract overseas, and deprive themselves of financial resources and essential learning experiences.

In countries as deprived as those in the Sahelian region, the only significant publishing sector is textbook publishing. And it is only by taking a more active role in this sector that local publishers will be able to grow and thus publish other general trade books such as literature and children's books.

Ensuring effective distribution

In all Sahelian countries, the inefficiency of the book distribution systems causes very large losses in both time and money. Typically the state takes on

174

responsibility for textbook distribution, but the state rarely has the skills and the required human, material and financial resources to fulfil the role adequately. The state also underestimates the costs of distribution because its own employees handle it and the costs are absorbed into salaries.

On the other hand, foreign publishers have no reason to be concerned with distribution. They are paid regardless of whether the books get to schools. And funding agencies also seem to have little interest in the distribution issues. For instance, the World Bank seems to favour the financing of production over the improvement of distribution.

It is our view that for the distribution situation to improve, the publishing chain must be seen as a whole. It is pointless for French publishers to produce, and for funding agencies to pay for, books that are not delivered to their intended end-users. No publishing development within Sahelian countries is likely unless:

- The state takes responsibility for curriculum development and author selection.
- The private sector takes responsibility for textbook origination, production and distribution.
- The funding agencies support the development of local publishing industries and the establishment of an efficient distribution network.

Case study J: Francophone West Africa

By Mamadou Aliou Sow, MD, Editions Ganndal, Conakry and Etienne Brunswic and Jean Valérien, Danaé-Sciences, Paris[76]

The countries in Francophone West Africa are Bénin, Senegal, Guinea (see Case study E), Côte d'Ivoire, Togo and Cameroon. Ten years after the world conference on Education for All in Jomtien in March 1990, the average book to pupil ratio in basic education throughout Francophone West Africa – except for Côte d'Ivoire – doesn't achieve the hoped for 1:1 ratio. According to French book trade figures[77], the annual book market in these countries amounts to around US$5m, 90–95% of which is made up of textbooks.

French imports, to the value of approximately US$3m per year (about 60% of the textbook market), essentially originate from the Hachette group (Hatier, and Edicef), the Havas group (Nathan) and the religious group, Saint Paul (*Les Classiques Africains*). Belgian publishers (*de Boeck* in the Democratic Republic of Congo) and Canadian publishers (Hurtubise in Côte d'Ivoire, Senegal and Mali) also export significant numbers of books to this region. World Bank loans funds 85% of the market with tenders ranging in size from US$2.5–5m.

Publishers from both the north and the south agree that textbook publishing in this region is the key to a book industry that is set to grow dramatically over the coming years.

Bénin

Basic facts
- Located between Latitudes 6–12° N and Longitudes 2–4° E.
- Bordered by Niger and Burkina Faso to the north, Nigeria to the east, and Togo to the west, All Francophone except Nigeria.
- Population: 5,9 million (estimated to grow to 8,3 in 2010). The population is 46% urban.
- The main city is Cotonou, with a population of 530,000; other major urban centres include the capital city Porto Novo (180,000) and Abomey.
- 70% of the population adhere to traditional religions, 15% are Muslim, 15% Christian.
- A former French colony, independence was attained in 1960.

---

76 The assistance of John Hall in the preparation of this study is acknowledged with thanks.
77 *Livres Hebdo*, November 12, 1999.

- French is the official language; Fon and Yoruba are the most widely spoken local languages in the south.
- 37% of the population is literate (women: 26%).
- The economic growth rate is 3,3%.
- The main economic activities are textiles, tobacco processing and agriculture.
- Per capita GNP: US$410.
- The unit of currency is the CFA Franc (CFA). CFA 100 = US$0,147.
- School population: 475,000 for primary (857,000 projected in 2010), of which 27% are repeaters.
- Gross Enrollment Ratio (primary): 63%.

Bénin's after independence textbook policy was to supply free books to schools. To implement it, the MoE used two parastatal agencies: the National Institute for Curriculum Development (INFRE) that was responsible for curriculum, textbook specifications and manuscript evaluation and the National Centre for Textbook Production (*Centre National de Production des Manuels Scolaires*, CNPMS) that was responsible for the publication and production of primary and secondary textbooks. School distribution was carried out by Ministry of Education, via the inspectorates.

Soon, this system became impossible to implement. Rapid growth in enrollment and increasing economic difficulties demanded changes in the basic policy as follows:

- Free supply by the MoE has been progressively abandoned. Distribution is increasingly carried out by booksellers, of which there are around twenty in the country, including ten in Cotonou and four in Porto Novo. There is also an informal distribution network.
- In order to achieve better textbook prices and to assist parents, the government has asked for financial assistance from the World Bank. It has already received grants from USAID, GTZ, and from bilateral agreements with French and Swiss development agencies. As a result of this, textbooks will be produced overseas. Neither local publishers[78] nor the textbook development department within the Ministry of Education, the *Centre National de Production des Manuels Scolaires* (CNPMS), are in a position to compete effectively for the World Bank tenders.

Although actual figures not available, the average book/pupil ratio is widely considered to be unsatisfactory.

---

78 *Les Éditions du Flamboyant* (1989), whose capital amounts to US$170,000 (Edicefs participation being 49%), have 20 titles (essentially trade) on their backlist. *Éditions Boya* are very recent.

Senegal

Basic facts
- Located between Latitudes 12–17° N and Longitudes 11–18° W.
- Bordered by Mauritania to the north, Mali to the east, Guinea and Guinea Bissau to the south. All these countries are Francophone except for Guinea Bissau which is Lusophone.
- Population: 9 million.
- The capital city is Dakar; other main urban centres include Saint-Louis, Thiès, Kaolack and Ziguinchor.
- 90% of the population are Muslim.
- French is the official language; Wolof is the main local language.
- A former French colony, independence was attained in 1960.
- 57% of the male population and 77% of the female population, are literate.
- The economic growth rate is 2,6%.
- Main economic activities are fishing, phosphate mining, tourism, agriculture.
- Per capita GNP: US$550.
- The unit of currency is the CFA Franc (CFA). CFA 100 = US$0,147.
- School population: 65% of the cohort age group, 1,034m for primary (2,4m in 2008) of which 16% are repeating.

Using the textbook component of a World Bank funded project, the Pedagogic Institute (INEADE) produced 31 primary textbooks between 1990 and 1997. Textbook development took place in Senegal but production was put out to tender and was then done by European publishers and printers.

Proceeds from the sale of these textbooks were supposed to feed into a National Education Textbook Publishing Fund (*Fonds d'Édition des Manuels de l'Éducation Nationale*, FEMEN), which would eventually become self-sustaining. However, when the scheme started, the selling price was set at a level such that only the basic production costs were covered; trade discounts and distribution costs were excluded. Distribution took place via the 60 retail outlets of the *Agence de Diffusion de la Presse* (ADP) that was granted a 48% discount off the retail price. ADP delivered books to the 'pavement' bookshops. At the same time, the Ministry of Education sold books directly to NGOs involved in a PTA-managed Textbook Revolving Fund, as well as to the Dakar municipality, which wanted to provide local pupils with free textbooks (although this particular measure later was abandoned).

In spite of all these efforts (books sold at one third of the actual price,[79] a motivating 35% discount, sales under state control for remote areas, regular

---

79 The French books are sold between CFA800–1,500, according to the grade, the maths books between CFA500 and 1,300, which amounts to less than US$2 in each case.

press campaigns, teacher training programmes), a recent survey indicates that only 51% of the pupils have a French book, only 22% have a maths book, and only 4% have a textbook in any other subject.

Faced with the failure of parent-funded financing and commercial distribution, the Basic School Development Plan (*Plan de Développement de l'École fondamentale*, PDEF) was considering introducing an overall loan scheme for the year 2000, which would require the government to finance annual reprints of more than 1,5m books to be distributed in more than 2,500 schools. This plan may be reviewed since the announcement that the World Bank may finance an education project, including textbook supply.

Côte d'Ivoire

> **Basic facts**
> - Located between Latitudes 4–10° N and Longitudes 2–9° W.
> - Bordered by Mali and Burkina Faso to the north, Ghana to the east, Guinea and Liberia to the west, all are Francophone countries except for Ghana and Liberia, which are Anglophone.
> - A former French colony, independence was attained in 1960.
> - Population: 13,6 million.
> - The legislative capital city is Abidjan (3m); other main urban centres include Bouaké (300,000) and Yamoussoukro, the political capital (100,000).
> - 65% of the population adhere to traditional religions, 23% of the population are Muslim, 12% Christian.
> - French is the official language; there are many local languages.
> - 60% of the population are literate.
> - The economic growth rate is 2,46%.
> - Main economic activities are food processing, agriculture and forestry.
> - The per capita GNP is US$690.
> - The unit of currency is the CFA Franc (CFA). CFA 100 = US$0,147.
> - School population: 69% of the cohort; 1,415m for primary (2,8m projected for 2010) of which 28% are repeating.

In Côte d'Ivoire, families buy textbooks published by the private sector. The system is self-sufficient and sustainable and more than two thirds of pupils have access to textbooks. Residual disparities remain and very poor families have difficulties in affording books. There are also varying levels of educational awareness. Some areas, such as Korhogo, in the north, are traditionally very reluctant to accept education. For the most remote villages, a co-operative project, managed by PTAs, sometimes constitute the beginnings of small rural bookshops.

Textbooks are manufactured according to first world standards and are thus expensive (US$8–10). Two publishers dominate the market. These are *Nouvelles éditions Ivoiriennes* (NEI), of which Edicef owns 49% and CEDA (40% owned by Hatier and 9% by Canada's Hurtubise). These two companies co-publish the best-selling French language collection for primary schools – *École et Développement*. Government withdrawal from any shareholding in these companies is almost complete. State-owned equity in NEI had fallen from 45% to 20% by the end of 1999, and will soon fall to just 5%.

Publishers have developed their own distribution networks, using fleets of vehicles. Booksellers are granted a 25–35% discount, and do a very good job delivering the books in urban areas.

An Ivoirian group, Pharmintex, has bought out the largest bookshop in the country, *Librairie de France*, which has many branches in Abidjan. Its turnover represents 15% of the national textbook market. *Société Anonyme de Librairie et de Papeterie de Côte d'Ivoire* (SALIPACI) has many retail outlets throughout the country. *Carrefour Siloë*, owned by the Abidjan archdiocese, has four retail outlets and achieves a turnover in the region of US$1,7 million, of which textbooks make up a very large share.

Edipresse, a 50% subsidiary of France's NMPP, operates seven freight lines that enable it to deliver books or magazines within 24 hours throughout the territory. However, it does not distribute textbooks.

Competition is fierce. Publishers will accept direct orders from schools, will sell to supermarkets (such as Hayat or Sococé) and will also supply 'pavement bookshops', which blossom during the back to school period.

Two rival associations defend booksellers' interests. These are the National Federation of Booksellers and Stationers (*Syndicat national des Libraires et Papetiers*, 1997) and the Association for the Promotion of the Profession of Bookseller in Côte d'Ivoire (*Association pour la Promotion du Métier de Libraire en Côte d'Ivoire*, 1998). More and more young Ivoirians are seeking careers in the publishing industry.

Textbooks still represent the lion's share of the Ivoirian book market. However, the reliability and profitability of this market has supported the emergence of other types of publishing including teaching aids, children's books and books for young adults.

Togo

Basic facts
- Located between Latitudes 6–11° N and Longitudes 0–2° W.
- Bordered by Burkina Faso to the north, Ghana to the west and Bénin to the east.
- A former French colony, independence was attained in 1960.
- Population: 4 million (7,4 million projected in 2010).
- The capital city is Lomé; other main urban centres include Sokodé and Lama-Kara.
- 50% of the population adhere to traditional religions, 20% of the population are Muslim, 30% are Christian.
- French is the official language; Ewe, Kabye and Kotokoli are the most widely spoken local languages.
- 67% of the male population and 37% of the female population are literate.
- The economic growth rate is 2,7%.
- The main economic activities are phosphate mining, cotton and subsistence agriculture.
- The per capita GNP is US$330.
- The unit of currency is the CFA Franc (CFA). CFA 100 = US$ 0,147.
- School population: 652,000 for primary (1,1m projected in 2010) of which 35% are repeaters.

Faced with an unreliable supply of free primary textbooks, a mutual insurance organisation run by Togo teachers has set up a textbook loan scheme, which makes books available to all pupils for a modest fee. The cash flow generated by this system has created the start-up capital for a distribution cooperative called LIMUSCO (*Librairie des Mutuelles scolaires du Togo*), which acts as a bookshop for the mutual insurance organisation.

When it started, the Ministry of Education strongly supported LIMUSCO. Teachers were temporarily assigned to open warehouses and retail outlets covering the whole country. Once this had been achieved, the government put an end to secondments and LIMUSCO became an independent and competitive company.

Togo thus presents a good example of controlled distribution. Today, LIMUSCO imports and sells basic stationery supplies, textbooks and teaching aids (grammars, dictionaries, etc.) at attractive prices. It is the sole distributor of some of Nathan's and Edicef's titles and it also distributes other Edicef and NEI/CEDA series.

Retail prices are the same throughout the country and these are set by marking the landed unit costs up by 30%. Prices range from CFA1,520 to 2,450 according to grade level for the *École et Développement* series – imported from Côte d'Ivoire – or from CFA2,230 to 2,875 for *Mon Livre unique de Français*, that is, an average price of US$3–4.

Cameroon

Basic facts
- Located between Latitudes 1–13° N and Longitudes 8–17° E.
- Bordered by Nigeria to the west, Chad and the Central African Republic to the east, Equatorial Guinea, Gabon and Congo to the south, all Francophone except Nigeria which is Anglophone and Equatorial Guinea which is Spanish speaking.
- Population: 14 million (21,2m in 2010).
- The capital city is Yaoundé; other main urban centres include Douala, Bamenda, Nkongsamba, Maroua and Garoua.
- 60% of the population are Christian, 20% adhere to traditional religions, 20% are Muslim.
- French and English are the official languages, there are many local languages.
- A former German, then joint French/British colony, independence was attained in 1960 (French part) and 1961 (British part).
- 75% of the male population, 52% of the female population, are literate.
- The economic growth rate is 2,9%.
- The main economic activities are mining (oil, gas, bauxite), forestry, cash crops (cocoa, coffee, banana), subsistence agriculture.
- The per capita GNP is US$680.
- The unit of currency is the CFA Franc (CFA). CFA 100 = US$0,147.
- School population: 1,964m for primary (3,3m in 2010) of which 29% are repeating.
- Approximately 88% of children go to school.

The Publishing and Production Centre for Teaching and Research (*Centre d'Édition pour l'Enseignement et la Recherche*, CEPER) is a state-controlled body in charge of producing textbooks. From 1995–1998, it was an empty shell. French publishers (mainly from the Hachette group, particularly Edicef, which had launched the 'Champions'[80] collection, covering 50% of the market) were supplying all of the primary school textbooks. Yet by 1999, only 10% of the pupils had textbooks.

In September 1998, CEPER was privatised and sold to a group of teachers. The new policy granted CEPER the exclusive right to publish textbooks and advocated organising the sale of textbooks in schools under PTA supervision thus bypassing the bookshops. CEPER became a company, with capital assets

---

80 For each of the six primary grades, in French and Maths, the titles available were pupil's books (sold at US$2–3), a workbook, which had to be renewed every year (US$1,3–1,7) and a teacher's guide (US$5).

of US$0.5 million. The main shareholders are the Mutual Insurance Cooperative for Cameroon's educators (*Mutuelle des Personnels de l'Enseignement du Cameroun*, MUPEC, whose President became CEPER's Director), *Agence internationale de la Francophonie* (which contributed US$85,000), and CASDEN-BP (the French *Banque Populaire*'s teachers'-only subsidiary which contributed US$35,000). On top of this, AIF gave subsidies to the value of US$35,000, and CASDEN-BP provided a loan of US$600,000.

For the 1999–2000 school year, six textbooks, covering three subjects (two million books) have been published for sale at prices[81] between US$1 to US$2. A new distribution system is also being established.

Five managers ('*Grands Opérateurs économiques*' or GOE) are responsible for each of the five regions, and supply 61 smaller zone managers (OE), each in charge of delivering books to schools in one of the 61 distribution zones in the country. Each manager has to pay a deposit or joining fee, matched by the discount it receives off the fixed retail prices. For GOEs, the fees are respectively US$10,000 and 20%. For OEs, the bonds are US$5,000 and 10%. In the field, PTAs and mutual companies carry out the final distribution to the pupils. These organisations are also entitled to a 10% discount.

Publishers belonging to the Hachette group (Edicef and Hatier) have refused to commit themselves to a partnership with CEPER. Concerned about losing market share, they have applied heavy pressure on the new organisation, mobilising local booksellers, the World Bank, the IMF and *Coopération francaise* against CEPER. Hachette group advisers, and even the entourage of the French President on an official visit to Cameroon, have raised the issue. In contrast, the Havas group (Nathan) and *Classiques Africains* have sealed partnerships with CEPER to supply junior and senior secondary schools.

The state of book distribution in Francophone Africa

The current situation. Growing enrollment figures and economic difficulties are increasingly leading governments to withdraw from state textbook production and distribution and the principle of free textbook supply, which used to be standard practice after independence, is being abandoned. The annual average unit cost of a pupil in Francophone West Africa is in the region of US$65, whereas it amounts to US$4,200 in France – a ratio of 1:65. However, French publishing standards (full-colour, cased bindings) are still applied. A textbook made to first world specifications is a luxury that is difficult to justify in Africa. As a result, textbooks are not widely available[82] (with the exception of Côte d'Ivoire) as basic teaching tools in education – this is despite the resolutions taken at UNESCOs Jomtien conference on the need to prioritise textbooks.

All the coastal Francophone countries are looking for solutions to enable textbooks to be supplied at prices that families can afford. Governments have

---

81 This price, between CFA650 and 1,150, is printed on the books, to avoid any speculation.
82 Estimated availability is less than one textbook per pupil (*not* one textbook per subject per pupil).

appealed to the solidarity of the international community, but even if every funding agency devoted their entire budgets to textbook supply, this wouldn't be enough to provide every pupil in the developing world with a textbook. Borrowing money from development banks has become more and more common and no real consideration has been given to what kind of investments would help countries achieve sustainable textbook supplies, and the economic benefits for national publishing industries, have remained negligible. Moreover, even if one considers that palliative solutions for production were essential (such as sub-contracting publishing and printing to overseas publishers), this has not solved the distribution crises.

The Ivoirian example – a transfer to the private sector – might seem promising for all countries, but remains difficult and seems to create apprehension in governments and funding agencies. Such a transfer cannot be improvised. Creating a national market means being able to address the country's needs while taking into account the resources of parents and PTAs.

Sometimes there seem to be as many possible solutions – even if they are often transitional – as there are countries. Governments want to 'repatriate' the textbooks used in their schools by aiming at national or regional production. Distribution, however, remains the weak link in the book chain.

Looking for medium term solutions

Promoting a national publishing sector. Negative experiences in the past have underlined the need to establish a medium-term perspective. The methods of implementation will be different depending upon the economic slant of the country concerned. It is absolutely necessary, however to endeavour to insert textbooks within a broader book development framework, for example, the creation of a national book committee, comprising representatives of all state and private sector players, and of the end-users.

The eventual goal should be to develop national publishing industries, a concept that is still weak in each of the countries surveyed. Long term policies are required to foster this development. Publishers indigenous to Africa need help to strengthen their assets. They should be granted financial and tax incentives, and training in the use of relevant technologies and other publishing and bookselling skills should be made more accessible.

Regional development. It makes sense for certain basic concerns to be dealt with from a regional viewpoint, for example:

- Gathering and spreading information on the situation in each country.
- Sharing strategies aimed at improving equity, for example, textbook or family-based funding subsidies (and working out how households should receive these and what budget line should support them).
- Developing common reference levels to create harmonisation among educational programmes and then working out strategies to co-publish thus using resources effectively.
- Exempting necessary raw materials from customs duties and granting

free circulation to books produced in neighbouring countries.
- Setting comparable prices to fight speculation.
- Initiating consultations to create a synergy between foreign funding agencies and national players.

Short-term measures to improve the existing situation

Co-ordinating responsibilities. It may be harmful to split up responsibility for textbook development. Research done by the Paris-based Institute for Educational Planning (IIEP) suggests that planning departments in the education ministries should handle textbook development. It is their view that information gathering and needs analysis have to be centralised. However, these planning departments should neither be responsible for curriculum development nor book production but they can make sure that dialogue between national players and funding agencies takes place within a national book policy. The planning departments should help their education ministries to reduce their financial commitments gradually while exerting national prerogatives over curriculum, the quest for better teaching quality and greater equity.

Adjusting agency intervention. Funding agency policies should aim to support national players. To assist local publishers and booksellers, a definite advantage should be given to local bidders. For example, tenders should be broken down into smaller projects that would better suit existing national capacities. Distribution reform should be a much higher priority for all funding agencies such that national infrastructures are developed, which are capable of supplying all schools throughout the various territories. For instance, a fund could be set up for a limited period (say five years) to supply local bidders with low interest loans, which would make up for the weakness of their capital base and would help them to secure the necessary investments.

Parents and teachers. PTAs at national or local level can influence the social demand for education and could educate the public about the importance of reading. It is thus in the authorities' interest to provide PTAs with increased financial support.

Distribution can also rely on PTAs, since these organisations are present in all schools and are concerned about their children's success. PTAs can make sure that distribution is actually carried out, by commuting between the school and the closest supply point. Moreover, parents are often able to set up local lending or leasing schemes, and to regulate the second-hand book market by organising annual book fairs.

Conclusion

Giving priority to basic education and leaving secondary and tertiary education to the private sector will enable publishers from the north to maintain their turnover and encourage them to invest in realistic partnerships with the local book industry. To have short and medium-term programmes running simultaneously, integrated strategies will be necessary. Immediate steps will be all the more efficient if they pave the way for a controlled future.

Chapter Four

CRITICAL ISSUES ON UPGRADING BOOK DISTRIBUTION IN AFRICA
By Tony Read

The emergence of reformed national book policies

The introductory essay and the individual case studies in Chapters One, Two and Three provided both a basic analysis and the raw data of book distribution issues and recent policy developments in various African countries. This analysis suggests that over the past decade, and most particularly in the past five years, there has been an upsurge of funding agency and government interest in market-oriented, private sector involvement in educational book supply.

In Anglophone Africa there have been a number of extremely important national book policy statements[83] which clearly affirm the position of local African book trades at the centre of educational book provision in the future, and which also emphasise the important role of the private sector in textbook distribution. Francophone Africa seems to be lagging behind in the area of national book policy development but there are encouraging signs that some national book policies might emerge in the region in the near future.[84]

Competitive publishing systems rooted in school-based choice and selection are now replacing monopolistic supply and supply-led distribution systems in a number of countries in Anglophone Africa. School-based textbook budgets are beginning to demonstrate that supply can be accurate and in accordance with school priorities and needs if schools (including primary schools) are permitted and trained to handle the management and the paperwork and make their own decisions. There have been problems as well, of course. The difficulties that Uganda experienced in getting primary schools to purchase textbooks in class sets and to use universal primary education funds properly are cases in point.

In funding agency and government policies, private sector educational publishing has been easier to fund and develop while private sector book distribution has been largely ignored in most countries. To date only Kenya, Côte d'Ivoire and Malawi of the case study countries[85] are making positive

---

83   The most important of these national book policy statements are Tanzania (1991), Uganda (1993), Kenya (1998), Malawi (1999, draft). National book provision/development policies are also in draft and should be finalised shortly in Ghana and Botswana.
84   There seems to be a need to create a forum where Anglophone and Francophone experiences in book development policies can be exchanged, shared and debated.
85   Uganda is planning a pilot project in de-centralised textbook procurement via local bookshops, for implementation in 2001.

and practical efforts to actively involve local private sector booksellers in primary schoolbook distribution. Private sector booksellers are very active in the coastal states of Francophone West Africa, but are not supported by active funding agency and government policies and rely instead on parental purchasing power. There are, however, encouraging signs that a number of other countries are also taking an interest in resolving the problem of re-creating national bookseller networks.

It is clear from the case studies that there is no universal solution to this problem. In Kenya and Botswana, and possibly in Côte d'Ivoire, there are strong existing booksellers. Therefore it should be possible to move quite fast in these countries. In Malawi, Tanzania and Uganda and in a majority of other African countries, where reliable local booksellers are scarce and generally financially very weak, one strategy would be to open up new markets to the commercial book trade school by school and district by district. This process should continue until skills, experience, management capacity, financial strength and public confidence have grown to the point where the brakes can be released. It is likely that the Malawi/Ugandan models will be more relevant to most other African countries than the Kenyan model, simply because few countries in Africa have the basic bookselling strength that exists in Kenya. It is perhaps more likely that a variety of models will emerge to suit specific national requirements.

Expanding retail bookselling networks to develop reading cultures

After decades of neglect, the importance of national networks of effective booksellers serving local needs throughout Africa is beginning to emerge as a significant regional and national strategic issue. Basic reading standards in both international and local languages are perceived to be falling in many countries throughout the continent. There is also great concern about declining performance among primary school leavers in particular.

At least part of the reason for the decline in reading standards is the non-availability of books of the right type in most locations outside the capital cities.[86] Effective bookshops and book outlets are now frequently found only in big cities and do not exist at all in rural and outlying areas. Although educational publishing (usually only core textbooks and teacher's guides) has generally been quite strongly supported by governments and funding agencies over the past decade, children's books and adult fiction and non-fiction in both local and international languages have received very little support.

This type of publishing is central in providing the kind of books that children and adults would wish to read for pleasure, thus supporting a much wider wish to read. This, surely, must be the basis for the creation of the much-

---

86 There is an obvious connection between the widespread decline in reading standards and the perceived decline in the academic ability and performance of school-leavers. If students can't read, how can they learn?

quoted 'reading societies'? Teaching reading at school *must* be supported by the provision of other books and reading materials which enable new readers to find subjects of interest that will not just provide them with additional, highly-motivated reading practice but will also encourage a love of reading as an end in itself.

Support for school library systems in most African countries has been very patchy and has usually been funded through large, one-off, centralised procurements. The opportunity has rarely been taken to channel at least some of the funding through the local book trade via consumer-based purchasing power.[87] The one country (Uganda) that has attempted to do this, via the provision of UPE funds for additional teaching and learning materials direct to schools, has largely failed to create significant additional business for booksellers. The retail book trade was too weak to cope and district based accounting systems could not control fund diversion and misappropriation by many of the schools.[88]

The lack of effective retail book outlets *plus* the widespread decline of national public library systems, which frequently lack even the most basic acquisition budgets, have created a situation where trade and children's book publishers have no market outlets for their publications except for a very limited sale via a few metropolitan bookshops. As a result of publishing largely for metropolitan needs, many local publications are often not as relevant to local needs as they might be. There are not enough new books in local languages and they are frequently too expensive for local purchasing power because of low print runs and the inability of local publishers and booksellers to take risks by investing in larger but more speculative print runs.[89] Thus, in a majority of countries there are simply few (or even no) new books available to meet contemporary local interests at the right price in the right languages.

Most children in school in Africa have no access to any books (except for a part share in an often grubby, much used textbook) through school libraries, public libraries or local retail book outlets. A majority of children in Africa

---

87 Only the issue of consumer based textbook procurement is covered in detail in this essay, but it is also recognised that school libraries (or even classroom book boxes) suffer from very considerable management and usage problems in a majority of schools and particularly in primary schools. These problems are not intractable, but they do require very precise and realistic solutions.

88 A visit to Uganda in June 2000 suggests that the local book trade is beginning to get to grips with UPE funding at the level of individual schools. However, the tendency now is for publishers to sell direct to schools and to ignore the local booksellers completely. Almost inevitably, and largely because of their greater financial resources, the publishers are beginning to reap the benefits of the UPE funds while the booksellers are once again left watching the game from the sidelines.

89 It should be noted that religious bookselling is an honourable exception to this trend. Many religious publishers in Africa publish extensively in local languages and at affordable prices and also make books available very widely via alternative distribution channels rooted in the very widespread network of churches and church activities. A significant proportion of non-textbook reading among children in Africa is probably related to reading religious books and pamphlets.

probably pass through primary school (and often through secondary school) without having read any book except the maths and language textbooks.[90] In these circumstances, how is it possible to develop a reading habit and a love of books for their own sake?

Most educational systems in Africa are attempting to provide education without a sound basis in reading.[91] This is a very critical issue, which must have a major impact on performance at school and which should therefore lie at the heart of government/funding agency educational strategies in every African country. Effective education, however defined, must be based on fluent reading and comprehension skills and these in turn require something more than just basic textbooks. The failure of governments and funding agencies to support school and public libraries and national retail bookshop networks has seriously reduced local, affordable publishing capacity by undermining the natural markets for local publications. Thus national bookselling networks not only support much wider book availability. They also provide one of the critical markets that support local publishing for local needs at locally affordable prices.

Every country in Africa should have its own publishing industry capable of serving its own educational, literary, scholarly, cultural and linguistic requirements with a capacity at least to export and sell important books (or the rights in important books) to other African countries and the rest of the world. The existence of such a publishing industry is critical to a sense of national and ethnic identity.

The case studies in this volume demonstrate some encouraging progress and the emergence of some definite strategies intended to support local book publishing and distribution capacity, and particularly private sector capacity. The issue of private versus state sector book publishing and distribution capacity is also vital in terms of support to democratisation. If the only available bookselling outlets are owned by the state, then it is almost inevitable that only publications supportive of state policies will be disseminated. If the state has a monopoly of 90% of the available national book markets (and this is typical of systems based on state publishing and state distribution in most of Africa), then only the state has the financial capacity to publish and distribute effectively in other market sectors. To be effective and democratic, information provision at any level in the system must be pluralist. Monopolistic information provision cannot support current pro-democracy policies.

---

90 An informal reading survey was conducted in Mendulo CDSS in Mulanje District in Malawi in 1999. It revealed that none of the Form 3 secondary school students had read a complete book for pleasure within memory until the CDSS was provided with a school library with a fiction section containing contemporary African novels and stories. Within weeks of the establishment of the new library many students were borrowing and reading two or three novels or stories a week.

91 A recent (as yet unpublished) research study carried out in the Mangochi and Balaka Districts of Malawi by Save the Children Fund (US) and financially supported by USAID concluded that 48% of students in the fourth year of primary school were not fully knowledgeable about the alphabet in either English or Chichewa.

Key problems in private sector book distribution in Africa

The case studies and the introductory essay have identified a number of fundamental weaknesses in book distribution capacity common to many African countries. In 2000, these weaknesses apply almost equally to private and public sector book distributors.[92] They must be noted and taken into account in the design and implementation of any strategies aimed to develop national book distribution capacity. The most critical inhibiting issues can be summarised as follows:

- Most booksellers[93] in most African countries lack the financial capacity to hold stocks of the most important titles in sufficient quantity to service school needs. Interest rates are often high and booksellers do not represent good loan risks as far as local banks are concerned. To be able to stock, most booksellers either need pre-payment from their customers or they need credit facilities from their suppliers.
- Most booksellers cannot afford to take risks. They have little interest in speculative stocking. They want firm orders from schools with payment in advance before they will order from the publishers. Faced with reluctance of many booksellers to stock or order firm without pre-payment from the customer, an increasing number of publishers may supply direct to schools in competition with the booksellers. The only speculative stocks maintained by a majority of booksellers are limited quantities of a few titles with known demand.
- Maintaining stock at locally convenient locations is normally essential to support school textbook ordering and sales of supplementary reading materials.
- Most schools do not trust most local booksellers enough to provide pre-payment. Most suppliers do not trust most local booksellers enough to provide significant credit facilities.

Examples of good practice

It is clear from the above that there is a self-perpetuating financing problem and that something is needed to break the circle of financial constraints that inhibits the growth of reliable and effective book distribution. Among the current experimental strategies designed to break through the kind of barriers described above are the following:

In Malawi, the MoESC/Danida provides matching funds against secondary school textbook fees collected by schools from the parents. But these matching funds are not provided to the schools. Schools place orders with one of ten

---

92   In Tanzania, for example, the state-owned TES now has exactly the same financing and credit problems as most of the private sector booksellers.
93   There are, of course, good, well-financed booksellers with excellent credit records in most of the case study countries but they are generally based in capital cities and cannot serve the whole country.

nationally approved private sector textbook suppliers.[94] The suppliers are selected by the MoESC/Danida on the basis of an agreed set of operational criteria and currently provide a national coverage. A school cheque drawn in favour of the supplier selected by the school must accompany the school textbook order. Bearer cheques or cash payments are not permitted. The school can order up to double the value of the school cheque. The MoESC/Danida provides the matching funds direct to the bookseller. The matching funds are released to the bookseller only when the supplier provides invoices plus completed delivery notes signed and stamped by the school to the MoESC/Danida office. This system has the following advantages:

- The achievement of nationally approved textbook supplier status confers significant potential economic benefit. All of the current list of suppliers are aware that failure to service school orders correctly or to pay suppliers in acceptable time will lead to the cancellation of this status. Thus booksellers are motivated to pay their bills in full and on time to the publishers and to provide good service to schools. The system is fully monitored to ensure full compliance and the development of good practices.
- The list of nationally approved textbook suppliers was compiled to ensure a book outlet in every significant town in Malawi. There are currently ten approved booksellers with a total of 33 retail outlets covering 72 school districts. Thus the basis for genuine national coverage has been established. It will be upgraded and expanded every year.
- The nationally approved textbook suppliers are expected to compete with each other for school textbook supply contracts. This has provided all schools with competitive discounts off fixed retail prices[95] and with free delivery direct to the schools. Competition has already improved standards of service to schools, including information on books provided by both publishers and booksellers.
- Any school can only double its order value if it orders via one of the nationally approved textbook suppliers and if it provides its cheque for 50% of the order value in advance. Thus, booksellers know that they have guaranteed turnover if they get a school to sign a supply contract and schools are motivated to sign a contract with a nationally approved supplier because this is the only way that they can access the matching funds and thus double their order value. Thus school business is directed

---

94 The nationally approved suppliers are all booksellers. Neither publishers nor wholesalers are currently permitted to be nationally approved textbook suppliers.

95 Current discount levels offered by approved textbook suppliers to schools are between 5–12%. Each year a national 'Approved List of Textbooks and Supplementary Books' is produced by the BPAM in association with the MoESC. This list contains full price information. Publishers cannot increase prices without the approval of the MoESC and this can only be given if there is clear evidence of significant devaluation/currency depreciation of more than 15% since the price list was published. The Approved List is sent to every school, divisional office, district office and bookseller. To date there have been no examples of price mark-ups from either publishers or booksellers.

through the approved suppliers. This creates reliability and predictability. The schools also must pay their cheque in advance, which guarantees some pre-financing to booksellers. This assists the booksellers in financing their ordering from the publishers. The pre-payment financing is used to part pay publishers for stocks. Publishers know that the only way that they can get their books sold to schools is via the nationally approved suppliers, so some level of publisher support to the suppliers is also guaranteed.[96]

- The matching funds are paid direct to the nationally approved booksellers but only on production of evidence that the school order has been supplied in full. Schools therefore trust the bookseller more because they know that if the bookseller does not supply their order accurately they do not have to sign the completed delivery note and this is the only way that the bookseller can collect the matching funds.[97]

- Only a limited number of the available secondary schools are eligible in any one year for supply via the booksellers. Thus, in 2000, only a named 216 out of 700 state-funded secondary schools in the country were eligible for supply via the booksellers. The rest of the schools submitted their cash and orders direct to the education ministry who in turn organised consolidated supply via a local freighting company. The list of schools is thus maintained at a level that fits the financing and management capacity of the local booksellers. If the 2000 orders are handled well, then the booksellers will have earned additional profits (which in turn will increase their financing capacity) and will have gained experience, which in turn will enable the number of 'direct supply' schools to be increased in 2001. Early indications suggest that the official booksellers have coped very well with their 216 schools and that it will be possible to increase the number of direct supply schools in 2001. It is hoped that booksellers will supply all secondary schools direct within two or three years.

- Because the matching funds cannot be redeemed by publishers but only by the nationally approved textbook suppliers, the only way that the publishers can achieve school orders and thus increased turnover is to support the nationally approved textbook suppliers.

- The introduction of the system described above created for the first time in many years a substantial school market for private sector booksellers. As a result, local and overseas investors combined to form a private sector textbook wholesaler. The wholesaler is not permitted to be one of the nationally approved textbook suppliers but works closely with the approved suppliers and provides systems, consolidation and distribution

---

96   One of the criterion for nationally approved textbook supplier status was that the bookseller had to be supported by the national publishers association as a (to some extent at least) creditworthy bookseller.

97   In June 2000 in the first year of operation booksellers had received orders and pre-paid cheques from 200 out of 221 direct supply schools (90%). This was a significantly better performance than the parallel collection rate achieved by the divisional offices of 65%.

capacity and assistance with financing against a commission on orders supplied. The wholesaler has probably made it possible for far more of the schools to be supplied via the booksellers.

In Kenya, the system best evaluated by the RNE pilot project in 1998 was the provision of cash to school bank accounts to create a school purchasing power capacity for textbooks. A list of approved textbooks was created to guide school purchasing and all schools were provided with official order forms, a specially written management handbook and sample contract forms to sign with the bookseller of their choice. All local booksellers were eligible to participate provided that they could persuade publishers to provide them with stocks of the books ordered by the schools. There was fierce competition among many booksellers[98] for school contracts and free supply direct to the school premises, competitive discounts off retail prices and even premium offers to schools emerged as the major inducements offered to schools to sign contracts. All schools were instructed not to pay booksellers until their orders had been fully and correctly delivered.

- The type of system developed in Kenya is probably only possible where there is a strong existing book trade. The cash based system and the unregulated selection of booksellers by schools would almost certainly not be appropriate or workable in most other African countries with weak bookselling infrastructures.
- The booksellers' cause was greatly assisted in Kenya by a critical policy decision taken by the KPA that all KPA members would support the KBPA and only supply schools via booksellers. As a result, there were virtually no examples of publishers supplying the pilot schools direct in competition with the booksellers. Kenyan publishers reached this decision because they were far-sighted enough to see the enormous benefits that would accrue to publishers from a strong local bookselling sector.
- The KPA also agreed to support booksellers with extended credit. The implementation of the project was delayed for some months (not the fault of schools or the book trade) and the publishers eventually finished up providing almost six months of extended credit to the booksellers. There were very few bad debts from booksellers to publishers but the pilot project would have failed if the Kenyan publishers had not had the financial resources to cope with very long periods of extended credit.
- All pilot schools operating on direct supply from booksellers against cash based ordering were extremely pleased with the discounts, free delivery and premium offers received from the booksellers. They compared the service received extremely favourably with previous state organised deliveries where most schools had to collect books from district stores (sometimes at considerable cost) and where many supplies were incorrect.

---

98 Booksellers from within but also from considerable distances outside the two pilot districts competed for school contracts.

Schools commented particularly on the speed of correction of supply errors by the private sector book trade, motivated largely by a desire to be paid.

- Most of the pilot primary schools were not capable of maintaining simple cash books to account for their expenditure but virtually all schools kept good transaction records so that a clear audit trail was available. Thus the pilot evaluation was able to judge that funds had been well and correctly spent and that the books supplied coincided with the orders and the order values. There were occasional examples of pressure on schools by district education staff to place their school textbook contracts with specified suppliers. There were also occasional examples of prices charged above those established in the approved book list. In general, however, there were remarkably few examples of corrupt practices and unacceptable mark-ups and profit taking.

- A comparison between the cost of supply from booksellers and the cost of supply from district based central competitive procurement and consolidated delivery indicated that the private sector booksellers were up to 6% cheaper than centralised procurement and delivery.

- The pilot project was successful at directing substantial ordering from schools through private sector booksellers. This in turn created profits and increased financial capacity in local booksellers and generated a much greater interest in the potential of the school textbook business. Several local traders, who were previously only occasional book suppliers, rapidly emerged as significant and permanent bookshop accounts.

- The pilot project was so successful that, in 1998, the government of Kenya published a new national textbook policy which established the basic principles of future textbook supply via competition, choice, school based purchasing power and school based decision-making through local booksellers wherever possible.

- It is interesting that the DFID-funded SPRED 3 project and the World Bank education reform project in Kenya will also support the de-centralised model of textbook supply through local booksellers which was pilot through the RNE project.

In Uganda a third approach to the supply of textbooks to primary schools via local booksellers is currently at the planning stage. The Ugandan model is also a pilot that will be implemented in three or four districts during 2001. In Uganda, schools will be provided with a per capita textbook budget from the local DEO. The purchasing budget will be provided in the form of Local Purchase Orders (LPOs), which will entitle schools to purchase only textbooks and teacher's guides from the official list of approved textbooks up to the stated value of the LPO. The LPOs will only be reclaimable by local booksellers who have been officially approved as the district textbook suppliers. To get DEO approval, local booksellers will have to meet a stringent set of criteria. These will include letters of approval from publishers, premises and storage of a minimum size and standard, the maintenance of sample copies of all approved

195

textbooks and a publicly displayed price list stamped and signed by the DEO to guarantee that the prices are correct. At least two suppliers will be approved in each district to ensure competition and good terms and service to schools. Schools will be instructed not to sign off the LPOs to booksellers until all orders have been fully and accurately fulfilled. Orders given by schools to non-approved suppliers or direct to publishers cannot be reimbursed by the district office. The advantages of this approach are as follows:

- Schools can only get their books by purchasing through the official suppliers. Thus ordering is forced through known local booksellers who meet basic criteria. Official suppliers know that they will get good turnover as a result of their approved status.

- Approved status confers economic benefit. Approved status will be lost if booksellers fail to supply to schools or fail to pay their bills. Thus good habits will be established so that the official suppliers can maintain their favoured status.

- Officially approved suppliers must meet the basic criteria, including financing capacity. This will create booksellers at district level who will have to upgrade their operations to meet good basic standards. Because there will be guaranteed turnover to the official suppliers it is expected that well-financed booksellers from Kampala or other districts might start to invest in district level branches and that other non-book businesses with adequate funds might also start to take an interest in district level bookselling.

- Publishers will only be able to achieve sales to primary schools by working constructively with the official suppliers. As in Kenya, publishers should become motivated to establish good working relationships with the official suppliers.

- Publishers will know exactly who the approved suppliers are and will be able to concentrate their marketing and sales efforts through known outlets that can be expected to generate good turnover and profits and thus enhanced financing capacity in future.

- Schools should benefit as in Kenya and Malawi by the improved service resulting from competition for school contracts.

The three examples of innovative practice provided above do not need major projects or major finance as basic requirements. Any government or funding agency can introduce these approaches on a small-scale pilot project basis in just one district or even at sub-district or zonal levels. The Kenyan model probably requires a well-established book trade as a pre-condition. The Malawi and Ugandan models are well-suited to underdeveloped local book trades and both stimulate the right conditions for the growth of bookseller/publisher co-operation, enhanced financing capacity, the development of credit facilities and the provision of good service to schools. Both systems support good habits of reliable supplier payment and reliable school order fulfilment. Both systems can apply to textbooks or to supplementary reading materials or to reference books. They can be oriented to primary school or secondary school supply or even to public library supply. All that is required is consumer-based purchasing power in some form plus good planning and preparation and some good practical experience in the way that the book trade works.

Basic conclusions on book distribution capacity

At this stage it is probably possible to outline some basic conclusions about the current state of book distribution in Africa. The key issues can be summarised as follows:

- The health of the national book distribution systems in most African countries is completely dependent upon access to the key school textbook markets.
- The form and nature of government and funding agency school textbook provision policies will determine absolutely the nature, size and viability of the book distribution systems, not just for school textbooks, but for all other market sectors as well.
- State monopolistic textbook publishing and distribution policies generally have not performed well in Africa, although there are a few reasonably adequate systems (for example, primary textbook systems in both Botswana and Lesotho).
- The destruction (in Anglophone Africa) or the failure to develop (in Francophone Africa) of national networks of effective and viable bookshops has had a marked and adverse impact in many countries on the development of cultural output and has undermined efforts to create reading and literate societies. The lack of bookshop outlets has had a much greater impact in rural than in urban areas.
- State-owned textbook distribution systems are not necessarily cheaper, nor are they more efficient, nor do they provide schools with better service. They may sometimes appear to be cheaper because many of the operational costs are concealed under diverse budget heads.
- A majority of state-run textbook distribution systems currently do not have the systems, information, facilities, expertise or finance to operate effectively and efficiently.
- In recent years, many of the traditional state book distributors in Africa have either failed or have ceased to be effective as government/funding agency support budgets have been reduced or removed.

Competition, choice and school-based decision-making on book selection can be supported via the local book trade by the use of consumer funding strategies, which in turn tend to create demand led 'pull' provision systems. Demand led textbook provision systems are inherently more accurate and less wasteful and are more likely to meet the actual needs of schools effectively.

The active involvement of the local book trade in the core school textbook market and in important associated markets, such as the provision of supplementary reading materials, is likely to create the financial strength within the private sector on which all other types of book distribution activity can be developed. Demand-based financing policies are more likely to support local, private sector, bookshop development than supply-side financing policies. It also needs to be emphasised that constant changes in policy approach are inimical to the development of effective textbook distribution systems and, by extension, to all kinds of national book distribution.

Creating (or re-creating) effective national bookselling and book distribution networks cannot be achieved overnight and requires the establishment of genuinely supportive and enabling environments. This in turn requires a close and professional understanding of the local book trade and its strengths, weaknesses and needs. The lack of investment finance, credit problems, an inability to cope with risk, poor co-operation between publishers and booksellers, inadequate management and systems and poor physical facilities are common problems that have to be taken into account in project design. Successful and innovative approaches have to create conditions that directly address the problems and provide motivation to change. Training programmes, by themselves, are never sufficient to solve these very basic structural inadequacies. The kind of support programme required in Kenya is likely to be very different to the support programme required in Chad.

In the development of reformed and effective textbook distribution systems there are three key principles, predictability, reliability and responsiveness:

- *Predictability* and *reliability* are fundamental. Government, funding agencies, the book trade, schools, parents and students must all know in good time what is expected of them. Sudden and frequent changes in policy and system should be avoided wherever possible. Systems should be in place for long enough that everyone can become familiar with their operations. Any significant changes need to be sign-posted, publicised and explained to the affected constituency well in advance. Similarly, the system *must* be reliable in the sense that the financing, resources, facilities and information necessary for its effective operation are guaranteed to be available every year, on time. If private sector involvement and investment are required as part of the system then reliability is critical. No significant investment can be expected in highly volatile situations or in countries where textbook finance is occasional and irregular.
- Systems also need to be *responsive* in the sense that they should be supervised and monitored so that problems can be clearly identified and thus speedily resolved. If textbook provision is indeed predictable, reliable and responsive to needs then it is very likely to be trusted and thus effective.

All of the above may sound very self-evident and basic but there are relatively few textbook distribution systems in Africa where all three requirements operate. As indicated above, experimentation in new approaches does not have to be on a large scale nor does it require large scale funding but it *must* be well planned and based on a thorough understanding of the local dynamics.

A decision tree for policy-makers

The decision tree on page 205 is intended to provide a convenient guide to the critical decisions and options that policy-makers need to consider in the construction of a national textbook policy, and, by logical extension, the essential framework for a national approach to delivery and fulfilment. The decision tree has six main stages. These are:

1 Essential preparation for policy-making.
2 Decisions on affordable and sustainable sources of textbook financing.
3 Decisions on the point of application of textbook financing.
4 Decisions on the type of funding.
5 Decisions on competition and choice and the location of decision-making.
6 Decisions on supply routes (including different types of tendering and their implications).

Brief notes on each of the six stages are provided below to assist in the use of the flow chart. More detailed explanations and analysis are provided in Chapter 1.

Stage One: essential preparation for policy-making

There is an obvious link between curriculum and teaching and learning materials requirements. Every curriculum should specify both the optimum and the minimum teaching and learning materials requirements needed to adequately deliver the curriculum objectives. These should include not just core textbooks and associated teacher's manuals but also reading books, essential reference books (dictionaries and atlases) and basic teaching aids. The fundamental assumptions relating to teaching and learning materials provision (language(s) of instruction, physical and content specifications including formats, extents, number of colours, etc, plus book life, book to pupil ratios, loss and damage rates, predicted enrollment growth, etc.) should also be stated.

On the basis of this information the annual recurring cost implications of the minimum levels of provision must be calculated and subjected to a rigorous assessment of affordability and sustainability. This in turn will require realistic assessments of sustainable potential government contributions, the level and extent of commitment and the reliability of funding agency support and the capacity for cost sharing and contributions from parents (if required). If the recurrent cost implications are considered to be beyond realistic and affordable financing capacity then the teaching and learning materials requirements and/ or curriculum specifications may need to be revised downwards or subjected to standard cost reduction strategies.

These might include a curriculum review to reduce the number of subjects requiring core textbooks, the extension of book life via improved physical specifications, or improved storage and management in schools, higher book to pupil ratios, a reduction in colour, reduced extents and formats, etc. The revised minimum teaching and learning materials profile should then be re-costed and assessed against the realistic financing capacity. This process of costing and revision may need to be repeated several times until a minimum affordable package of teaching and learning materials provision is agreed.

There is a fairly common viewpoint that it is wrong to submit curriculum specifications to detailed cost and affordability analysis and that any attempt to do so (and any attempt to reduce curricula requirements as a result) is simply subjugating educational outputs to the lowest common denominator of financial expediency. On the other hand, it is surely a pointless exercise to create curricula that are so demanding of support from teaching and learning materials (and other inputs) that they can never be afforded and are thus never provided.

The most common curriculum problem is probably the specification of too many subjects to be taught in primary schools, which in turn leads to increased needs for textbooks and other teaching and learning materials. It is curious, for example, that the current policy in Kenya is to shift from an eleven to a six subject primary curriculum. In Uganda, at exactly the same time, the policy is to shift from a four to a ten subject curriculum. There is an argument that the introduction of too many subjects in the primary curriculum can overburden largely under-trained teachers and can also divert critical teaching/learning time away from the acquisition of the key skills of literacy and numeracy.

Stage Two: decisions on affordable and sustainable sources of finance

The most fundamental policy decision at this stage is whether basic teaching and learning materials provision will be:

- Free to parents.
- Totally funded by parents.
- Cost shared between parents and the government.

In the ideal world all teaching and learning materials would be free to parents. Experience in Africa (and elsewhere in the developing world) demonstrates that the cost to parents of purchasing teaching and learning materials is one of the major factors that inhibit primary school enrollments. But there are numerous examples also where 'free' provision results very quickly in 'no' provision and this in turn can lead to parental and student disillusionment with UPE and free provision systems. This can also often lead to rapid changes in textbook provision policy as funding agencies come in to offer financial support for relatively short periods and then switch to concentrate on other priorities.

Free textbook provision policies require combined government and funding agency funding to be made available at the specified levels over the long haul, and this in turn requires long term funding agency and government commitment. If this long-term commitment isn't in place, some form of parental contribution may be necessary.[99]

There are two broad parental financing options. Parents can contribute by direct purchase (where books are owned by the student) or by the payment of rental fees to the school (where books are owned by the school). Rental fees tend to be cheaper than direct purchase and can also be more equitable. Most communities prefer rental fees to be maintained in, and managed by, the school rather than remitted back to central government. Rental fees remitted to central government are often used to support supply-side procurement and distribution policies. Rental fees retained for use by schools become the basis of demand-based systems.

Subsidising parental purchase usually requires some form of producer support in which funds are provided to publishers (for example) in order to reduce prices. Where publisher subsidies are restricted to single titles there can be significant market distortions, which prevent effective competition. Subsidising rental fees can be achieved by matching fund systems which can be applied to the consumer (ideally to the school rather than to the student or parent) and which therefore support demand side systems and retail bookshop development

Stage Three: decisions on the point of financing
The next critical policy decision that will have an impact on teaching and learning materials distribution systems is where the available funding is spent. There are two basic choices. Finance will either be applied to the producers or to the consumers. Funding by procurement direct from commercial publishers may well support private sector publishers but usually implies state distribution systems and the neglect of private sector distribution channels. Funding the publication and printing of textbooks usually implies the classic state centralist publishing/printing model. Once again, this type of producer funding will tend to support supply-side, statist models of distribution.

Consumer funding can be applied at the level of districts or sub-districts (the type of model that might emerge in Tanzania), or can be provided to individual schools (as in Uganda or Kenya). School based consumer funding can consist of government/funding agency funding only (free book provision), or parental fees only or matching funds (in which the state meets a proportion of the contributions made by parents). Consumer funding can also comprise household-based subsidies, but these are notoriously difficult and expensive to target and deliver. School based consumer funding is the basis for all demand-led distribution systems and it best supports competitive textbook provision and choice. District based funding tends to have all of the disadvantages of producer funding with few of the advantages of school based funding.

Stage Four: decisions on the type of funding
Producer funding is typically made via direct remittance to the producers concerned. Only in consumer funding are there different ways of making the funding available. Thus this level of policy decision is only applicable when

---

99   The cost of basic textbook provision is not large in comparison to total educational budgets and many authorities urge governments and funding agencies to always absorb the costs of free textbooks, at least for basic primary education.

basic consumer-based approaches to textbook provision have already been agreed. Chapter One provides a description and the pros and cons of the different types of consumer funding which are available.

In all cases, the basic systems support demand-led distribution and make possible the involvement of the private sector book trade. They all support choice and competition. The main differences lie firstly in the level of parental contribution required and secondly in the management skills and accountability of the schools. Order form systems provide the maximum control over funding and allow for centralised procurement and centralised delivery of the books ordered by the schools. LPOs and cash systems are easier and cheaper to administer but imply less control and accountability over the funds and therefore the need for higher levels of management skills in schools.

Stage Five: decisions on competition and choice

This policy stage requires decisions as to whether there should be competitive textbook supply and choice for schools on the books that they wish to use. The various types of competition and choice available are specified in Chapter One and the advantages and disadvantages of each are provided there. Only the 'no choice' option maintains the typical and traditional state centralist approach to textbook provision.

Stage Six: decisions on supply routes

The choices at this stage are straightforward. They are:
- The use of state owned/funded distributor.
- The hiring in via competitive tender of warehousing, consolidation and delivery services (these can be contracted at central, regional or district levels as required, although there are management costs and problems in moving towards multiple simultaneous tendering systems).
- The use of a limited number of officially approved private sector retailers (combined state and private sector operations are possible in this option. Also, approved retailers may be organised to compete with each other or to operate through geographic monopolies).
- The use of any retailer. This is the system that currently applies in Kenya and is only an option if there is already a strong and diverse retail bookseller sector.

Only the last two of the options provided actively support the development of private sector, national, bookshop development.
The combined policy decisions of the six stages described will create a national textbook provision system and will define the type of teaching and learning materials distribution system.

The future

This survey and analysis of trends in book distribution in the case studies suggests that there is already a policy change underway among a number of governments and funding agencies in their approaches toward national textbook distribution. This change is more apparent in Anglophone than in Francophone countries and is by no means universal even in Anglophone countries. But the reaction against the inefficiencies, the lack of a service culture and the typically high cost operations of state centralist policies is now almost ten years old.

In 2000 there are a number of countries where interesting and highly relevant strategies are beginning to emerge that are worthy of serious study and perhaps emulation. Among the case study countries Kenya, Uganda, Malawi and Botswana are already adopting positive policies towards radically increased private sector involvement in school textbook distribution and the re-creation of national bookshop networks. The potential profits from renewed access to the national school textbook markets (and particularly the primary textbook market) could re-finance the sector over the next few years and thus support the kind of provincial and district level bookshops that were a feature of many countries only 40 years ago.[100]

Unfortunately, the provision of access to the markets, by itself, will not be enough. The wholesale and retail book trade in many countries is now very weak. Even the old state distributors that have survived (TES in Tanzania is the most notable example) no longer have the investment finance once provided freely by government to buy stock and to cope with risk. Few publishers currently would provide significant credit to very many booksellers – state or private – in most of the case study countries.

Management capacity might respond to training initiatives, but practical solutions to the twin problems of financing capacity and creditworthiness have to be found if the book trade is to play a full role once again in textbook distribution on a national scale. Booksellers must start to pay their bills promptly to gain access to all-important credit facilities and they must take care of their reputations so that schools are more willing to provide pre-financing with their orders. And the private sector book trade also has to face up to the responsibility of having to supply the whole market and not just the profitable pieces of it that are easy to reach. This means that local booksellers will have to take on board the need to supply the remote and difficult access schools as well as the easy urban schools. It is encouraging that in both Kenya and Malawi the local booksellers appear to be willing to accept this challenge.

There is also a key role in all of this for the national and regional book trade associations, which must support and encourage more pro-active

---

100 Danida introduced consumer-based, matching fund support for secondary textbook purchases via the local book trade in Malawi early in 2000. As a result, the CLAIM bookshop in Mulanje achieved more turnover from one textbook order placed by a local secondary school than it managed to achieve in the whole of the previous year from trade sales alone to the general public. This graphically illustrates the enormous impact of access to school markets on local bookselling and the potential for local business profits and growth represented by this access.

developmental policies among their membership. There is also a need for a tougher trade association stance on the defaulters who spoil the market for the reputable traders who are trying hard to build a responsible and reliable business

Getting access to the core textbook markets and providing genuine service in supply to schools will create the kind of profits that should re-establish competent national bookshop outlets, at least down to district levels. This, by itself, will create additional markets for both publishers and booksellers. Good retail bookshop outlets throughout any country are one of the critical supports to the establishment of a reading society. But none of this can happen without the right policies and strategies and the creation of a supportive and enabling environment. This is the critical role of governments and funding agencies. But governments and funding agencies must recognise in turn that their approaches to these issues will have an impact that extends far beyond basic efficiencies in school textbook supply. Good policies and implementation strategies will support reading within the wider society and this will have an impact on democratisation and good governance.

APPENDIX 1

Current membership of the Ghana Book Publishers' Association

1   Ghana Publishing Corporation
2   SEDCO Publishing Limited
3   Afram Publication (Gh.) Limited
4   Waterville Publishing Company
5   Educational Press
6   Oshiaperm Publishing Company
7   Adwinsa Publications
8   Ghana Universities Press
9   Business Publications
10 Baafour & Company
11 Bureau of Ghana Languages
12 Black Mask Limited
13 All Good Books Limited
14 Frank Mask Limited
15 Minerva Book Limited
16 Asempa Publishing Limited
17 Africa Christian Press
18 Weoli Publishing Services
19 Unimax Publishers Co Ltd
20 Sam-Woode Limited
21 Onward Publishing Co Ltd
22 Quick Services Books Limited
23 Pearl Publications
24 Wavelight Publications
25 Sub-Saharan Books
26 Bible Society of Ghana
27 Ghana Institute of Linquistics' Literacy & Bible Translation
28 Aman Publications
29 Sebewie Publishers
30 Dela Publications & Design Services
31 Alter International Ltd
32 Academic Publications Ltd

33 Academic Publications Ltd
34 International Bible Society
35 Newgen Bookshop & Publishers Ltd
36 Eurrekka Industries Ltd
37 Studio Brian Communications
38 Anansesem Publications
39 Degraft Graphics & Publications
40 Advent Press
41 Afrique Publications Ltd
42 Golden Wings Publication Ltd
43 Triumph Publication and Book Depot
44 Osei Kwadwo Enterprise
45 AMAA Books Publications
46 Book Industry Publication Unit
47 ADAEX Educational Publication
48 Ahenpa Publishers Limited
49 National Science and Technology Press (NASTEP, CSIR)
50 Graphic Corporation
51 F. REIMMER Book Services
52 STEP Publishers
53 KOBRA Prints Ltd
54 Readwide Publishers
55 Royal Gold Publishers
56 K 'N' AB Ltd
57 NORCENTO PUBLISHERS Ltd
58 Beginners Publishers
59 E.C.G. Publications
60 Klo-Amanie Enterprise
61 Merit Educational & Professional Books Ltd
62 Tony's Guide Book Producing Ent.
63 Yetoda Publishing
64 IFA
65 OTB Services Ltd
66 OLIVE Publications
67 Advanced Legal Publications
68 Bentil Books Ltd
69 Jeta Quality Consult.
70 OBFES Publications
71 Mayan Books Limited
72 Dyno-Media Ltd
73 Sankofa Publications Ltd
74 Ghana Legal Iteracy & Resource Foundation
75 Smartline Limited
76 Amorin Publishing
77 Adomsiman Publications Ltd

APPENDIX 2

Main bookshops in the major towns of Kenya

Town	Bookshop
Nairobi	Chania Bookshop
	Laxmi Booksellers
	Savannis Book Centre
	Book Distributors
	Book Corner
	Catholic Bookshop
	Text Book Centre
	Premier
	Book Point
	Prestige
	Keswick
	Kesho
	SU Christian Centre
	University of Nairobi Bookshop
Mombassa	Kant Bookshop
	Hussein Limited
	Bahati Bookshop
	Amir's Book Centre
	Coastal Emporium
	Bahari Bookshop
Kisumu	Anvi Emporium
	Text Book World
	Kesho Bookshop
	United General Stores
	Lolwe Agencies

Nakuru	Ereto Bookshop
	Rift Valley Stationers
	Flamingo
	Peruman
	Catholic Bookshop
Eldoret	Students Choice
	Eldoret Emporium
	Kerio Stores
	Vitabu
	Conart
Nyeri	Kimji
	Chamken
	Watani Bookshop
Kakamega	Union Bookshop
	New Kakamega Bookshop
	Vaghela Bookshop
Meru	Catholic Bookshop
	Dabuem Bookshop
	Uzima Bookshop
	Bhatt Bookshop
Embu	CPK Bookshop
	Diocesian Bookshop
	Ropey Supplies
Thika	Thika Bookshop
	Mwendia Ltd
Kitale	Kitale Printers
	Mwalimu Cooperative
Mandera	Frontier Bookmen
Nanyuki	Juttson Stores
Machakos	Maisha Mapya
	J.K.Stores
	Mutula Bookshop
	ABC Bookshop
	Stanbook Emporium
Bungoma	Bungoma Fancy Stores
	Bungoma Booksellers

GLOSSARY

Words and acronyms common in education, development and the book trade

In almost all developing countries and in many transitional economies the core of the national book trade is in educational publishing and distribution. In many of these countries more than 90% of the potential market for books and other types of publications is provided by educational institutions and is often supported by funding agencies. The educational book market is, therefore, dominated by educational and developmental policies and strategies and by donor financing. The ultimate viability of publishers, booksellers and printers in the developing world often depends on the policies of government and funding agencies toward education in general and toward teaching and learning materials provision in particular. But the book trade is often deprived of hard information on educational and developmental policies and strategies and frequently does not fully understand the concepts, processes and practices of development aid.

The education sections within the funding agencies have their own terminology and jargon that can be as opaque to the publisher, printer and bookseller as book trade technical vocabulary is to the education professional and the funding agency. As an aid to improved understanding, this glossary attempts to bring together in one place the commonest terms and acronyms of the book trade, education and development in so far as they are relevant to each other.

In the interests of brevity, self-evident terminology (e.g. *book*) is not included. Nor are the most technical terms from computers, DTP, pre-press, printing and binding. The technical vocabulary and specialised usage are already voluminous in these areas and there are a number of excellent technical dictionaries already available that cover these subjects in much greater detail and with greater precision than is possible here. For similar reasons, most of the technical vocabulary relating to computers is omitted. This glossary is intended primarily for those who are regularly working, planning and surviving at the interface between the three disciplines of teaching and learning materials, education and development aid and who need access to reasonable but not overwhelming definitions and detail. To make the glossary suitable for practical use the definitions have attempted to avoid jargon and in some cases are more detailed than those normally found in technical word lists. Some examples are provided where relevant.

Words or phrases in *italic* in the definitions are also listed as headwords and are defined elsewhere in the glossary. Words that are used very often in the glossary that is 'publisher', 'bookseller', 'manuscript', etc. are not necessarily italicised.

211

A-series. The international *ISO* range of paper sizes.

abbreviation. A shortened version of a word or phrase.

ABC. The African Books Collective; a collective of African publishers established to promote and distribute the sales of books and journals published in Africa to countries outside the African continent.

abridge. To create a shortened version of a book or manuscript.

abridgement. A shortened version of a book or manuscript.

absorbency. The degree to which paper takes up moisture as measured by a standard test.

account. A company, organisation or individual with which a supplier maintains a trading relationship, often used by publishers to refer to their bookseller customers.

accountability. The responsibility to report to others about the intended and actual use of resources and the achievement of results.

accounts. A statement of the financial position of a company, organisation or individual.

acknowledgement. A statement of thanks for assistance given in the making of a publication; also a written note, generally in the *prelims*, of permission received by the owners of any copyright material (text or illustrations) reproduced or quoted in the publication.

ACP. Africa, Caribbean and the Pacific. A geographical definition or description used to describe those countries that have a special relationship with the European Union.

actual book life. A concept most commonly used in relation to schoolbooks; the average length of time a book actually lasts in use in the classroom. This is generally established by test sampling of schools or institutions in a system. See also **assumed book life** and **book life.**

adaptation. The result of amending a book (often a textbook or reference work) by altering, adding or deleting text and/or illustrations to make the book suitable for a different audience or market from that for which it was originally intended.

ADB. See **AFDB.**

addendum. Additional material added to a text after printing, often on an inserted slip of paper.

ADEA. (Association for the Development of Education in Africa) An association of funding agencies, African Ministries of Education and other interested groupings which has the objective of developing co-operative strategies to improve educational provision and performance in Africa. It has several working groups including one specifically concerned with books and other teaching and learning materials, which is led by the *DFID* in London. ADEA has its headquarters in Paris.

Adjustable Programme Loan. *(APL)* A type of development financing used by the World Bank in which a longer term financial commitment is broken down into a series of shorter phases, each with its own targets and objectives. The sequence of shorter phases is intended to provide flexibility and the opportunity to review progress more regularly and thus to be able to respond more quickly to changed circumstances or altered priorities.

advance. An agreed pre-payment against a contract. In publishing terminology it generally refers to an advance against royalties paid by a publisher to an author or by a publisher to another publisher when reprint or subsidiary rights are involved. Advances may be paid at different stages of a contract, for example, on signature of a contract, on delivery of the manuscript or on publication. See also **royalty** and **rising royalty.**

advance copies. The first copies of a printed book sent to the publisher prior to the delivery of *bulk stock*; usually used for checking the quality of the printing.

advance sheets. Folded and collated sheets supplied to a publisher for approval prior to printing.

AFDB. (African Development Bank) The multilateral development agency for the Africa region. Also sometimes referred to as *ADB*. The headquarters of the organisation are in Abidjan in Côte d'Ivoire.

against the grain. Folding or cutting at right angles to the grain of the paper.

agent. An individual, company or other organisation, not in the direct employment of the principal, which represents the defined interests of the principal in a specified geographical area or market sector; an *agent* is usually paid on the basis of a percentage commission on the value of sales achieved. An *agent* normally performs sales, marketing, promotion or representational functions.

agreement. A document stating what has been agreed between two or more parties. An agreement is not necessarily legally binding although it can also be used as an alternative word for contract.

aid co-ordination. The co-ordination of aid assistance from different sources. It differs from donor co-ordination because it does not indicate who is responsible for the co-ordination.

annex. See **appendix**.

annotate. To make notes relating to the text directly on the relevant page of a publication. *Annotations* may be informal (i.e. made by the reader in handwriting on the page for personal use) or they may be a designed feature of a publication or text. For example, *annotated* editions of the Bible or Shakespeare provide notes or comment on the text as an aid to understanding.

anthology. A published collection of works or excerpts selected by an *editor* from different sources, usually on a defined theme.

APL. See **Adjustable Programme Loan.**

APNET. (African Publishers Network) A professional association of African publishers and publishers' associations, representing 42 countries with headquarters in Harare.

appendix. Additional material, considered to be of interest to the reader but too detailed or tangential to be included in the main body of the text. *Appendices* are normally added at the end of the main text.

appraisal. A part of a funding agency investment cycle in which an overall assessment of the relevance, feasibility and sustainability of various kinds of support is made prior to final decisions on funding and implementation.[1]

art board. Wood-free board coated and polished to a high finish for fine printing of *half-tones*.

art paper. Paper coated with china clay and polished to a high finish and used for high quality photographic or art printing.

artwork. (a/w) Illustrative matter in the text *or* original illustrations from which *scans* are made are made prior to printing.

assign. To formally and legally transfer ownership. Thus, in copyright, it refers to the legal transfer of copyright ownership to another party.

---

1   Grateful acknowledgements are made to Danida for the use of this definition (and a few others) which have been adapted from the List of Abbreviations and Key Concepts in the 'Danida Guidelines for Sector Support Programmes (May 1998, Revised Edition)'.

assumed book life. A term frequently associated with school textbooks and library books, which is used as the basis for budgetary projections when calculating the costs and timing of textbook provision and replacement. See also **actual book life** and **book life.**

auction. In the publishing context an *auction* is a competitive public sale of a publication right in which the rights are awarded to the highest bidder. Publishing auctions are generally conducted via the submission of bids or proposals in sealed envelopes prior to a stated deadline.

author. The writer of the book or manuscript. See also **co-author.**

author's agent. A specialist representative of the interests of authors, normally reimbursed on the basis of a commission on the author's earnings. See **agent.**

author's contract. The legal agreement between publisher and author which establishes the terms and conditions of publication and the exploitation of neighbouring and subsidiary rights.

author's copies. The number of copies provided free by the publisher to the author, as specified in the *author's contract.*

author's corrections. Corrections made by the author on *page proofs* that have already been typeset.

a/v. Audio visual.

backlist. The previous publications of a publisher; generally used to distinguish between new titles and existing, already published titles in a *catalogue* or *on an order form.*

back-up. Printing on the reverse side of a sheet.

bad debt. A debt that is considered unlikely to be paid. *Bad debts* are generally written off in the company *accounts* at the end of a financial year.

bank. A grade of lightweight printing and writing paper often used for printing multi-part sets.

bar code. A machine readable code used for product identification purposes which consists of a printed pattern of vertical black and white stripes or lines of varying widths.

basic education. Usually used to refer to primary and junior secondary (middle school) form that is the first eight years of education.

baud. The number of computer bits transmitted per second over a data communications channel.

BEFA. (Basic Education For All) An alternative term for *Universal Primary Education* although the two terms are not, strictly speaking, synonymous because Basic Education can include junior secondary grades.

Berne Convention. The international convention, revised or updated from time to time, which defines the currently agreed international standards of copyright legislation and defines international copyright relationships. Countries that are signatories to the Berne Convention agree to maintain the defined minimum copyright standards and to extend reciprocity to other signatory countries.

bestseller. A publication that has achieved unusually high levels of sales.

bibliography. A list of books and articles organised according to a theme and intended to guide further or deeper study of that theme. *Bibliographies* typically contain information on author, title, publisher, country of publication, date of publication, *ISBN* and a brief description of the contents. In addition, journal articles used in bibliographies would contain the name of the journal, the *ISSN* and the volume and issue references.

bid. (1) A competitive request for submissions, usually for educational books or manuscripts or for supply and/or consolidation services or for printing and/or publishing services, usually organised by a government and/or funding agency. *Bids* can be for printing only, for authorship, for publishing services on existing manuscripts, for existing titles off-the-shelf, for full origination services, for consolidation and distribution or for a combination of the above. (2) A *bid* may also be known as a *tender*. (3) The proposal prepared and submitted by a *bidder* in response to a request for *bids*.

bidder. A company or organisation preparing and submitting a *bid*.

bidding. The process of preparing and presenting a *bid*.

bill of exchange. A written instruction, usually produced by a bank, to pay a stated sum on a given date to a drawer or a named payee if stated conditions are complied with.

bill of lading. A ship-master's detailed receipt given to a consignor.

binder. The machine, company (or even individual) which (who) performs the *binding* process.

bindery. The place where the *binding* process is performed; usually a part of a print shop or factory.

binding. The specialist manufacturing process of attaching the *cover* to the *book block*.

bi-wall carton. A *carton* manufactured with two thicknesses of *kraft board* for additional strength.

blad. A manufactured *dummy*, usually with one or two printed sections, intended to demonstrate the final appearance of a publication; normally used as a sales aid, often in association with the sales of co-editions or co-publications.

bleed. A printing term meaning to cut into the print area during the trimming process; also a page design term meaning to extend the print area to the trimmed edge of the page.

block. Letterpress printing surface made from etched metal for printing illustrations.

blocking. A binding operation in which an impression is made into a book cover and filled with metal foil.

blow-up. To enlarge photographically (usually some part of an illustration).

blues. A photoprint made from the assembled films used in making offset plates also known as dyelines.

blurb. The brief description of the contents of the publication, which is printed on the *cover* or *dust jacket* or is used for advertising and marketing purposes.

boards. Rigid material, usually pasteboard, used to make the *case* of a book.

bold. A style of printing which uses a thick black typeface.

bond. A range of printing and writing papers over 60 *gsm*.

book bank. A scheme, generally associated with universities and higher education institutions, in which multiple copies of core textbooks are purchased by university libraries for loan or rental to students. The scheme aims to make good textbooks available to all students at an affordable cost. Makerere University in Kampala, Uganda has a well-established and successful book bank scheme.

book block. The block of trimmed text pages excluding the *cover*. Also known as text block.

book club. An organisation that sells selected books on special terms to subscribing members.

book jacket. Protective wrap-around cover on a book, usually made of paper and also known as a *dust jacket*.

booklet. A book with a limited number of pages, usually *self covered*.

book life. The period of effective usage of a book. The term is commonly used in association with textbooks as the basis for annual and/or projected budgetary assumptions. Thus there is an *assumed book life,* a *target book life* and an *actual book life.*

book loan. A form of textbook provision in which *textbooks* are provided to students on loan but without charge. *Book loan* schemes require good production specifications to achieve acceptable book life and sufficient stock to enable all students to be able to borrow. Loans can be made on a daily, weekly, termly or annual basis. See also **book rental.**

book paper. Paper made principally for the manufacture of books, pamphlets and magazines as opposed to newsprint, cover card, *kraft,* etc.

book to pupil ratio. The ratio used to express the average number of pupils who are required to share a textbook in the classroom. Thus a maths *book to pupil ratio* of 1:3 indicates that there is one maths textbook for every three pupils.

book rental. A form of textbook provision in which *textbooks* are provided to students on loan against the collection of an annual rental fee.

bookseller. A trading company, organisation or individual with a significant part of their business activity concerned with selling books. A *bookseller* need not operate from a bookshop, hence the terms *briefcase bookseller,* pavement bookseller or *verandah bookseller.*

bookshop. A retail establishment open to the public in which the sale of books and book-related items is the dominant activity.

book token. A certificate or voucher usually purchased as a gift, which can be exchanged for books at a wide range of bookshops up to a specified value.

book trade. The totality of all of the organisations and individuals involved in the business of creating, manufacturing, publishing, promoting, selling and distributing books.

book value. The value of capital assets and/or stock that is entered into the company balance sheet.

break even. The point at which a company, publishing project or book title has earned (or will earn) sufficient income to cover but not to exceed its costs.

briefcase bookseller. A bookseller with no permanent premises and no stock who operates on very low overheads and low margins by only placing orders with publishers once firm institutional orders have been achieved; a term in common use in the *book trade* of the Indian sub-continent and, increasingly, in Africa.

brightness. Measure of a paper's reflectivity to a standardised light source.

bromide or bromide print. A print made onto a photographic printing paper coated with silver bromide emulsion.

budget support. A development term in which finance is provided by a *funding agency* direct to the Ministry of Finance to provide general recurrent budget financial support, as opposed to project specific financing, in which the development financing has to be used for more or less closely defined purposes and/or activities. Budget support is generally an integral part of a *SWAp.*

bug. Computer term for a defect interfering with a computer operation.

bulk. The thickness of paper measured as the number of sheets per unit of measurement.

bulk order. An order for a large quantity of stock.

bulk purchase. The purchase of stock in larger than normal quantities; the term is generally associated with special prices or extra discount to the purchaser because the supplier derives financial benefit from sales security and faster than normal cash flow.

bulk stock. The majority (or a large portion) of the print run. *Bulk stock* may be maintained in special warehouses as a stock reserve that is drawn upon as required. See also **forward stock.**

burst binding. A form of *unsewn* binding in which the signature folds are not cut flush (as in *perfect binding*) but are pierced with small holes to enable the adhesive to run through and form a stronger bond between the *spine* and the *book block.*

buying around. Avoiding the prohibitions of a *closed market* agreement by arranging the purchase of goods from an alternative supplier who is not the exclusive distributor and who is not party to the *closed market* agreement.

C.A.D. (Cash Against Documents) A freighting abbreviation denoting that documents enabling a consignment to be released will only be provided to the purchaser on payment of the invoice. The same acronym can also stand for Computer Aided Design and Computer Assisted Design.

C.A.L. (Computer Assisted Learning).

calliper. The thickness of a sheet of paper or board measured with a micrometre.

camera ready copy. See **CRC.**

caps. Capital letters (upper case).

caption. The title or brief description attached to an illustration and usually set above it. See also **legend.**

card. Thick stiff paper used for paperback book covers.

carriage. Delivery.

carriage paid. Delivery costs paid by the supplier.

carton. A *kraft* container used for packing and transporting book stock. See also **bi-wall carton** and **tri-wall carton.**

cartridge paper. A type of heavy paper often used for drawing.

case. (1) Originally the box in which type was kept hence *upper case* for capital letters and *lower case* for small letters. (2) A cover or binding made by a case-making machine and usually printed or labelled before it is fixed to the *book block.*

casebound. A book bound using covered boards for the front and back covers; a hardback book.

cash on delivery. See **C.O.D.**

cash with order. (C.W.O) A trading relationship in which a supplier will only supply goods if cash to the correct value accompanies the order. This style of trading relationship indicates high levels of supply risk.

cast-off. To estimate the space that a *MS* or *TS* will occupy in print.

catalogue. A list of titles in print providing bibliographic information, current prices, a brief description of contents and intended audience and a list of relevant distributors, agents, etc. with contact details. A catalogue can cover the whole of a publisher's or distributor's list (a general catalogue) or it can be specific (schoolbook catalogue, science catalogue, children's book catalogue, etc.).

centre notes. Notes placed between columns on a page.

certificate of origin. A certificate required by funding agencies and the customs departments of some countries that specifies the origin (the country of manufacture or assembly) of the goods supplied.

character. A letter, numeral, symbol or mark of punctuation. In printing type characters vary in width.

check digit. The final digit of an *ISBN* or *ISSN*, which has a mathematical relationship to the other digits and can therefore be used to check that the other digits are correct.

chemical pulp. Pulp obtained from wood or other plant sources by chemical processes rather than by mechanical processing.

CIDA. (Canadian International Development Agency) The arm of the Canadian government responsible for overseas aid.

c.i.f. (cost, insurance and freight) A freighting abbreviation which denotes that all freight, clearance and insurance charges up to the point of destination are covered by the shipper.

clearance charges. The costs associated with clearing goods through customs.

closed market. A territory where all of a supplier's sales and exports have to pass through a single exclusive local distributor. The market is thus 'closed' to all other importers.

close up. To reduce the spacing between characters of type.

clothbound. A book protected by a rigid cover, usually cloth wrapped around boards.

coated paper. A paper which has been given a chemical finish (usually with china clay) to produce a glossy or semi-glossy surface suitable for printing *half-tones*. *Coated papers* are typically used in magazines and in art books.

co-author. One of two (or more) authors who have equal status in the writing of a book or publication.

C.O.D. (Cash on Delivery) Denoting that supplies will only be released to the purchaser on payment of cash at the point of delivery.

CODE. A Canadian funding agency.

co-edition. A publication in which more than one publisher contributes to costs and participates in at least some of the editorial decisions. There are benefits in reduced costs through enlarged and shared printings.

collage. An illustration made by pasting photographs and other types of illustrations, etc. in combination.

collate. To put the folded sections of a book in correct sequence before binding.

collophon. A printer's or publisher's identifying symbol, usually printed on spines and title pages, also known as a *logo*.

colour separation. The process of separating artwork colours into the constituent three prime colours (cyan, magenta and yellow) plus black prior to film making, plate making and printing.

colour swatch. A sample of a specified colour.

colour transparency. A full colour photographic positive on film.

commission. A percentage of *Net Sales Value* (usually excluding freight charges and any unpaid bills) usually paid by a publisher to an agent for marketing and promotion services.

commission agent. An agent who works for a supplier, usually engaged in sales, promotion and marketing activity, who is reimbursed entirely through *commission* earned on sales.

commissioning editor. An editor in a publishing house primarily concerned with *list building* by the identification and commissioning of new titles and authors.

competitive bid. A submission or request for submissions to take part in a competition according to rules, procedures and evaluation methodologies established by the government/funding agency responsible for launching the *bid.*

competitive textbook evaluation. See **evaluation.**

composition. Setting a manuscript in type, or, the assembling of type and spaces to make up the page to be printed.

conditions of sale. The conditions imposed by a supplier on a purchaser as part of a sales transaction. For most publishers the dominant *conditions of sale* are the copyright obligations, which are normally printed on the *title verso.* In most countries, *conditions of sale* cannot legally override a customer's statutory rights as defined in any applicable consumer protection legislation.

consignment. A form of supply (usually from publisher to wholesaler or retailer) in which the purchaser does not have to pay for stock supplied until the purchaser has sold it. *cf* with *sale or return. Consignment* is used to make certain that good stocks are available with booksellers when a major title is launched or as a method of moving excess stock by making sure that it is available at the point of sale. In cases of bankruptcy, *consignment stock* is the property of the supplier *not* the purchaser and cannot be used to defray debts. There is normally a fixed time period during which *consignment terms* apply.

consignment stock. The stock which is subject to *consignment terms.*

consignment terms. The terms and conditions on which *consignment* applies.

consolidation. The process of collecting supplies from many different suppliers and sorting and re-packing them into packages for end-users. In the educational book trade this usually refers to the procurement and collection of books from many (several) different publishers and re-packing them into packages for individual schools or institutions. Consolidation sometimes implies procurement and delivery services in addition to pure consolidation activities. Large-scale consolidation is normally considered to be a specialist activity.

consolidator. An organisation that specialises in the provision of consolidation services.

consumable book. A book that is designed to be written in and so can only be used by one student and therefore has a limited life expectancy.

consumer funding. A term usually related to educational supply in which the funds for textbook or library purchase are provided by government or *funding agency* direct to the consumer, which is generally a school or educational institution.

contact print. A photographic print made by placing a negative directly on to sensitised paper and then illuminating it.

container. A large, box-like receptacle, made of steel to standard dimensions, used for the secure transport of goods.

containerisation. The process of packing and shipping goods using containers.

content. The subject matter of a book or publication.

contents list. The list of main headings with page numbers, which provide a summary of the contents of the title.

contents page. The page in the *prelims,* usually a *recto,* on which the contents list appears.

contract. A legal agreement between two or more parties.

contraries. Unwanted material in pulp or paper.

contrast. A range of tonal gradations.

contributor. A person who contributes articles or chapters or photographs, etc. to a publication.

co-production. A publication where the production process is shared by two or more publishers.

co-publication. A publication that is undertaken by two or more publishers simultaneously.

copy. The written text, including illustrative matter, of a publication or advertisement.

copy editing. The process of *editing* the *copy*, that is getting it ready for press.

copy editor. The person who *edits* the *copy*.

copy preparation. The process of preparing copy for a publication or advertisement.

copyright. The legal right to copy, publish, perform, broadcast or adapt works of intellectual creation, for example, writing, music, software, artwork, etc. and to authorise others to do so.

copyright fee. A fee payable for the use of copyright material.

copyright law. The national legislation that defines copyright and other related rights in all its forms and which determines, applies, regulates and governs the use of copyright material.

copyright notice. The statement in the prelims, usually on the title *verso*, which identifies and asserts the copyright ownership and which contains the universally recognised copyright symbol, ©.

copyright page. The *verso* of the title page of a book on which copyright information and the copyright symbol is placed.

copywriter. The person who writes the *copy*.

correction. The act of correcting a mistake. In editorial terms, a change intended to correct an error in a manuscript or set of proofs.

corrigenda. Things that need to be corrected in a printed book.

cost benefit. The relationship between the cost of any activity and the perceived benefit resulting from the activity.

cost cutting. Reducing costs to achieve lower prices or better margins.

cost effectiveness. The relationship between the cost of any activity and the effectiveness of that activity.

costing. Establishing the projected costs of a publication.

cost of sales. The costs incurred in achieving a sale. This includes the costs of manufacture and expenses incurred to achieve a sale.

cost price. A price calculated to cover the costs of development, origination and production without achieving a profit.

cost recovery. An educational/development term meaning that all or part of the cost of educational book provision (typically textbooks) should be recovered via contributions from parents, either by purchase or by the collection of rental fees.

cost sharing. An educational/development term meaning that the costs of education (typically textbook provision) should be met partly by government and partly by parents or communities.

course book. A book designed to cover a course of study; an alternative term for a textbook.

cover. Literally, something fitted to provide protection. In publishing terms the *cover* now has a dual purpose to provide protection and to create interest via the *cover design* or *blurb*. Covers are no longer a term applied specifically to books. Record sleeves, audio-cassettes, CD ROMs, etc., also have covers.

cover board. A rigid board used as the basis for a *casebound* book.

cover card. A thick stiff card used for paperback or soft-bound books. Cover card can come in a variety of different qualities from strawboard to art card and is typically used in *grammages* of between 120 *gsm* to 320 *gsm*.

cover copy. The *copy* for the front and back covers of a publication.

cover design. The artistic design of a *cover* incorporating text and illustrative material which is intended to attract interest and to assist sales.

covering costs. Achieving sufficient income to cover actual costs of publication.

covering power. The measurement of the opacity of ink on paper.

c.p.i. Characters per inch.

c.p.l. Characters per line.

CRC. *Camera ready copy*. This is text and illustrations typeset, designed and laid out ready for camera work and film-making.

credit. (1) (noun) An agreement to receive supplies before payment. (2) (verb) To provide a positive balance in a financial account.

credit account. An account with a supplier which can be used to obtain goods before payment.

credit ceiling. Also known as *credit limit*. This is the maximum credit that a supplier will allow to a purchaser. Credit ceilings can be adjusted upwards if the purchaser has a good payment record, or downwards if the supplier has a slow payment record.

credit control. The supplier's process of monitoring and controlling the credit extended to a client.

credit controller. The staff member responsible for controlling credit.

credit limit. See **credit ceiling.**

credit period. The period, usually expressed as the number of days from date of invoice or the end of the month, that a supplier allows to a purchaser before invoices fall due for payment. Credit is normally only provided by a supplier to a purchaser who has a good payment track record.

credit rating. A commercial estimate of a customer's suitability to receive credit.

credits. A list of individuals and organisations annotated to indicate the roles that they have played in the development of the publication, usually inserted into the *prelims*.

credit-worthy. To be considered trustworthy in terms of being able to pay a supplier on time (and therefore to receive credit).

crop. To cut down the size of an illustration in order to improve the appearance or relevance by removing unwanted material. Cropping is usually performed by masking or digital manipulation rather than by physically cutting the illustration.

cross-cutting issues. Issues that are perceived by funding agencies and governments to be of such importance that they must be addressed in every activity and at every level. Current examples of common *cross-cutting issues* are gender equity and participation, human rights and good governance and environmentally sustainable development. HIV/AIDS is also a common *cross-cutting issue*.

cross-reference. An instruction to a reader to refer to another point in the text for the information required, or for additional information on the same topic.

customer. The client served by the supplier. Thus a bookseller is the customer of a publisher and an individual or a school is a customer of the bookseller, etc.

customer file. A record maintained either manually or electronically, which records all historic and current transactions between a supplier and a customer. It also often records the terms and conditions of supply.

GLOSSARY

customer services department. The department within a supplier's organisation, which is responsible for ensuring prompt, accurate and courteous service to a customer.

customs. The department of government responsible for collecting import taxes and controlling the importation of banned or restricted goods.

customs clearance. The process of passing goods through customs checks and controls, whether or not duty is payable.

customs duty. A tax levied by a government on certain specified goods at the point where they are imported.

customs of the trade. A set of assumptions that apply automatically to all jobs performed by a printer without having to be specified in detail. The *customs of the trade* are usually agreed and published by national printing trade associations.

cut and paste. A method of document preparation, usually in preparation for camera work, in which a number of components are cut out from different sources and combined by pasting them together on a prepared backing sheet.

cut flush. To cut level with or to cut evenly.

C.W.O. See **cash with order.**

Danida. Danish International Development Agency – the arm of the Danish government responsible for overseas aid.

data. Information held in a computer store.

database. A collection of organised information held on a computer that may be retrieved selectively.

deadline. The date by which a specified activity must be completed.

dedication. Inscription made by an author and usually included in the *prelims*, which dedicates the book to a named individual(s).

definition. The degree of sharpness in an illustration.

delete. To remove type or to strike out unwanted manuscript or typescript.

delivery date. The date promised or scheduled by a supplier for delivery to a purchaser; often used specifically by publishers to denote the arrival of bulk stock from the printer.

delivery instructions. The instructions relating to all aspects of delivery which are provided by a purchaser to a supplier. The instructions may cover the type of transportation to be used, the package marking system, packing instructions, size of individual parcels and required documentation.

delivery note. A receipt offered by a delivery organisation for signature by a customer as evidence that the consignment has been delivered accurately as ordered and without damage. The delivery note also records the date of delivery, which can be important in avoiding damages for late delivery in funding agency or government-funded contracts.

depreciation. An annual write-down in the balance sheet on the value of capital goods and stock maintained by the company. Different types of capital goods will have different rates of depreciation. Thus heavy printing equipment may have a ten-year write-down period, whereas computers and vehicles may have only three or four year depreciation periods.

design. The arrangement or layout of a publication.

designer. The person responsible for the design.

desktop publishing. The processes of typesetting, page lay-out and design, the placement of illustrations and editing performed using specific software packages and computers. There is a widespread misunderstanding, common among many funding agencies, that the provision of computer hardware and a DTP software package is sufficient by itself to ensure high quality publishing output.

development agency. See **funding agency.**

DFID. Department for International Development – the arm of the British government responsible for overseas aid.

die. A device for stamping a particular shape.

die stamping. The process of embossing text paper or book covers using a *die*.

dimensions. The height and width of a book.

direct mail. A method of selling based on mailing catalogues/brochures direct to targeted end-users, usually associated with some form of premium offer (for example, a prize draw restricted to those who purchase or take goods *on approval*).

direct selling. To market sell direct to the end customer without going through intermediaries such as *wholesalers* or *retailers*.

direct supply. In the context of the book trade this is the supply of books by the publisher direct to the end user without using the services of intermediaries such as *wholesalers* and *retailers*.

discount. The difference between the price of a book sold to a book *wholesaler* or *retailer* and the price at which the same book is sold to the end user. The discount is usually expressed as a percentage reduction off the retail price. The purpose of the discount is to provide the operating margin by which a *wholesaler* or *retailer* can cover their operating costs and create profits.

display. To make books easily and attractively visible at a point of sale and thus more likely to sell.

display matter. Text matter which is picked out by being set in larger or different type or on lines by itself for example, chapter headings or the title.

display stand. A free standing unit which enables titles to be easily seen.

distribution. The process by which goods are moved efficiently and cost effectively from the supplier to the purchaser.

distribution costs. The costs associated specifically with distribution. These costs generally incorporate warehousing and storage costs as well as transportation costs.

distribution system. The totality of facilities, equipment, systems, staffing, transportation, etc., which enables a supplier to deliver goods effectively to the total market. Individual companies have *distribution systems* and the effectiveness of these systems determines the profitability and thus the future of the company. Many governments also have monopolistic *distribution systems*, often for textbooks, but different rules apply to government and commercial *distribution systems*.

distributor. Company or organisation which is responsible for the transportation of books from the warehouse to the customer. Distributors often also take responsibility for payment and for packing, documentation and records connected with the transport.

donor. See **funding agency.**

door-to-door. Doorstep selling.

double column. Text set in two parallel columns on a page; the columns are generally of equal width.

double page spread. A form of page design in which the total page layout uses two facing pages designed as a single unit.

down time. The period when a machine or a piece of equipment is not in use. In general, high levels of *down time* imply poor cost amortisation. It is the very short periods of *down time*, which make some printers very price competitive.

DP. Data processing.

d.p.i. Dots per inch.

draft. A preliminary written version of a text or project.

DTP. See **desktop publishing.**

due date. In the context of the book trade this generally refers to the date on which an invoice becomes due for payment.

dues. The accumulated orders for a publication which is awaiting publication or a new edition or which is temporarily out of stock.

dues building. Delaying a decision on a reprint until orders have accumulated to the point where it is likely that the reprint will be successfully sold out.

dummy. A prototype of a book consisting of a bound copy which is faithful in terms of raw materials and processes, extent, format, etc. to the look of the final book and which may also have a printed signature bound in to demonstrate the page design, layouts and treatment, etc. Dummies are generally manufactured as a sales aid. They are also often a compulsory requirement as part of a publisher's *bid submission* in response to an *ICB* or *NCB* in order to be able to demonstrate intended production specifications.

dump bin. A container manufactured by a publisher for promotional purposes and intended to be displayed at the *point of sale,* in which a variety of books can be placed to encourage browsing and searching by potential customers.

durability. The characteristic of being hard wearing and long lasting. A desirable characteristic in school textbooks intended for use in severe rural environments in many developing countries because it enables extended *book life* and thus the possibility of amortising costs.

dust jacket. A paper jacket for a book which protects the book from dust and dirt but also serves as a promotional tool by drawing attention to the contents and qualities of the book.

ECD. Early Childhood Development.

edit. Check, correct and rearrange copy prior to publication.

editing. The process of preparing a *ts* or *ms* for publication.

edition. All the copies of a book printed from the same type or the same plates plus subsequent copies printed from offset plates prepared photographically from the original typography. An *edition* may consist of many different printings or *impressions*, provided only that the book is reprinted in its original or only very slightly different form for example, corrected reprint; also an extensively revised version of a book or a book issued in a different form or a book differently bound and intended for a different audience.

editor. A specialist who selects and/or prepares for publication the written texts presented by authors. See also **commissioning editor, copy editor,** etc.

educational contractor. A bookseller who specialises in winning contracts to supply educational materials (usually to school boards or educational authorities).

educational management information system. (EMIS) The essential data collection system necessary to provide accurate and timely statistics on all aspects of the education system for planning purposes; as important for the private sector book trade concerned with education as it is for government and funding agencies.

electronic publishing. Publishing in electronic form as opposed to print on paper. *Electronic publishing* can include electronic databases, computer software, CD ROMs, Internet publishing, etc.

ellipsis points. Spaced periods or dots used to indicate an omission in quoted matter.

em. A unit of measurement of width in printing usually equivalent to 12 points of the point size of the type in use.

emboss. In printing, to make figures so that they stand out on a surface.

EMIS. See **education management information system.**

en. A measurement used in typesetting denoting half of an *em*.

end matter. The text that follows the main text in a publication. Typical *end matter* can be *endnotes*, a *bibliography, appendices,* an *index, etc.*

endnotes. Explanatory notes to the text inserted at the end of the chapter or at the end of the whole text.

endpapers. Folded paper, usually stronger than the *text paper* and often coloured and/or decorated, which is pasted to the insides of the front and back covers of a book to provide extra binding strength.

EPOS an. Electronic point of sale system using barcodes to log sales and control stock.

erratum (errata). Errors discovered in a book only after it has gone to press and which are considered sufficiently serious to warrant correction via the use of an *erratum (errata) slip.*

erratum slip. A slip of paper inserted into a book that corrects errors discovered in the text only after the book has gone to press.

estimate. A quotation or costing for a specified job or piece of work; normally a printing or production function in response to a request from a publisher or editor.

estimator. The specialist responsible for providing estimates; this is usually a printing or production function.

EU. European Union.

evaluation. (1) An assessment by an independent group of a number of different textbook proposals or submissions in order to determine whether or not a textbook is suitable for use in the context of a specified curriculum and syllabus. *A threshhold evaluation* occurs when any book that reaches a pre-determined level of acceptability is approved for use in schools. *A competitive evaluation* is a form of textbook approval system in which publishers compete with each other against fixed criteria, usually established by a Ministry of Education, to achieve approval status for a textbook submission. In a competitive system there is a limit on the number of titles that will be approved. (2) An independent examination and assessment of a programme aimed partly to determine its results, efficiency, effectiveness, impact, relevance and sustainability, and partly to draw lessons that may be more widely applicable.

exclusion clause. A contract clause that specifically excludes a particular act, territory or subsidiary right from the activities permitted under the terms of the contract.

exclusive contract. A contract that provides for the granting of exclusive rights. In an authors contract this would normally guarantee the publisher the exclusive right to publish and/or to exploit the copyright and subsidiary rights; in a distribution contract it could guarantee that the distributor had exclusive rights to stock and sell in a defined territory. Alternatively, the distributor might guarantee to the publisher that it would not stock and sell the list of any rival publisher. Exclusivity is valuable and is generally recognised by higher rates of payment.

exhibition. A display of artistic or industrial products.

exhibitor. A company or individual that exhibits at an exhibition.

expiry date. The date on which a contract or agreement (or even a specific clause in a contract or agreement) terminates.

export. Sales and delivery outside of national borders.

export edition. A special edition of a publication intended for sale only outside of national borders.

export packing. Heavy-duty packing, often shrink wrapped for water proofing, to provide extra stock protection for books which are intended for export.

extended credit. A *credit period* longer than that normally given by a supplier to a purchaser. *Extended credit* may be offered to support an unusually large order, or to provide time to pay in unusual market conditions (for example, after a currency devaluation).

extent. The length of a publication, either in terms of number of words or number of pages.

extract. Special text matter set off typographically or by the use of indentation from the main body of the text.

fastness. The resistance of printed colours to fading.

favoured account. A distributor, wholesaler or retailer provided by a supplier with additional trading privileges (e.g. additional discount, longer credit, etc.) because the account is considered to be commercially or strategically important or because it is required to undertake a particular additional task. For example, a *favoured account* may be created to establish significant local stocks in an *open market territory* where competition among suppliers would normally inhibit investment in large stocks.

fee. A sum of money paid to an individual or organisation for undertaking a particular task or for the use of specified copyright material.

f&g. Folded and gathered, used in relation to printed sheets in the process of book *binding*.

fibre. The cellulose constituents of wood pulp and paper.

figure. A line illustration, chart or diagram.

file copy. A copy of a book held on file for future reference and use and in which corrections or comments may be recorded for future incorporation into a corrected reprint or new edition.

film make-up. The process of positioning pieces of film ready for platemaking.

film mechanical. *CRC* composed in film rather than on paper.

film rights. A subsidiary right of copyright that provides for the payment of copyright fees or royalties in the event that a work or portion of a work is used as the basis for a film. *Film rights* are closely associated with television rights.

filmsetting. Creating type on film by means of a photosetting system.

final proof. The last set of page proofs before a book or publication is approved for printing.

fine papers. High quality printing paper.

FINIDA. (Finnish International Development Agency) The previous name for the arm of the Finnish government responsible for overseas aid. This role is now carried out by the Finnish Ministry of Foreign Affairs.

finish. The lamination or varnishing of a cover *or* the type of surface of paper or card.

finishing. The process of cover lamination or varnishing.

firm. Definite or confirmed, as in *firm order*.

firm order. An order that cannot be revoked.

first edition. The first printing of a book. If the book is very successful the first edition may become very valuable.

fixed costs. Those costs which do not vary with the print run for example typesetting, artwork, pre-press costs, etc. See also **running costs.**

flat sheets. Cut and printed sheets before they have been folded.

flooding. An excess of ink on a printing plate.

Florence Agreement (and Nairobi Protocols). An international convention monitored by *UNESCO*, in which ratifying states guarantee the free flow of books and information (and the raw materials from which books are made) between countries without duty, license or tariff barriers.

flush. A typesetting term meaning the absence of indentation, e.g. flush right meaning type justified to the right-hand margin; also used in *binding* to indicate 'level' for example, *cut flush*.

flyleaf. Any blank leaf at the front or back of a book, except for endsheets which are pasted to the inside of the covers.

FOB. Free on board, a freighting term meaning that the costs of shipment (by sea or air) will be paid by the consignee.

fog. Unintended light penetration into photographic film.

folded sheets. Sheets that have been folded and are awaiting collation and binding.

folder. The machine used to fold sheets prior to collating and gathering. Folding, collating and gathering can be performed as part of the same process.

fold-out. Folded sheet in text which opens out beyond the page-size.

folio. An (obsolete) imperial paper size in which a standard paper size is folded once to form two leaves or four pages; also a page number usually placed at the outside of the *running head* at the top of the page.

font. A complete collection of a specific design and size of type, including capitals, small capitals and lowercase together with figures, punctuation marks, ligatures and commonly used signs and accents. The *italic* of a specified font is usually considered to be part of the font.

foot. The bottom of the page or book.

footnote. An explanatory note to the text inserted at the foot of the page on which the subject of the note is located.

foreword. A short introductory piece of text, generally included in the *prelims* of a non-fiction book, which is generally written by someone other than the author(s). See **preface.**

format. The *dimensions* of a book; also the shape, size, style of a book as determined by type and page design.

forthcoming. A title not yet published.

forward stock. Relatively small quantities of stock held close to the *picking* and *packing* area of a warehouse for immediate usage in the fulfilment of customer orders. Forward stock is topped up from *bulk stock* at regular intervals to make certain that there is sufficient stock for immediate needs.

four-colour. In printing terms this means the three primary colours (yellow, magenta and cyan) plus black.

four-colour printing. The use of the three primary colours plus black to achieve the full range of colour possibilities. Four-colour printing requires four sets of film, four sets of printing plates and four impressions. It is thus significantly more expensive than one or two colour printing.

FPE. (Free Primary Education) Currently a target of most developing countries and *funding agencies*.

freelance. A specialist who is employed on a contract basis rather than as a permanent employee.

free primary education. An educational/development objective to provide primary education free of charge as an encouragement to parents to send their children to school. See also **Universal Primary Education.**

freight. Transportation from supplier to purchaser.

freight charges. The charges made for transportation by the supplier to the purchaser.

freight costs. The costs of transportation.

frontispiece. An illustration, often *tipped-in,* positioned to face the *title page.*

front matter. A printing and editorial term meaning all of the text preliminary to the main text and including the *title* and *half title* pages, *title verso, contents, preface,* etc. See also **prelims.**

fulfil. The process of supplying an order. An order has been *fulfilled* when the books ordered have been delivered to the purchaser.

full colour. Generally taken to mean four-colour (see **four-colour***).*

funding agency. (also known as a donor or aid agency) A financial institution, government department or charity that exists to provide assistance to developing or *transitional* countries via the provision of *grants* and/or *loans* for specified developmental purposes. *Aid agencies* fund the development and procurement of a significant proportion of *teaching and learning materials* in developing countries and *transitional* economies and can have a profound impact on the form, nature and viability of the *book trade* in these countries.

fungibility. The ability to substitute one form of income or expenditure for another. For example, the provision of book donations as a form of aid may lead to the removal of library acquisition budgets. Continued support for textbook provision can lead to the permanent loss of the textbook line from the national education budget. Government funds may well be increased in sectors not receiving funding agency funds but may be decreased in areas in receipt of funding agency funds.

galley. Originally, an oblong tray for set type.

galley proof. Also **galley.** Proof in the form of continuous single column strips of type not divided into pages or page designed. Usually the first proof pulled.

gather. A binding term meaning the act of *gathering.*

gathering. A binding term meaning the process of collecting together the leaves of signatures of a publication to form the text block prior to binding.

general books. Books intended to be of interest to the general adult reader.

ghosting. An unintended faint printed image on the page caused by poor inking on a printing press.

glossy. A photograph with a hard shiny finish that is used for reproduction.

glue. The adhesive used to fix the *book block* to the book *cover.*

g/m². See **gsm.**

graded readers. Supplementary reading books in which the vocabulary and language structures are graded for difficulty according to broad age and reading ability bands.

grain. The direction of the fibres in a sheet of paper or card. Paper or card resists folding or bending against the *grain* and thus good printers take care to make sure that the *grain direction* runs parallel to the *spine* of the book.

grain direction. The direction in which the fibres lie in sheets of paper or cover card; it is desirable to prevent warping by ensuring that the grain direction is parallel to the spine of the book.

grammage. (*gsm*) The weight of paper and cover card, expressed in grams per square metre.

grant. The provision of finance, usually for a specified purpose, which does not require repayment and does not accrue interest or service charges.

gratis. Free.

gratis copy. A free copy of a book sent for review, marketing or presentation purposes or as a condition of receipt of copyright permissions.

green. Paper, cover card or cover boards which have been insufficiently dried and which in consequence still have a significant moisture content. Green paper or boards may stick on the printing machine or may warp.

green boards. Cover boards which have not dried adequately before being used in the binding process and which may therefore *warp* badly as a result.

gross margin. The *gross profit* expressed as a percentage of *net income*.

gross profit. The profit achieved after the deduction of the *cost of sales* from net income but before the deduction of overheads and administration costs.

gsm. Grams per square metre – a measure of paper weight.

gutter. The space occupied by the two inner margins separating the print areas on the facing pages of a book or publication; specifically the margin allowed for binding.

half-title. The short title of a book usually standing alone on a separate page and also usually printed on the *recto* preceding the *title page*.

half-tone. A photoengraving process in which a screen is used to print illustrations as a continuous tone; used for the reproduction of photographs or other kinds of illustrations which have continuous tone.

hand binding. Book binding performed manually rather than by machine.

hand-setting. Type setting performed by hand rather than by machine.

hardback. A *case bound* book.

hardback rights. A license to publish a book in *hardback* style.

hard copy. Text and/or illustrations reproduced on paper as opposed to being available on screen.

hard loan. A loan at close to commercial interest rates and terms of repayment. The International Bank for Reconstruction and Development (IBRD), a part of the *World Bank*, is the major source of hard loans for *Newly Industrialised Countries* (see **NIC**) and some developing countries.

Harvard system. A system of bibliographical references used in a text.

head. Top of a page or a book.

heading. A title at the head of a page, section or chapter.

headline. A large heading at the beginning of an article or at the top of a page, especially in newspapers.

head margin. The white space above the first line of a page.

headword. The main entry in a dictionary or glossary.

heat sealing. Closing plastic wrapping materials by melting the plastic.

Heavily Indebted Poor Countries Initiative. (HIPC) An international programme intended to provide debt relief to the poorest and most heavily indebted countries.

hickey. Spot or defect on a printed sheet caused by dust, lint or ink imperfections.

highlight. The lightest tonal values in a half-tone.

HIPC. See **Heavily Indebted Poor Countries Initiative.**

hot metal. Type set either by hand or by machine (Linotype or Monotype) using cast metal.

house style. The set of rules governing punctuation, spelling, capitalisation, hyphenation, the use of captions and running heads, etc. which are adopted by a particular publishing house or printing house to ensure uniformity and consistency of appearance on the page and within a publication. See **style.**

ICB. See **International Competitive Bidding.**

illustrator. A person who produces drawings and *artwork* for publication.

image scanner. See **scanner.**

impact. The positive and negative changes directly or indirectly produced by a *project*, programme or component, whether intended or not.

imperial. Pre-metric paper sizes, still used in North America.

import. A purchase made from an external supplier that has to be brought into the country of the purchaser.

import duty. A tax payable on the value of the goods imported.

import license. A license required, usually from the local Ministry of Trade, before a specified item may be imported. Countries which are signatories to the *Florence Agreement* generally do not require import licences for books and other kinds of publications but other related items such as paper, card, other printing raw materials, print machinery and spare parts often do require import licenses and this can have an inhibiting impact on the operation of the local *book trade.*

imposition. The process of arranging the made up pages of a printing sheet so that when the sheets are printed and folded the pages will be in the correct order.

impression. All the copies of a book manufactured during one printing.

imprint. The name of the publisher under which the title is published. Many imprints are still used even though the original publishing house has been purchased and fully absorbed into another company and no longer exists in any operational sense.

in copyright. A book, text or illustrative material that is still within the legal period of copyright and thus liable to permission, copyright fees or royalties before use is permitted.

indent. (1) To set a line of type so that it begins or ends inside the normal margin. (2) An order from an importing bookseller direct to a publishing house or wholesaler with whom the bookseller has an operational credit account and where the bookseller will remit funds direct to the publishing house in payment of the invoice without going through a local agent or intermediary.

index. Alphabetical list of subjects contained in a work, together with their page numbers.

India paper. An expensive but specialised *text paper'* incorporating low *grammage* but high strength, *durability* and *opacity*; traditionally used for bibles or other expensive reference books where long life is a requirement.

indicator. Either a quantitative or qualitative statement used to describe existing situations and to measure changes or trends over a period of time. Indicators are often used to measure the degree of fulfilment of stated objectives, outputs, activities and inputs.

in-house. Any activity performed within a publishing house by the staff of that publishing house.

infringement of copyright. The use of copyright material without permission.

initial print run. The first print run of a book.

in print. A title that is available for purchase from the publisher. It should be noted that a title may be *in print* but *out of stock,* that is the title is available to purchase but the publisher is temporarily out of stock and may have to wait before an order can be fulfilled.

inspection copy. A free or discounted copy of a textbook sent by a publisher at the request of an educational institution so that the institution can inspect the textbook with a view to bulk purchase or recommendation.

institutional linkage. The creation of long term, formal links between institutions in the developed and developing worlds as a means of increasing information and technology transfer.

in stock. Publications in the warehouse, which are immediately available for sale and supply.

international competitive bid. (ICB) A competitive bid in which suitably qualified local, regional and international companies may participate.

International Standard Book Number. See **ISBN.**

International Standards Organisation. The organisation that co-ordinates the drawing-up of internationally accepted standards.

ISA. International Standards Authority.

ISBN. (*International Standard Book Number*) An internationally recognised identifying number allocated to each edition of any book title.

International Standard Serial Number. See **ISSN.**

inventory. An up-to-date listing of stock quantities for every item maintained in stock.

ISSN. (International Standard Serial Number) An internationally recognised identifying number allocated to magazines, journals and other serial publications.

IT. (Information Technology) A term which refers to the use of computers, computer networks, telecommunications mechanisms such as modems, email, the internet, etc. The term is sometimes extended to ICT (information and communication technology).

jacket. See **dust jacket.**

jobber. A wholesaler.

joint venture. A business agreement whereby the inputs and outputs are shared in a fixed proportion according to legal and contractual agreements.

journal. A newspaper or *periodical.*

journal subscription agent. A company specialising in the identification, procurement and supply of specialist journals (academic, professional and popular).

justification. The process in which lines are *justified.*

justify. To adjust the spacing in a text so that every line finishes at the same margin.

juvenile. A book for children (US).

k. An abbreviation for kilo, that is one thousand.

key plate. In colour printing, the plate (usually black) containing the outline, which is used as a guide for the other colours.

keyword. A headword in a dictionary or a word that can be used to guide searches in a database.

kill. To purposely omit text or illustrations in a revision or new edition of a publication.

kraft board. A heavy duty brown paper or board used primarily for making cartons and other packing material.

kraft paper. A heavy duty paper used for making wrapping and covering materials.

laminate. In book-binding, the sealing or bonding of the cover card with a clear plastic sheet (laminate) for the purpose of achieving enhanced protection.

lamination. The process by which a book cover is laminated.

landscape format. A book format in which the dimension of the width is greater than the height.

large print. Books printed in large, bold typefaces on white paper to assist partially sighted people to read.

launch. To introduce formally a new product to the market; generally accompanied by as much publicity as possible.

layout. The way in which a printed page is arranged or a rough sketch or plan of a book design.

lc. Lower case.

lead time. The estimated advance warning required before an activity can be satisfactorily performed.

leaf. A single thickness of paper; in a book, two pages are equivalent to one *leaf.*

leaflet. A folded sheet of paper, generally unstitched, issued free for the purposes of publicity or information.

learned journal. An academic journal which is published for the purpose of providing scholars with access to the latest research in their fields.

Learning and Innovation Loan (LIL). A type of loan, typically associated with the World Bank, which is intended to provide limited funds over a short time frame (typically no more than three years) to provide immediate support and which will lead to a policy framework and agreement which can be used as the basis for further larger scale and longer term financial support.

legend. (1) The title for an illustration, chart or table and usually set below it. See also **caption.** (2) The key to the symbols of a map or chart.

library supplier. A company specialising in the procurement, consolidation and supply of books and other related software to libraries. Usually has high level bibliographic capacity and can often offer specialist library services for example, computerised cataloguing, catalogue cards, jacketing and reinforcing, spine labeling, etc.

license. Agreement granted by the holder of the rights in a work to another party to manufacture and distribute a literary work or to exploit the work in another form.

LIL. See **Learning and Innovation Loan.**

limited edition. An edition, often a fine binding, with a fixed number of copies. Often the copies of a limited edition are individually numbered to increase the potential demand from collectors and thus the selling price.

line artwork. Illustration copy for reproduction consisting of only solid blacks and whites, which can be reproduced without gradation in tone.

line drawing. A drawing consisting of only solid blacks and whites, which can be reproduced without gradation in tone.

line length. The designed length of a line of text on a page. This may have significance for young children in the early stages of reading where eye scanning over a long line can prove difficult for some children. In the former Soviet Union, the line lengths and type fonts and sizes were considered to be of such importance in the development of reading skills and eye care that they were prescribed by law for school textbooks.

lint. Loose surface fibres released from paper during printing.

list building. The process of developing a list of popular and significant publications with good sales and income generation potential.

list price. The publisher's catalogue price of a publication.

literal. A typographical error.

literary agent. An individual or company who, for a fee or commission, looks after the interests of an author. Literary agents may look after a great many authors at the same time. They are responsible for submitting manuscripts to publishers, negotiating on the author's behalf and managing the authors' rights, including translation rights, serial rights, film rights, etc. In developing countries literary agents tend to work far more on general trade than on educational books.

loan. The provision of finance, usually for a specified purpose, which has to be repaid in a specified period at agreed rates of interest.

local purchase order. (LPO) A form of voucher that is commonly used by government departments or district bureaucracies to provide purchasing power to organisations or individuals as an alternative to cash.

logframe. See **logical framework.**

logical framework. A presentational tool for the development, planning, management and monitoring of projects and/or programmes used by most funding agencies.

logo. One or more words or other combinations of letters displayed as a unified entity in order to provide a distinguishing appearance for a company or product.

lower case. The uncapitalised letters of the alphabet (*lc.*).

LPO. See **local purchase order.**

lump sum. A single sum payment to fulfil a financial obligation.

lump sum contract. A contract where payment is in the form of an agreed sum for the completion of the job and where detailed accounting for monies spent is not required.

machine readable codes. Bar codes which can be 'read' by optical scanning or optical character recognition (OCR) devices.

machining. Manufacturing.

madrassa. Private school for Islam studies (also known as 'medersa').

mailing lists. Specialised lists of addresses organised according to target groups, either maintained in-house or purchased from specialised mailing list companies and used for advertising and promotional purposes.

mail shot. A piece of advertising sent by mail.

make ready. To prepare printing machines for a specific print job.

make-up. Forming typeset material into pages.

management accounts. The regular monthly financial information required to manage satisfactorily the affairs of a company or organisation.

manufacturing costs. The costs incurred in the manufacturing of a book or publication. For books, these costs commonly cover raw materials (mostly text paper and cover card but also thread, glue, ink, laminate, etc) plus printing, binding and finishing costs.

manuscript. The *text* of a publication prior to *typesetting*; originally this meant handwritten work but now the word is synonymous with typescript.

margin. An area of white space left around the printed matter on a page.

mark down. A reduction in the retail price of a publication, usually to achieve better or faster sales and improved cash flow.

market. The geographic area or the sector into which titles may be sold or rights negotiated.

marketing. The activity of promoting and selling titles. Most commercial publishing houses have marketing departments.

market research. In the context of the book trade, research into a market (geographic) or market sector (for example, computer book opportunities) or a combination of the two as the basis for investment in new title or new list development, or planned expansion into a new market area.

mark up. (1) An increase in the retail price of a publication to achieve better margins and additional profitability. Mark-ups are common in export markets where local distributors often do not consider that the discounts offered are sufficient to meet the costs of freight, and stock holding with the risks of non-sales and potential devaluations. In these circumstances retail prices may be *marked-up* by a percentage over and above the prevailing exchange rates. (2) Instructions on a layout for the compositor to follow when typesetting or making-up.

mass market paperback. A paperback, usually popular fiction, intended for high quantity sales through the specialised systems and outlets utilised by mass market paperback publishers and distributors.

mass media. Television, radio, daily newspapers and popular magazines, etc. that is those means of public communication which are regularly accessed by the general public.

matching funds. Funds provided by funding agencies/development partners in fixed proportion to funds made available by governments. Alternatively, funds provided by funding agencies and/or governments in fixed proportions to contributions made by parents and/or schools. Matching funds are a technique used to encourage local contributions, local ownership and involvement as well as cost-sharing and cost-recovery.

matt. Non-shiny, relating to text paper, cover card and photographs.

mechanical paper. Paper made almost entirely out of softwood pulp created by grinding rather than by chemical treatment. Mechanical papers are cheaper papers, which are often not suited for school textbook use.

mechanical pulp. Pulp made dominantly from softwood by grinding rather than by chemical treatment.

misprint. A typesetting error.

misregister. The failure accurately to match up one or more colour impressions on a printing sheet; usually resulting in a somewhat blurred image.

moisture content. The amount of moisture in paper, expressed as a percentage of the weight.

monitoring. Continuous or periodic surveillance of the progress of a *project*, programme or component.

monochrome. Single colour.

monotone. Illustrative material in one colour.

montage. A photograph in which several images are combined photographically.

ms(s). Manuscript(s).

MTEF. See **Medium-Term Expenditure Framework.**

multilateral donor. A development partner funded or managed by a number of different countries.

multilingual. A society in which many languages are spoken. Where the medium of instruction of the early years of primary education is in a number of different local or dominant languages, textbooks may be required in several different language versions. This situation has financial and organisational consequences.

multinational. An international company with branch, associate or subsidiary companies and offices in many countries.

National Competitive Bid. (NCB) A competitive bid which is advertised nationally (rather than internationally) and which is primarily intended for national (as opposed to international or regional) bidders.

NCB. See **National Competitive Bid.**

negative film. A transparent photographic film on which light values are reversed (the black shows as white, left is right, etc). Used in preparing an offset plate.

net line value. See **net sales value.**

net profit. The surplus of income over expenditure after the deduction of costs of all costs of sales including overhead and administration costs.

net receipts. The actual income received by a publisher after the deduction of all freight and discounts.

net sales value. (NSV) Also variously known as NSV, net line value or NLV. This is the cash actually received by a supplier from a transaction after the deduction of discounts, commissions, bonuses, freight or carriage charges, etc.

new edition. A substantial correction of a book, usually a textbook or reference book, in which the information is completely reviewed, corrected and up-dated and in which much new and original material may be inserted. The book is usually published under the original name and with the original authors' or editors' names, even if the new work is the result of new authors and editors.

newsprint. Paper used for newspaper production characterised as low grammage and low durability; sometimes used for textbooks but not often recommended because durability is poor.

NFE. Non formal education.

NIC. Newly industrialised country.

NLV. Net line value. See **net sales value.**

non-book. Publishing product not in book form, for example, audiotapes, CD ROMs, electronic databases etc.

non-bookshop outlets. Sales outlets for books made via non-specialist retail channels for example, supermarkets, garden centres, pavement kiosks, churches, etc.

NORAD. Norwegian Agency for Development.

notched binding. A similar binding style to *burst binding* but instead of the adhesive flowing through perforations in the signature fold it flows through triangular notches cut out of the signature folds. See also **slot binding.**

NSV. See **net sales value.**

OCR. Both *optical character reader* and *optical character recognition.*

octavo. An Imperial paper size.

offprint. A printed copy of an extract or journal article that once formed part of a larger publication.

offset. A printing process in which ink is transferred from a plate to a uniform rubber surface and from there onto the paper.

on account. A preliminary payment in advance of full settlement.

on approval. Goods supplied, which may be returned if not satisfactory.

on credit. Goods supplied, which will be paid for at a later date agreed between the supplier and the purchaser.

on demand publishing. A publishing and printing methodology which permits text to be selected and mixed from a variety of sources to create a custom designed publication which may be printed economically in very short *print runs.*

one-sided art paper (card). A smooth-coated, high quality paper or card, which has been treated to receive print on one side only.

only to order. A title which is not maintained in stock but which will be supplied only on the basis of a *firm* customer order. The abbreviated form is *OTO*.

on stop. The situation in which a supplier will no longer supply a purchaser on credit terms.

OP. See **out of print.**

opacity. A descriptive characteristic of paper that describes the degree to which light will pass through the paper and thus the degree to which print on one-side of the paper is visible from the other side. See also **show through.**

opening. Facing pages.

opening stock. The stock in the warehouse at the beginning of an accounting period (for example, the beginning of the financial year).

open market. A geographical *market* or *territory* in which the supplier will sell to any bona fide distributor without restriction because there is no exclusive agreement which restricts the *territorial* sales to one supplier only. See also **closed market.**

operating costs. The costs associated with the actual running of a company. Operating costs do not normally include the *cost of sales*.

operating loss. A financial deficit incurred as a result of normal trading activities during an accounting period.

operating profit. A financial surplus incurred as a result of normal trading activities during an accounting period.

optical character reader. A device that uses photoelectric means to recognise printed characters.

optical character recognition. The identification of printed characters by photoelectric means.

option. The right to purchase a copyright license within a specified period during which no other party may purchase the license. It is normal to pay for an *option*.

order. A request/requirement for goods to be supplied, normally provided in written form; the quantity of goods supplied.

order book. A book in which orders received are recorded.

order form. A printed form used for the specific purpose of writing out orders.

origination. The processes involved in initiating a book or publication. These normally include writing, artwork, picture research, illustrations, permissions, design, page layout, etc.

origination costs. All of the costs associated with the processes of *origination*.

orphan. A single line of text at the bottom of a page isolated from its succeeding paragraph. It is usually avoided by making changes to wording or spacing, which either eliminate the single line or lengthen it. See **widow.**

OS. See **out of stock.**

OTO. See **only to order.**

outlet. A place or premises where goods may be sold.

out of copyright. A publication that has passed beyond the legal term of copyright and is therefore in the public domain. Although the title may be *out of copyright*, the typesetting and treatment may well be *in copyright*. Thus, Shakespeare's plays are *out of copyright* but the Arden edition of Shakespeare's plays is very much *in copyright*.

out of print. A publication is *out of print* if there is no stock available to purchase and the publisher has no plans to make further stock available through another printing. Under these circumstances the license to publish will generally revert to the author after a set period of time and the author may seek an alternative publisher.

out of register. The failure of one or more colours on a printed page to be exactly positioned. This generally results in either a blurred image or in colours overlapping their defined print areas on the page.

out of stock. A publication is *out of stock* if there is no stock available to purchase but plans for additional stock are in hand. When a publisher reports *out of stock* with a date for stock availability it usually means that a reprint is in hand or that additional stock is being called from another location. Out of stock – no date often means that the publisher is uncertain whether or not there should be a reprint and is waiting to see how potential orders *(dues)* are developing. See **dues building.**

outside reader. A publisher's or literary agent's manuscript reader who is not employed within the company but who works on a job-by-job basis. Few publishing houses now maintain in-house readers. Specialist manuscripts are almost inevitably sent to *outside readers.*

outstanding. An unpaid bill or account.

overdue account. A purchaser who has not paid outstanding debts to a supplier on the *due date*.

over-ink. To apply too much ink to a printing press.

overprint. To print further matter on a sheet that has already been printed.

overrun. The act of printing more copies of a book than are required for immediate demand.

overs. Additional copies to those ordered from a print run caused by the time taken to halt a printing machine in operation. The printer normally gives *overs* to the publisher free of charge. See also **spoilage.**

overstocks. Copies in stock that are surplus to immediate requirements.

ownership. Acceptance of responsibility for a policy, activity or plan. *Ownership* implies formal or real authority to act or take decisions.

ozalids. A proof, made from assembled film, that is used to approve the final lay-out of text and illustrations prior to printing. See also **blues** (US usage).

packager. A company which originates book titles up to film or finished copy stage that will be sold to publishers for publishing, marketing, sales and distribution.

packing. The material used to wrap and pack a consignment for delivery.

PAD. See **project appraisal document.**

page. The pieces of paper making up a book are called leaves. One side of a leaf is a page.

page break. The point at which one page ends and another succeeding page begins.

page make-up. Assembly of the elements in a page into their final design.

page proofs. Manuscripts typeset or otherwise made into pages.

paginate. To put into page order.

pagination. Page numbering.

pallet. A wooden frame on which books (and other goods) are stored or transported in order to keep stock off the ground and to facilitate handling by the use of fork lift trucks.

palletise. Packing stock for transportation on *pallets.*

pamphlet. Booklet comprising only a few pages.

paperback. A book bound in stiff paper or card covers.

paperback rights. The right to publish a work in a paperback style.

paper engineering. The special skills of designing and manufacturing the three-dimensional images characteristic of *pop-up books.*

paper merchant. A paper and card wholesaler buying different types, qualities and sizes of paper from different mills in different countries and selling on to local publishers and printers.

paper mill. A factory which manufactures paper and card.

parental contribution. An education/development term meaning the contributions in cash or kind which parents make toward the education of their children; in the context of *teaching and learning materials* provision, the cash contributions either via book purchase or rental fees which parents make toward the costs of educational book provision.

parentheses. Text material set in closed brackets.

part delivery. A partial delivery of an order to a purchaser.

part payment. A partial payment for an order from a purchaser.

part mechanical paper. Paper containing up to 50% of mechanical paper with the balance of chemical pulp.

partwork. A title published not as a single volume at one time but as a series of, usually, weekly parts which can be collected together by a purchaser into a binder or folder.

pass. One run through a printing machine.

pass for press. The final clearance from the publishing house after scrutiny of *final page proofs* that manufacturing can commence with no further changes required.

paste-up. A document prepared for copying by combining and pasting different components of text and illustration onto a backing as a guide to the printer for make-up.

penalty clause. A clause in an agreement or contract, which specifies the punishments (penalties) to be imposed in the event of any failure to perform according to the terms of the contract.

PER. See **Public Expenditure Review.**

perfect. A printing term meaning to complete a sheet by printing the reverse side. See also **perfecting press.**

perfect binding. An unsewn paperback binding style characterised by cutting flush the gathered signatures and applying adhesive to the fanned edges that are then glued directly onto the spine.

perfecting press (perfector). A printing press that prints both sides of a sheet simultaneously.

performance discount. An additional discount offered by a supplier to a purchaser if pre-determined sales performance targets are achieved.

performing rights. The right to perform; specifically for music, dance, drama, etc.

periodical. A journal or magazine published at regular, pre-determined intervals (for example, monthly, quarterly, etc).

permission. A formal permission from the copyright holder to use copyright material in a publication, often dependent upon the payment of a fee.

permission fee. A fee paid to a copyright holder for permission to reproduce copyright material.

permissions department. The specialist department of a publishing house with the responsibility to identify the copyright owners of all copyright materials to be used in the book and to achieve permissions after payment of the necessary fees.

pH. A measure of the acidity of paper.

photocomposition. Typesetting using characters on a photographic film.

photo-offset. Offset printing using photographic plates.

phototypesetter. The piece of equipment that produces *photocomposition*; also the operator of the machine.

picking. Selecting stock from stock shelves in a warehouse as the first part of customer order fulfilment.

picture library. A library of photographs organised into categories and themes for easy reference in which the photographs are available for use by publishers against payment of an appropriate fee.

picture research. Research aimed at identifying the source of illustrations specified and required for a publication.

PIF. See **Policy Investment Framework.**

piracy. The illegal reproduction and sale of copyright material, typically books, without seeking permission or paying remuneration to the legal copyright owner or licensee.

pirate. The individual, organisation or company undertaking the act of piracy.

PIU. See **Project Implementation Unit.**

plagiarism. Passing off the thoughts and words of another person (specifically in this context, an author) as one's own.

plant costs. The non-recurring expenses in the manufacture of a book, such as composition and plates.

plate. The surface from which a printing impression is made. Also, a full-page illustration on a smooth or coated paper printed separately and inserted into a book as a *tip-in* or wraparound.

PMU. See **Project Management Unit.**

Policy Investment Framework. (PIF) A sector policy document prepared by government and considered by government and funding agencies as the basis for funding agency/ government investment in the total sector; often the preliminary activity required prior to the initiation of a *SWAp*.

point of sale. (POS) The point at which the purchase of something takes place. Often a retail outlet.

pop-up book. A book containing three-dimensional figures that rise when the book is opened. See **paper engineering.**

portrait format. A set of book dimensions in which the height is greater than the width.

POS. See **point of sale.**

positive film. A photographic image on paper or film which corresponds to the original subject.

pp. Pages.

PR. Public relations.

preface. A formal introduction to a book, usually setting out the aims, scope and style of treatment of the contents.

prelims. The preliminary text of a book prior to the main text. Prelims can consist of *the half title, the title page, the verso, the contents list, a list of tables, figures and plates, a dedication, a list of acknowledgements, a foreword, a preface,* etc.

pre-press. The activities that have to be completed before a publication goes to *press.* Thus, typesetting, artwork, design and lay-out, film-making, etc.

pre-press costs. The costs of *pre-press* activities.

pre-publication. The period prior to the publication date.

press. The machine used for printing.

press costs. Printing costs.

press release. Any statement issued to newspapers, radio, TV, etc.

price fixing. A conspiracy between one or more parties to artificially fix the price of a commodity or commodities above the price at which the commodity would normally sell in free market conditions. Thus, a group of bidders might agree to respond to a request for bids by fixing the minimum price that will be offered in response to a bid.

price list. A list of published and available titles with their current prices, usually made available to customers and potential purchasers as an aid to sales and marketing.

pricing policy. A statement of policy that applies to the establishment of prices for a range of products. Pricing policies may be public documents intended to attract publicity and to increase public profile, or they may be confidential company documents intended to inform internal pricing decisions only.

printer. A factory or company that has printing as its main activity.

printing press. The piece of equipment which performs the printing.

print run. The quantity of books to be printed.

process colours. The four basic colours used in printing to produce any other colour. The process colours are cyan (blue), yellow, magenta (red) and black.

production. The processes of manufacturing including (in the case of books) all *pre-press* activity, raw materials selection and procurement and manufacturing.

production cost. The total cost of manufacturing up to the delivery of bulk stock of the finished copies.

production department. The department of a publishing house which is responsible for the procurement, cost control, quality control and on-time delivery of finished bulk stock via the processes of manufacturing.

professional books. Those books catering for the interests of professional disciplines such as marketing, auditing, accounting, etc.

profit. The surplus of income over expenditure after the inclusion of all costs.

profit and loss account. An account that shows all income generated, the costs of achieving that income and the overhead and administrative costs of the account. If the income is greater than the expenditure the company is in profit; if expenditure is greater than income then the company has made a loss.

pro forma. A dummy invoice, which serves as a quotation and is normally used to obtain payment in advance of supply or as the basis for a customer to obtain a letter of credit.

programme aid. Funding agency assistance provided for the purpose of general financial support to the economy or to a specified sector of a country. The term is often used interchangeably with budget support, balance of payments support or import support. When used in relation to general financial support to a specified sector (for example, education) it can be an alternative term for a *SWAp*.

project. A development term implying a package of specified activities agreed between government (or other body) and *funding agency(s)* to be completed in an agreed time period in pursuit of a limited number of agreed development objectives for which finance is provided by the *funding agency(s)* and, on occasions, by the government.

project aid. Funding agency assistance provided in support of a package of specified activities agreed between government and funding agency(s) which are scheduled for completion within an agreed time frame and in pursuit of a limited number of developmental objectives.

project appraisal document. (PAD) The detailed description of a proposed project that is used by funding agencies and governments to appraise and evaluate a project prior to final approval and financial negotiations and agreements.

projected sales. The forecast of future sales of a publication.

project implementation unit. A special unit established in a government ministry or department and funded by a funding agency to manage or assist in the implementation of a funding agency funded project. See also **project management unit.**

project management unit. (PMU) An alternative name for a *project implementation unit.*

promotion. The process of publicising and selling.

promotion copies. Early bound copies of a publication intended to be used for promotional and publicity purposes and particularly, in the case of books, for sending out as *review copies.*

proof correction marks. The marks made on a set of proofs to inform the typesetter of any necessary corrections.

proof read. The task of reading a set of proofs to detect and correct spelling, grammatical, stylistic and presentational errors and inconsistencies.

proofreader. The person who proof reads.

proofreader's marks. The special marks made on a *ms, ts* or set of proofs to enable required corrections to be made accurately.

pseudonym. A fictitious name used by an author to conceal their true identity.

publication date. The date on which a book is scheduled for publication. Publicity, promotion and marketing activity is often planned around this date and great efforts are often made not to change the *publication date.*

public domain. Not subject to copyright; something that belongs to everyone.

Public Expenditure Review (PER). A review of the efficiency and effectiveness of government expenditure either in total or specific to one or more sectors.

publicity. The process of advertising and achieving exposure to increase recognition and thus to maximise sales potential.

publish. The process of organising the development and production of a publication for distribution and sale.

publisher. A company or organisation (or sometimes an individual) who organises the development and production of a publication for distribution and sale.

pulp. The raw material consisting largely of cellulose from which paper and cover card is manufactured.

pulp fiction. Low quality, mass market, paperback fiction.

purchase ledger. A record of all purchases.

quality control. The processes of ensuring that manufactured goods meet and maintain the quality standards required by the client or purchaser.

quantity discount. Additional discounts offered by a supplier to encourage bulk purchasing.

quarto. An Imperial paper size.

quire. One-twentieth of a ream.

quotation. (1) Excerpt from a published work, which is included in a manuscript and attributed to the original creator, and usually shown in quotation marks. (2) The price given for the provision of services or for the sale of goods, etc, which is used as the basis for negotiation.

raw materials. Natural or processed substances used as part of a manufacturing process to make something else. Thus the basic raw materials for a book are paper and card or boards plus ink, thread, glue, etc.

reading copy. A gratis copy of a book sent for the purpose of reading prior to a decision to purchase bulk stock or translation or subsidiary rights.

ream. A package of 500 sheets of paper of the same quality, size and format.

rebind. Binding up a set of stored sheets.

recommended retail price. Retail price recommended but not enforceable by a publisher.

recto. The right hand page of a book when opened flat.

reel. A printing term; a large cylinder around which a continuous sheet of paper is wound.

reel fed. A method of providing paper to a printing machine in which the machine receives the paper in a continuous sheet from a *reel*.

reference book. A title that is not intended to be read from cover to cover but which will be referred to for information purposes as and when required for example, a dictionary or atlas, etc.

register. The accurate printing on top of each other of two or more of the four process colours to produce a clear final colour image.

reissue. A reprint issued after a title has been unavailable or out of print for a period of time.

rejection. The notification from a publisher informing an author that a submitted manuscript is not considered suitable for publication by that publishing house.

remainder. Unsold stock that the publisher sells off in bulk at below cost price to specialist *remainder merchants* in order to generate such cash income and to make space in the warehouse. *Remainders* are usually restricted to trade, general and children's books.

remainder merchant. A specialist wholesaler of remainder books.

repaginate. To redo the page numbering at proof stage, usually because additional text or illustrative material has been added or because there has been a revised page design and layout.

representative. An individual who represents the interests of a company, institution or organisation. Often used to denote a sales person (for example, sales representative).

reprint. A second or subsequent printing of a title with no (or minimal) corrections.

repro. An abbreviation for the reproduction of illustrations and the process of generating film. A 'repro house' is a company that undertakes this kind of work.

reproduction rights. The right to produce or reproduce a literary work.

retailer. A shop or outlet that sells goods to ordinary customers at *retail prices*.

retail price. The price at which a publication is sold in single copies to ordinary customers. See also **wholesale price** and **special price.**

returns. Stock returned by a purchaser to a supplier, either within the *terms and conditions of supply* or simply because the stock cannot be sold.

returns policy. A publisher's policy on acceptance of *returns*.

reverse out. The type or illustration matter in white surrounded by solid colour or black is *reversed out*.

reversion of copyright. The return of contracted rights to the original copyright owner at the termination or expiry of a copyright licensing agreement or contract.

review. A comprehensive assessment of the progress of a programme, project or activity. *A review* is generally formal and takes place at fixed and pre-determined periods during the life of a programme, project or activity.

review copy. A free promotional copy sent to a newspaper or specialist journal or magazine for the purposes of achieving a favourable review which will assist marketing and sales efforts.

reviewer. The person who undertakes a *review*.

revision. A reprint with corrections, which is nevertheless not substantive enough to justify the appellation of 'new edition'.

rights. The legal rights of intellectual property that subsist in a literary work. This right can be sold by the copyright owner or by the copyright licensee for publication, sale or exploitation in a variety of forms.

rights manager. The staff member of a publishing house responsible for the sale and maximisation of income from the subsidiary rights owned or licensed by the publishing house.

rising royalty. A royalty agreement in which the percentage paid increases with the number of copies sold. Also known as a sliding royalty. See also **royalty.**

royalty. A payment made by a publisher to a copyright holder as remuneration for the right to publish and sell. It is a performance linked payment, which takes the form of a percentage on either the retail price value of the number of copies sold *or* more frequently the NSV of the number of copies sold. Royalties are normally paid annually or bi-annually in arrears. See also **advance.**

royalty statement. The statement of sales and thus royalties due, usually provided either annually or bi-annually, by a publisher to the author.

rrp. Recommended retail price.

running costs. Those costs that vary according to the size of the print run. Running costs include raw materials, machining, royalties, etc. See also **fixed costs.**

running head. The line at the top of a printed page, which normally shows the book title and the chapter title and sometimes the page number.

run on. Additional copies printed as part of a print run but printed as additions to the number of copies required by the publisher from the print run.

run on price. The price of printing additional (that is, run-on) copies on top of the regular print-run. Run-on prices may often be costed on the basis of marginal profitability.

saddle stitch. A wire stitch binding in which all the signatures are gathered together within each other and the stitches are inserted through the signature fold. As a result there are limitations on the number of pages that can be accommodated within a saddle stitched binding. The normal limit varies with the thickness of the text paper but is generally somewhere between 96 and 124 *pp.*

sale or return. A form of supply (usually from publisher to wholesaler or retailer) in which the purchaser may return any copies of a book for credit to the purchasers' account, which have not been sold by a specified date. *Sale or return* implies that the original supplies have been paid for in accordance with the normal *terms of supply* agreed between supplier and purchaser. This is a different arrangement from *consignment.*

sample pages. A selection of pages submitted for approval or as an example.

sc. Small capital letters.

scanner. The equipment that breaks down tone images into dots for the purpose of printing.

scanning. The electronic process of reading a document into digital memory from which it can then be retrieved when required.

schedule. A programme of tasks to be accomplished and deadlines to be met to achieve publication.

school books. Books intended for use in schools. Often used to mean *textbooks*.

score. A line scratched on the surface of a paperback book cover parallel to and 6–8 mm from the spine in order to form a hinge that enables the cover to open without placing pressure on the binding.

screen. A transparent finely-ruled plate or film used in half tone reproduction.

screen printing. A printing process in which ink is forced through a prepared sheet of fine material.

SDP. See **Sector Development Programme.**

secondary colour. The colour made by a mixture of two primary colours.

second colour. The second printing colour used after black.

sector. A discreet area of government or economic activity, for example, education, health, energy, agriculture, trade, finance, etc., are all *sectors*.

Sector Development Programme. (SDP) A term used by some funding agencies to denote a *SWAp*.

Sector Expenditure Programme. (SEP) A term used by some funding agencies to denote a *SWAp*.

Sector Programme Support. (SPS) A modality of providing funding agency support, which is longer term than a *project*. It is generally conceived as a more flexible approach, which will normally include a variety of modalities at different levels within agreed objectives and management procedures. It is a term used by some funding agencies to denote a *SWAp*.

Sector Wide Approach. See **SWAp.**

see-safe. A condition of supply which enables a purchaser to buy with security because the goods can be returned for credit if they are not sold and are still in mint condition. *See-safe* differs from consignment because in a *see-safe* transaction the purchaser must pay for the goods.

self-cover. A book in which the first and last pages of the *text block* are used as the front and back cover of the book; in other words, no special cover card is used. This form is typical of *pamphlets* and *booklets*.

SEP. See **Sector Expenditure Programme.**

serial. A story that is published in instalments; a periodical or journal.

serialisation. The process of publishing in serial form.

serial publication. Any publication made available in regular instalments.

serial rights. The right to publish something as a *serial*.

series. A set of books usually published in a common format and on a common theme or supervised by a common editor; a set of successive issues of a periodical, of articles on one subject or by one writer.

sewing. The process of attaching together signatures using a sewing machine and thread stitches.

sewn binding. Any book-binding that uses thread sewing to hold together the individual signatures comprising the *text block* and to insert the *text block* securely into the *spine*.

sheet. A single sheet of paper.

sheet-fed press. A printing machine that is fed individual sheets of paper one at a time to take the printed image.

shelf life. The usable storage life of raw materials and book stock.

short discount. Lower than normal discounts.

short run. A low print run, often associated with academic books and monographs.

show through. The extent to which the text printed on one side of a page is visible (shows through) when the reverse of the page is read.

shrink wrapping. A thin plastic film wrapped around either single books or even paletted consignments which is heated to create a vacuum and then shrunk after cooling to tightly enclose the consignment and maintain it free from damage from damp or dust.

SIDA. Swedish International Development Agency.

side stitch. A form of binding in which the wire stitch is punched through the side of the book, usually with the head of the stitch on the front cover and the tails folded onto the back cover. *Side stitching* has often been used for cheap bindings for textbooks in many developing countries. However a side-stitched book will not lie open when flat and students tend to shorten the book life by pressing out the gutters and thus breaking the binding.

signature. A *folded* and *trimmed* printing sheet.

slip case. Cardboard case for a book that displays the spine.

slot binding. A similar binding style to *burst binding* but instead of the adhesive flowing through perforations in the signature fold it flows through rectangular slots cut out of the signature folds. See also **notched binding.**

smoothness. The evenness of the paper surface.

snowflakes. White dots on a piece of printing caused by water droplets.

soft loan. A loan at very preferential interest rates and usually with a significant grace period before repayments fall due. The International Development Association (IDA), a part of the *World Bank*, is one of the largest sources of soft loans. *Soft loans* are normally restricted to the poorest countries.

special price. An unusually low price usually offered in return for a large quantity order.

specifications. The complete set of instructions for the design and manufacture of a publication.

spine. The part of the book cover which encloses the fastening of the *text block;* the part of the book cover that typically faces outwards on a book shelf.

spine lettering. The lettering on the *spine* of a book that usually comprises the title, author and publisher's imprint.

spoilage. Waste incurred during printing or binding.

spread. A pair of facing pages.

SPS. See **Sector Programme Support.**

square spine. A book *spine* that has been squared as part of the binding process.

SRM. See **supplementary reading materials.**

stabbing. Wire stitching through the back margin.

stage. An interval or step in a planned programme. It usually serves to define intermediate decision-making or review points where results can be assessed and decide upon future action.

stakeholder. A person, group, organisation or other body who has an interest in the sector or component in receipt of interventions and/or assistance. *Target groups* are always *stakeholders* but *stakeholders* are not always *target groups.*

standing order. A regular order for a standard number of copies of all titles of a particular type, category or description. Thus a permanent order for a fixed number of copies of all titles published by a particular author.

stet. A *proofreading* term; literally 'let it remain'. The term is used when a false correction has been made and the *proofreader* wishes the *typesetter* to ignore the false correction.

stiffness. The rigidity of paper or card.

STM. Scientific, Technical and Medical publishing.

stock control. The process of controlling the level of stock to ensure that there is sufficient to supply customer requirements while simultaneously attempting to avoid tying-up funds unnecessarily in slow moving stock.

stock control system. The system, manual or computerised, which is used to control stock levels.

stock level. The current level of stock.

stock list. The list of titles maintained in stock and available for purchase.

stock turnover. The speed at which stock moves through the warehouse. This is usually expressed as an annual ratio between the average stock level and the total stock throughput over the period of a year. Thus, an average stock turnover rate of 3,5 means that the average stock level is being replaced 3,5 times each year. High levels of stock turnover generally imply good warehouse management.

stopped account. A purchaser to whom a supplier will no longer provide goods because previous debts have remained unpaid for an unacceptable period after the due date. A stopped account may be re-opened if the purchaser pays off previous debts.

storage. The act of storing or the state of being stored. Also, space used for storing things.

store. A place where stocks or supplies are kept. See also **warehouse.** A *warehouse* implies a building designed for storage purposes. A *store* implies a place where goods are stored, irrespective of whether it was designed for storage purposes. A store can also be a retail shop, for example, a book store.

style. The rules of punctuation, capitalisation, hyphenation, spelling, use of captions and running heads, etc. that ensure uniformity and consistency on the page and within a publication. See also **house style.**

sub-heading. A subsidiary heading or a division of a main heading. See **heading.**

submission. In the context of publishing or the book trade, the sending in of a proposal in response to a competitive bid for publishing, printing, distribution or consolidation services. Also refers to sending in textbooks for evaluation and approval for use in a national state school (or sometimes university) system.

subscription. The system by which title orders are taken from customers in advance of publication. Also a payment for a serial publication (for example, a journal or magazine) for a fixed number of issues within a fixed period (usually one year).

subsidiary company. A commercial company which is owned and controlled by another company and which is subordinate in terms of policy and decision-making.

subsidiary rights. Rights which are acquired by publishers from the authors for subsequent re-sale, for example, serial rights, translation rights, film rights etc.

subsidised textbook supply. A supply of textbooks in which money has been provided by government to reduce prices to the end-consumer. See also **subsidy.**

subsidy. A sum of money, usually provided by government, given to an industry to reduce final prices to the consumer either for political reasons or because the product is considered to be socially essential. Thus *subsidised textbook supply.*

subtitle. A subsidiary *title* for a book or publication.

supplementary readers. Reading books which are supplementary to main textbooks or course books; supplementary readers are usually intended for use in primary grades and often have graded vocabulary and grammatical structures; also, any reading books intended for classroom use which are not main textbooks. See **graded readers.**

supplementary reading materials. (SRM) All reading material including books, magazines, posters, books for reading aloud, etc. which are intended for school use to support reading development and which are not main textbooks.

supplier. An individual, organisation or company involved in supply goods or services to purchasers.

sustainability. The ability of a programme to continue to provide planned benefits after the termination of funding agencies funded assistance.

SWAp. (*Sector Wide Approach*) A development term used to describe a situation where a majority of *funding agencies* agree on a comprehensive set of sector policies, objectives and activities with government and then provide co-ordinated funding and support to achieve the agreed sectoral goals. In a *SWAp* the government partner must 'own' the agreed approach.

synopsis. A short version of a longer original. Thus, a summary or precis of a book. A *synopsis* is often required as part of a textbook *bid* or *tender* when new textbook proposals are requested for evaluation. The cost of developing an entire new publication, which might then not be accepted, would be a disincentive for many *bidders*. A *synopsis* plus other samples is a cheaper alternative.

talking book. An audio cassette or CD, which presents a dramatised reading of an abridged version of a well-known book or story. Originally intended for the blind, *talking books* now have a growing market for children and adults.

target book life. The *book life* that is aimed for as a means of reducing the annual recurrent costs of textbook provision. Enhanced conservation, improved storage and stock management and organised book repair are all methods used to extend *book life* and thus to achieve improved targets. See also **book life.**

target group. A specified group who are intended to benefit directly and in a measurable way from planned interventions.

teacher's book (manual). A book written specifically for teachers, which is designed to accompany a *textbook* and which generally provides additional subject information, ideas to assist teacher presentation of specific topics, suggestions for specific content related activities and suggested tests, etc.

teaching aids. *Teaching and learning materials* intended to assist the teacher in the presentation of the curriculum. Typical teaching aids can be teacher's guides, wall charts, wall maps, flash cards, science kits, slides, transparencies, audio tapes, educational software, etc.

teaching and learning materials. A generic term covering the full range of potential educational materials. The term can cover *textbooks*, teacher's guides, *workbooks*, *workcards*, audio-visual materials, *teaching aids*, etc.

tele-ordering. Ordering by electronic means.

tender. An alternative word for *bid*.

terms of payment. The stipulated methods and conditions governing payment for supplies in a trading agreement between a supplier and a purchaser.

terms of reference. The proposed outputs of a specified activity comprising objectives, results, required actions and activities. Usually used in relation to technical assistance assignments.

terms of supply. The package of terms and conditions agreed between a supplier and a purchaser, which governs the trading relationship between them. This package usually covers discounts, credit and payment terms, forms and methods of supply, etc but can also extend in some cases to performance and incentive discounts and marketing and promotion arrangements. Most suppliers have a basic *terms of supply* package, which can be amended to fit the specific requirements of particularly large or important customers.

territory. In the context of publishing or distribution a *territory is* a definable geographic area of the world, such as a country, group of countries (for example, the Former Soviet Union) or region.

territorial rights. The right to publish in a specified form in a defined geographical territory. Thus US rights are the right to publish within the geographical territory of the USA.

text. The words, as opposed to the illustrations, of a book.

text area. In the context of a page design, that part of the page which will be covered by the text.

textbook. A book intended for students, which is planned and written to cover the concepts, content and skills required by a defined course of study.

textbook approval system. A method of evaluating and approving for use in schools competing textbooks submitted by publishers.

textbook revolving fund. (TRF) A system of achieving sustainable textbook provision in countries with financial problems. The fund is established on the basis of contributions made by parents, which may also be supported or 'matched' by funds provided by funding agencies and/or government. The funds are allowed to accumulate over a period of years until annual expenditure on replacement purchases can be balanced by annual income from contributions. The most successful textbook revolving fund in Africa was managed by the School Supplies Unit in Lesotho.

text paper. The paper on which the text is printed, as opposed to the cover card.

thread sewn. A book in which the signatures are gathered together and sewn with thread as the basis for binding operation.

threshold evaluation. A method of textbook evaluation and approval in which certain minimum standards are established for the quality of textbooks submitted for approval. Only those titles meeting the standards can be approved but all titles meeting the standard may be approved. There is no competition between different textbooks for approval. See also **evaluation.**

thumb index. A set of lettered grooves cut down the side of a dictionary to provide easy reference.

tie-in. A publication linked to a media event that will provide additional exposure and thus increase sales; thus, the book of the film, the book of the TV series, etc.

tint. A solid colour reduced in shade by screening.

tip-in. A single leaf fixed in a book by pasting it on to the back edge of the adjoining page.

title. The name given to a publication.

title page. The page containing the book title and all associated information (for example, author and publisher and date of publication, etc. are commonly inserted onto the title page); the title page is always a *recto* page.

title verso. The reverse side of the title page.

trade association. An association of companies and organisations who are all engaged in broadly the same kind of business activity, for example, Publishers Association, Booksellers Association, Authors Association, etc. Trade associations can also operate on a market sector basis (e.g. the International Association of Scholarly Publishers or the Educational Publishers Council), on a regional basis (the European Publishers Association or the African Publishers Network) or on a world-wide basis (for example, the International Publishers Association).

trade book. A book of general interest aimed for sale through retail bookshops.

transitional economy. A country in the process of shifting from the economic policies of state centralism toward market oriented economic policies.

translation rights. The right to translate and publish a work in another language from the original language of publication.

TRF. See **textbook revolving fund.**

trim. To cut off the rough edges of a book along the three open sides after the completion of the binding process.

trimmed size. The final designed dimensions of a book after trimming.

tri-wall carton. A *carton* manufactured using three thicknesses of *kraft* board for additional strength.

ts(s). Typescript(s).

turnover. Net income.

TVET. Technical and Vocational Education and Training.

type. Originally a piece of metal with a raised character for use in printing.

typeface. A set of characters with a distinctive unifying design.

typesetter. The specialist responsible for typesetting.

typesetting. The process of composing or setting the manuscript or typescript into type ready for the camera. Once an entirely mechanical process requiring great skill, most typesetting is now handled electronically using *DTP* or even word processing packages.

type size. The size of *type*.

typo. A typographical error; more specifically, an error made by the compositor or typesetter and thus a printer's error rather than a publisher's or author's error.

typographer. A person skilled in *typography*.

typography. The art of printing. Also, the style and appearance of print on the page.

uc. See **upper case.**

unabridged. The full and unshortened text.

unbacked. Printed on one side only.

unbound sheets. Usually, sets of folded, collated and gathered sheets that are held in store awaiting binding. When both a paperback and hardback edition can be manufactured from the same set of sheets it is economical to hold bulk stock in unbound sheets so that bindings can be targeted to the edition required.

uncoated paper. Paper with no coating and therefore not suitable for high quality illustrated work.

uncorrected proof. A set of proofs which have not been corrected.

UNDP. United Nations Development Programme.

unearned advance. An advance paid to an author that is larger than the royalties achieved as a result of sales.

unit cost. The total cost of publishing or manufacturing divided by the number of copies produced; thus the cost of one unit.

universal copyright convention. (UCC) An international convention, similar but more recent than Berne, which also defines standard *copyright* terms and relationships. It is this convention which requires the © symbol together with the date of publication and the *copyright owner's* name to be included for reciprocal protection to apply. Most countries of the world are signatories to either Berne or UCC and many to both.

Universal Primary Education. (UPE) The development target that aims to have all children of school age in school and completing basic education. To achieve this goal there is increasing pressure to make basic education free of charge to parents so that one of the major barriers to full enrolment is removed, hence *FPE*.

unjustified. Text in which the right-hand margin is variable rather than standard.

unsewn. A book in which the signatures are not sewn together with thread.

untrimmed A book prior to trimming with top, bottom and outer edges with the guillotine.

untrimmed size. The dimensions of a book prior to trimming.

UPE. See **Universal Primary Education.**

upper case. Capital letters.

USAID. (United States Agency for International Development) The arm of the US government responsible for overseas aid to developing countries and transitional economies.

uv. Ultra-violet.

uv varnish. A form of varnish applied to a paperback book cover in which the varnish is chemically bonded to the cover card by the use of ultra-violet light; a strong form of varnished finishing, which is often used for textbooks to be used in harsh conditions.

value. The degree of lightness or darkness of a tone or colour.

variable costs. Those production costs that vary in accordance with the number of copies printed; variable costs include paper and cover card, printing and manufacturing costs and royalties. See also **fixed costs.**

varnish. A clear, chemical covering applied to the cover of a paperback after cover printing in order to provide enhanced protection and durability, particularly from damp.

VAT. Value Added Tax.

VDU. Visual Display Unit (a computer screen).

verandah bookseller. An alternative term for pavement bookseller in use in some countries.

verso. The left-hand page of a book when lying open flat.

volume. A book; also large quantities.

volume discount. An additional discount offered to a purchaser for buying in large quantities.

volume rights. The right to publish in book (volume) form.

vouchers. Payment orders issued instead of cash.

waiver. A decision or an *agreement* to ignore or not insist upon a rule, a *contract* clause or a previous agreement.

warehouse. A large building in which goods or materials are stored. See also **store.**

warp. The distortion of a book usually caused by uneven shrinkage or expansion of the raw materials. Warping in books is generally caused by using 'green' boards or by failing to maintain the grain direction of the *cover card* or *boards* parallel to the spine.

wastage. Losses as a result of machining and storage.

web. A continuous length of paper as opposed to a sheet.

web-fed. Paper supplied to a printing machine in the form of a continuous sheet of paper fed from a reel.

web offset printing. A printing process whereby the print is applied to a reel, or web, of paper resulting in folded sections of paper coming off the press.

web press. A printing machine in which the paper is supplied in the form of a continuous sheet of paper fed from a reel.

white space. The space on a page opening that has not received a printing impression. If there is too little white space on a page (particularly for textbooks) the text matter may seem overcrowded and daunting.

WHO. World Health Organisation.

wholesale price. The discounted price at which goods are sold to a trade customer.

wholesaler. An organisation, company or individual who buys goods in quantity from the original suppliers for resale to retailers.

widow. A single line of text at the top of a page isolated from its preceding paragraph. It is usually avoided by making changes to wording or spacing, which either eliminate the single line or lengthen it. See also **orphan.**

WIPO. (World Intellectual Property Organisation) The UN agency responsible for the protection and monitoring of intellectual property rights such as copyright, performing rights, etc.

wire stitch. A form of binding in which the cover is attached to the *book block* by wire stitches. See also **saddle stitch** and **side stitch.**

woodfree. Paper which contains no mechanical pulp.

wood pulp. Pulp made from wood.

word count. The number of words in a text.

workbook. Ancilliary material to a *textbook;* a consumable book in which the student is encouraged to write and undertake exercises and activities linked to the textbook.

workcard. A sheet of card, often laminated for protection and long life and usually printed both sides, containing educational or training exercises and activities intended for pupil use. *Workcards* can be used with any age group but are probably more often used with very young children.

working capital. The finance used or required to operate a business.

work in progress. Uncompleted work on which expenditure has been incurred but from which income has not been generated. Represented in the balance sheet as an asset.

World Bank. The largest of the multilateral Development Agencies providing financial assistance in the form of both hard and soft loans to developing countries and transitional economies.

wysiwyg. 'What you see is what you get' – an acronym which describes a visual display showing an exact replica of the final version.

NOTES